Learning
Windows 7

Ramesh Bangia
B.Sc., Dip. Comp. Sc.
Formerly: Managing Editor, Software Today
Formerly: Incharge Computer Centre, Hindustan Copper Ltd., New Delhi

KHANNA BOOK PUBLISHING CO. PVT. LTD.

Learning Windows 7
Ramesh Bangia

ISBN: 978-93-80016-59-7

Published by:
Khanna Book Publishing Co. (P) Ltd.
4C/4344, Ansari Road, Darya Ganj, New Delhi-110 002
Phone: 011-23244448 Telefax: 011-23244447
E-mail: contact@khannabooks.com
Website: www.khannabooks.com

Regd. Off: 1694-95, 1st Floor, Nai Sarak, Delhi-110006 (India)
Phone: 011-23283211 Telefax: 011-23256658

Printed in India by:
S.P.S Printers & Binders, Delhi

Preface

Learning of a software is both easy and difficult. It depends upto what level you are planning to learn. If you are learning only for the working use, then it is very easy. But, when you try to go deep into it, then you realise how difficult it is to master it.

Windows 7 is such a vast subject that it will take a lot of time to understand it fully. This book has been written in mind to make you aware of the options available in the software and how they can be used. It is like telling the child about the steps and stairs. You are the one who is to climb the stair. This book will just guide you how to use the stairs.

I am indeed debited to my publishers Khanna Book Publishing Co. Pvt. Ltd. for their suggestions and encouragement given in producing this book.

I would like to thank my family specially my wife Sadhna, kids Mayank and Samarth, for without their criticism this book would not have seen the day.

Suggestions for improvement of the book are indeed welcome.

Ramesh Bangia

Contents

1 Introduction to Windows 7

Introduction

Much hyped Windows 7 is here. It is the new version of ever popular operating system called Windows. Keeping in the trandition of the various versions given earlier by Microsoft, this one too has some advancements specially in the field of mobile computing, networking and other related topics.

To know more about the various new features, read on.

What's New in Windows 7?

Faster, more responsive performance

Nobody likes to wait. So we've focused on the basics that can impact the speed of your PC. Windows 7 starts up, shuts down, resumes from sleep, and responds faster.

Improved taskbar and full-screen previews

You can use the taskbar at the bottom of your screen to switch between open programs. In Windows 7 you can set the order of the taskbar icons and they'll stay in that order. The icons are larger, too. If you point to an icon, you'll see a small, preview version of the page or program. If you point to this preview, you'll see a full-screen preview. To open a program or file, click an icon or one of the previews.

Get the picture: See what's open with full-screen previews

Better on laptops

Windows 7 helps extend the battery life of your laptop with power-saving features, including dimming the display if you don't use your computer for a while. Another new laptop-friendly feature, location-aware printing, can automatically switch your default printer when you go

Jump Lists

With Jump Lists, you can quickly find files that you've worked with recently. Right-click a program icon on the taskbar to see a list of recently-opened files. You can also pin files that you use regularly to a Jump List. Some Jump Lists show commands for common tasks, like playing music or videos.

A leap in efficiency: Jump Lists provide quick access to common files and tasks.

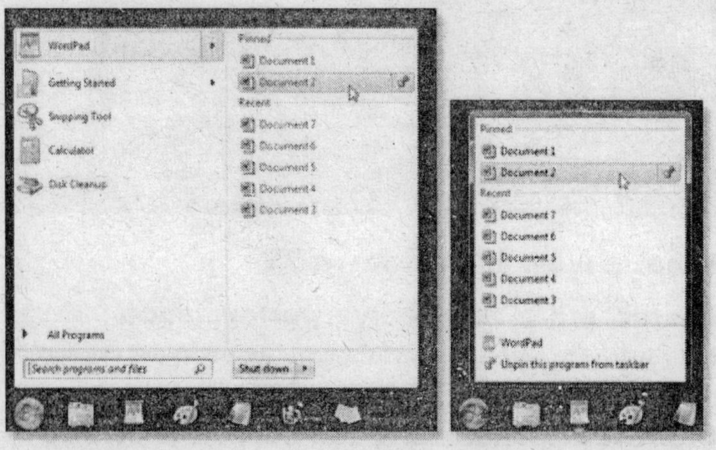

A leap in efficiency: Jump Lists provide quick access to common files and tasks

Find more things faster with improved search

Thanks to an improved search, you can find more things in more places—and do it faster—than in previous versions of Windows. Just type a few letters into the search box to see a list of relevant items, such as documents, pictures, music, and e mail. Search results are grouped by category and contain highlighted keywords to make them easy to scan.

Few people store all their files in one place anymore. Windows 7 is designed to search external hard drives, PCs on a network, and other locations. It also speeds up your search by displaying recommendations based on previous queries. Overwhelmed by the results? New dynamic filters can instantly narrow results by categories such as date or file type.

Easier ways to work with windows

Windows 7 simplifies how you work with the windows on your desktop. You have more intuitive ways to open, close, resize, and arrange them.

Maximize a window by dragging its border to the top of the screen, and return the window to its original size by dragging it away from the top of the screen. Drag the bottom border of a window to expand it vertically. To compare the contents of two windows, drag the windows to opposite sides of the screen. Each window will resize to fill half of the screen.

To see all of your desktop gadgets, drag your mouse to the lower-right corner of your desktop. The open windows will turn transparent, making your desktop, and the gadgets on it, immediately visible. Want to minimize all open windows? One click and it's done. If you've moved your taskbar, you can drag your mouse to a different corner of the desktop to make open windows transparent. It's a Snap: Dragging a window to the desktop edge resizes it to fill half of the screen—making it easier to quickly compare two windows.

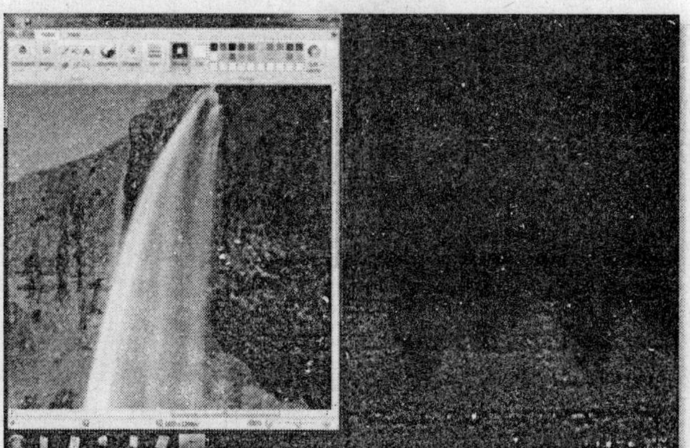

It's a Snap: Dragging a window to the desktop edge resizes it to fill half of the screen—making it easier to quickly compare two windows.

Better device management

Devices and Printers

In the past, you had to go to different places in Windows to manage different types of devices. In Windows 7, there's a single Devices and Printers location for connecting, managing, and using your printers, phones, and other devices. From here, you can interact with your devices, browse files, and manage settings. When you connect devices to your PC, you'll be up and running in just a few clicks.

Device Stage

Device Stage helps you manage cell phones, cameras, printers, MP3 players, and other devices connected to

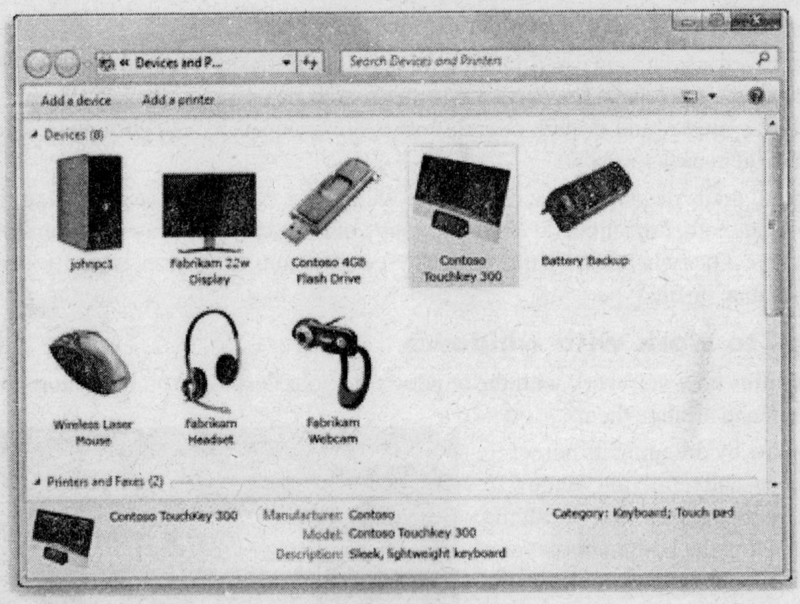

All together now: See all your devices in one place in Devices and Printers.

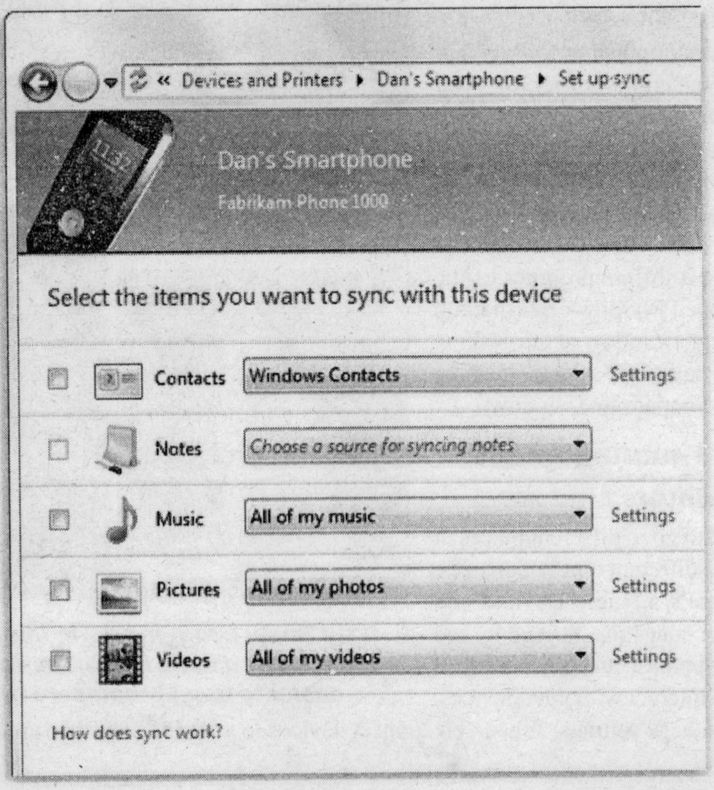

Center stage: The new Device Stage feature puts your favorite devices in the spotlight, making it easier to see status and perform common tasks.

By design: New themes and Windows backgrounds (shown above) give your desktop a personal touch.

your computer. When you plug in a compatible device, you'll see its status and a list of popular tasks. You'll even see a picture of your device.

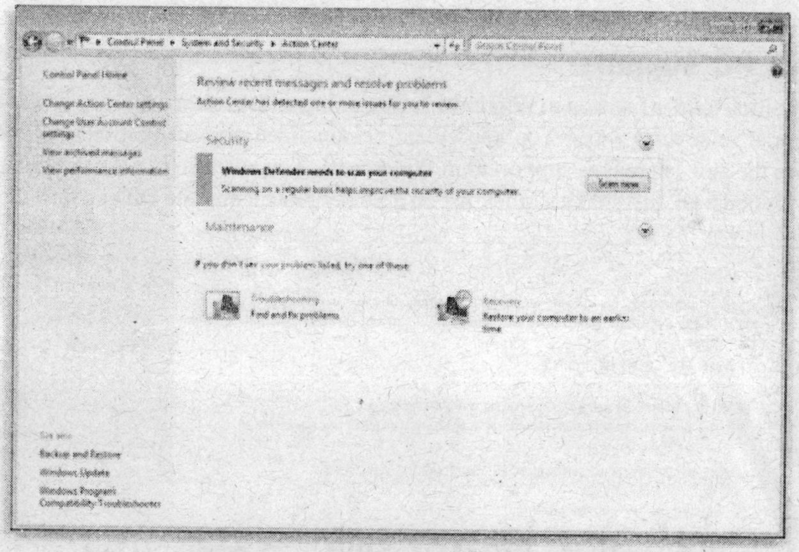

Bringing it together: Action Center cuts down on distracting pop-up messages by consolidating system notifications.

Windows HomeGroup

Windows HomeGroup makes it easier to connect to other computers running Windows 7 so you can share files, photos, music, and printers throughout your home. You choose what to share with other members of your homegroup.

Theme packages reflect your style

With Windows 7, you start with a clean desktop and get to decide how it looks. We provide the templates, or themes, and you can choose the color or format.

New theme packages include rich backgrounds, 16 window colors, sound schemes, and screen savers. You can download new themes and create your own to share with friends and family. There are plenty of ways to make it yours.

Take control of problems

In Windows 7 you get to choose the messages you want to see. Action Center consolidates notifications from multiple Windows features, including Windows Defender. When Windows 7 needs your attention, you'll see an Action Center icon in the notification area and can find out more by clicking it. No time to look at the alert right away? Action Center will keep the information for you to check later.

Share music and videos

After your pictures, videos, and music are all on your computer, it's natural to want to share them with other computers in your home. Windows 7 introduces new media sharing and streaming features that make your PC a great home entertainment hub. HomeGroup makes it easy to share music, pictures, and video with other computers running Windows 7.

With another new feature called "Play to," you can play your digital media on other devices in your home.

Introducing Windows Touch

Using a keyboard and mouse are great for many tasks, but they aren't always the easiest way to do things. If you've got a touchscreen, you can just touch your computer screen for a more direct and natural way to work. Use your fingers to scroll and zoom. Large touch-sensitive areas on the Start menu and the taskbar make Windows Touch easier to use.

Better Tablet PC support

Handwriting recognition takes a big step in Windows 7. Beginning with greater accuracy and speed, Windows 7 improves pen input in several ways. You can create personalized custom dictionaries for handwriting recognition and use the new languages supported in Windows 7. You can also use the new Math Input Panel to write math expressions. Or, just make a quick list on a Sticky Note using the tablet pen.

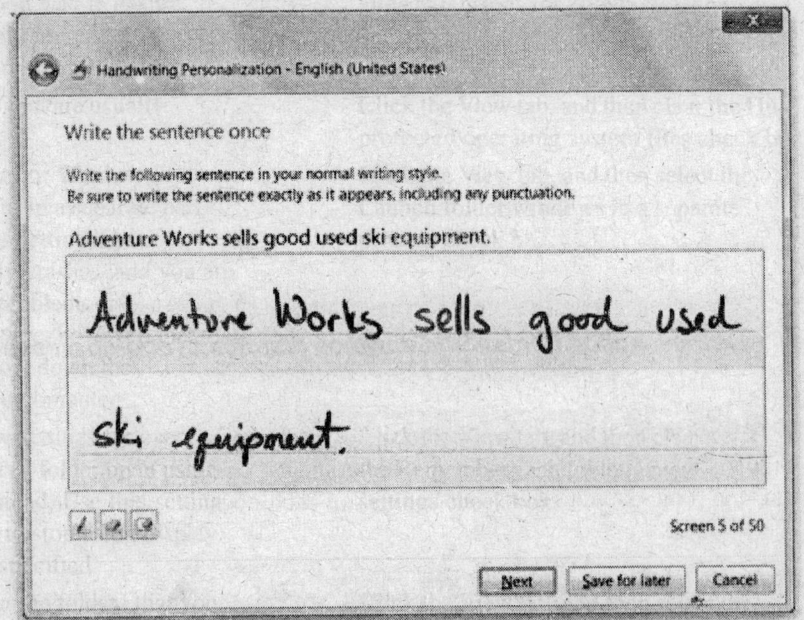

Just write it down: Handwriting recognition in Windows 7 is more accurate.

2 Desktop of Windows 7

Introduction

The desktop is the main screen area that you see after you turn on your computer and log on to Windows. Like the top of an actual desk, it serves as a surface for your work. When you open programs or folders, they appear on the desktop. You can also put things on the desktop, such as files and folders, and arrange them however you want.

The desktop is sometimes defined more broadly to include the taskbar. The taskbar sits at the bottom of your screen. It shows you which programs are running and allows you to switch between them. It also contains the Start button , which you can use to access programs, folders, and computer settings.

Working with desktop icons

Icons are small pictures that represent files, folders, programs, and other items. When you first start Windows, you'll see at least one icon on your desktop: The Recycle Bin (more on that later). Your computer manufacturer might have added other icons to the desktop.

Taskbar

Adding and removing icons from the desktop

You can choose which icons appear on the desktop—you can add or remove an icon at any time. Some people like a clean, uncluttered desktop with few or no icons. Others place dozens of icons on their desktop to give them quick access to frequently used programs, files, and folders.

If you want easy access from the desktop to your favorite files or programs, you can create shortcuts to them. A shortcut is an icon that represents a link to an item, rather than the item itself. When you double-click a shortcut, the item opens. If you delete a shortcut, only the shortcut is removed, not the original item. You can identify shortcuts by the arrow on their icon.

To add a shortcut to the desktop

Supposing you have a program loaded into the computer and you are quite often using it. So you would like to have a shortcut for it. For example, I use **PageMaker**, quite often, so I have created a shortcut for this and it is available on the desktop.

Supposing you are using a program called **Paint** quite often during your use of the computer. You would like to create a shortcut for it. Lets see how it is created. For this you follow the steps here.

1. Minimize all your opened programs.
2. Click at the right button of the mouse on the desktop to get a menu, as shown here.
3. Click at **New** to get the new menu, as shown. Click at **Shortcut** to create one.

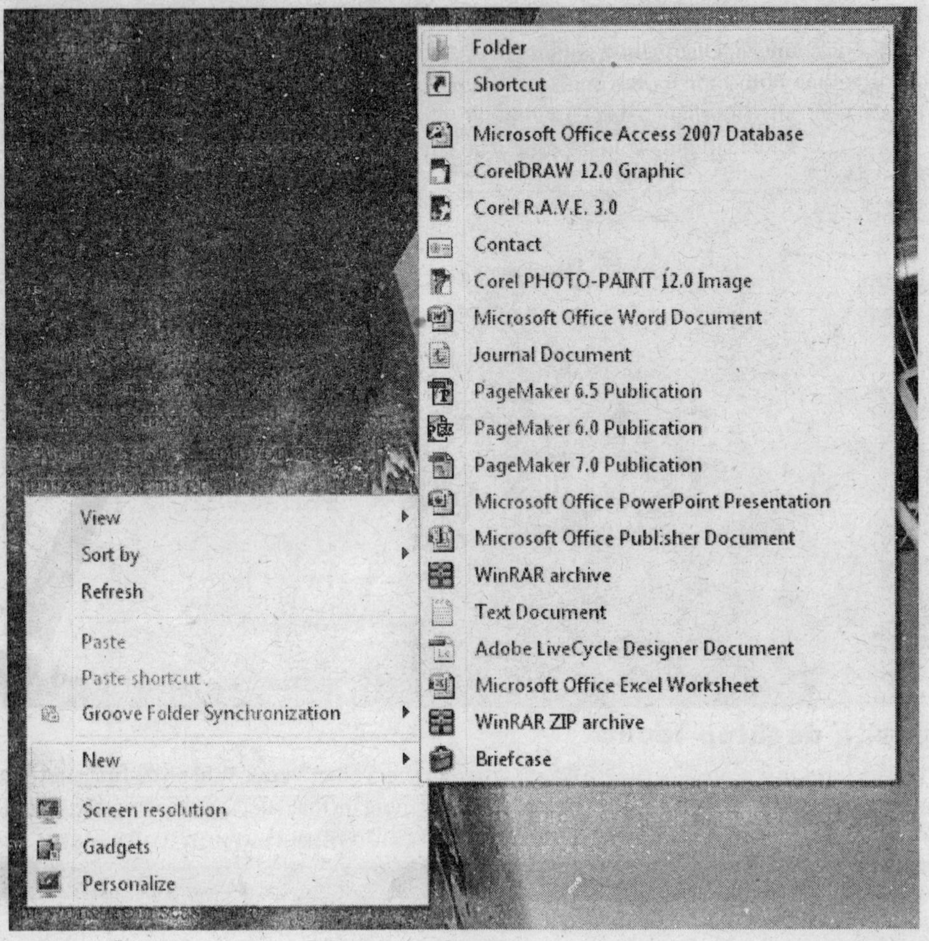

4. This will give rise to a dialog box, as shown. Side by side, you will notice that it has created a new folder with **New Shortcut** as the name.
5. Click at the browse button to locate the file associated with the new shortcut. In our case it will be **Paint** or **Paintbrush**. In this case, as the picture shows that the file is available in the Windows folder under the name **mspaint.exe**.

   Once selected it will be filled up in the File name column. Click it to open it. This will lead us back to the main dialog box of **Create Shortcut**.

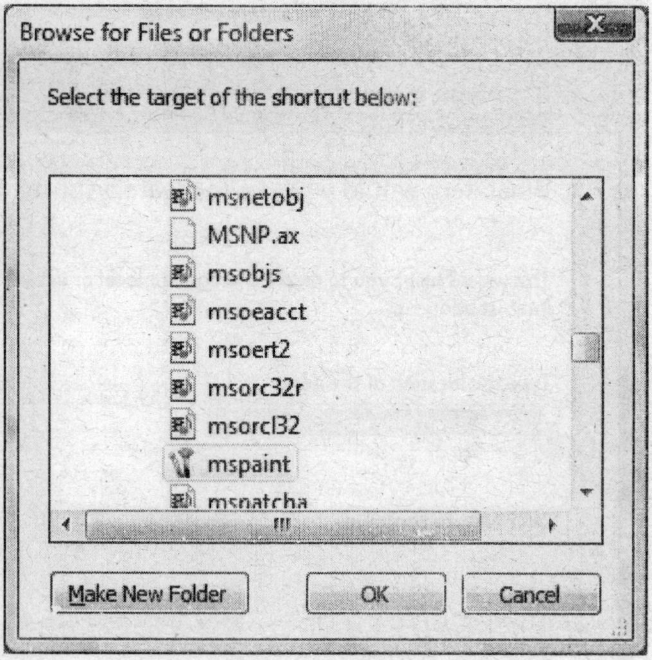

6. You will now see that the command line has been filled up with the exact location of the file which is to be Run for launching of this shortcut from the desktop.
7. Click at **Next** to get the next dialog box. This will ask you fill up the name you want to give to the shortcut. Here we have given it as **PAINT**.
8. Clicking at **Finish** will end the procedure to create the shortcut. Once done, it will create a new shortcut named **PAINT**on the desktop. You can now use it to launch Paint.
9. This can be seen on the next page.

To add or remove common desktop icons

Common desktop icons include Computer, your personal folder, the Recycle Bin, and Control Panel.

Right-click an empty area of the desktop, and then click **Personalize.**

In the left pane, click **Change desktop icons.**

Under Desktop icons, select the check box for each icon that you want to add to the desktop, or clear the check box for each icon that you want to remove from the desktop, and then click OK.

To move a file from a folder to the desktop

1. Open the folder that contains the file.
2. Drag the file to the desktop.
3. To remove an icon from the desktop
   - Right-click the icon, and then click Delete. If the icon is a shortcut, only the shortcut is removed; the original item is not deleted.

Moving icons around

Windows stacks icons in columns on the left side of the desktop. But you're not stuck with that arrangement. You can move an icon by dragging it to a new place on the desktop.

You can also have Windows automatically arrange your icons. Right-click an empty area of the desktop, click View, and then click Auto arrange icons. Windows stacks your icons in the upper-left corner and locks them in place. To unlock the icons so that you can move them again, click Auto arrange icons again, clearing the check mark next to it.

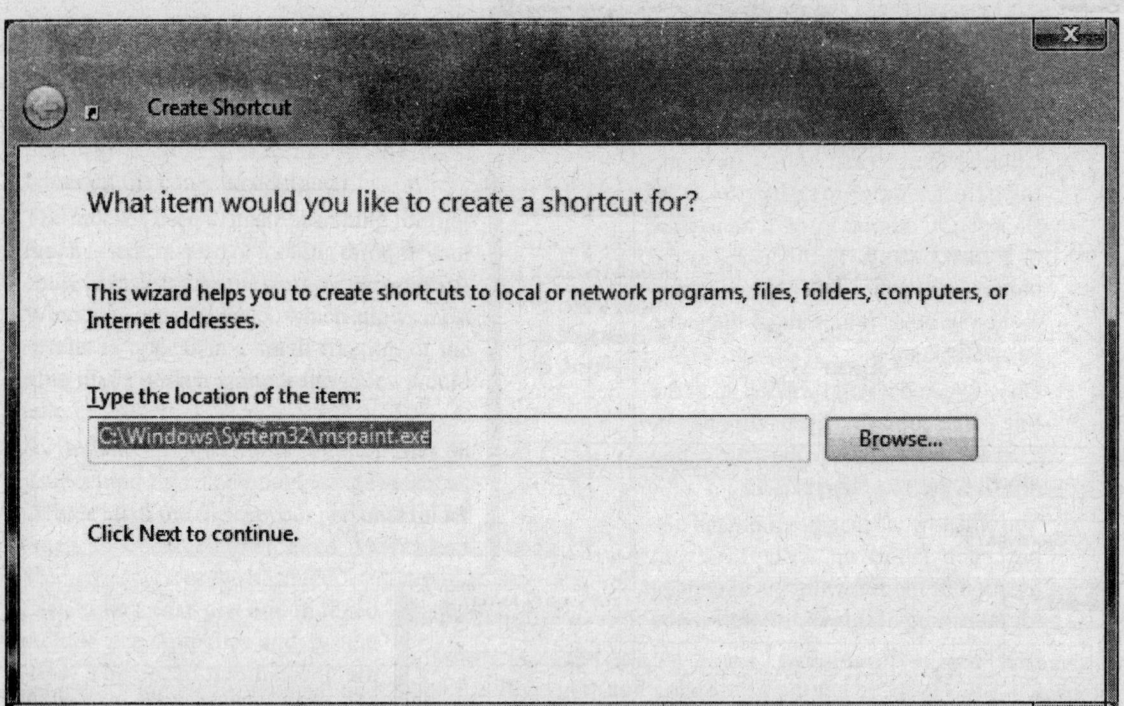
Create Shortcut
What item would you like to create a shortcut for?
This wizard helps you to create shortcuts to local or network programs, files, folders, computers, or Internet addresses.
Type the location of the item:
C:\Windows\System32\mspaint.exe
Browse...
Click Next to continue.

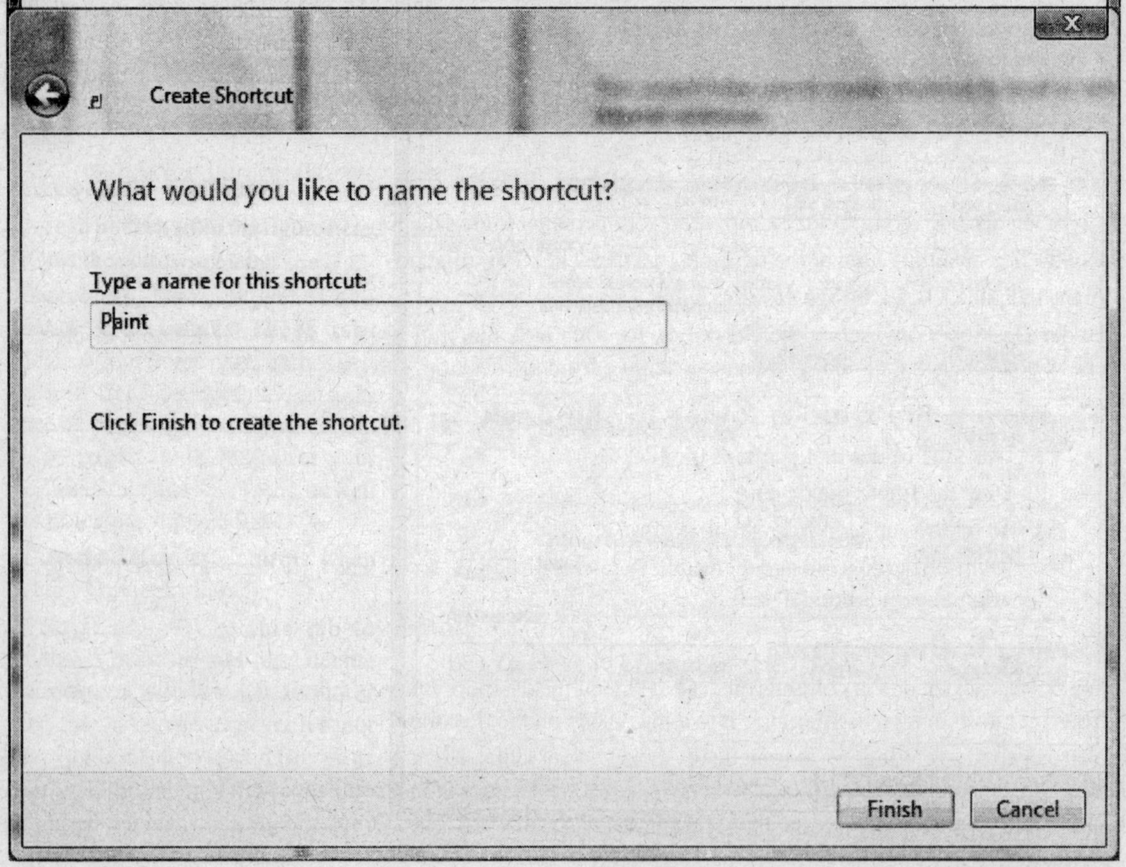
Create Shortcut
What would you like to name the shortcut?
Type a name for this shortcut:
Paint
Click Finish to create the shortcut.
Finish
Cancel

- By default, Windows spaces icons evenly on an invisible grid. To place icons closer together or with more precision, turn off the grid. Right-click an empty area of the desktop, point to View, and then click Align icons to grid to clear the check mark. Repeat these steps to turn the grid back on.

Selecting multiple icons

To move or delete a bunch of icons at once, you must first select all of them. Click an empty area of the desktop and drag the mouse. Surround the icons that you want to select with the rectangle that appears. Then release the mouse button. Now you can drag the icons as a group or delete them.

Select multiple desktop icons by dragging a rectangle around them

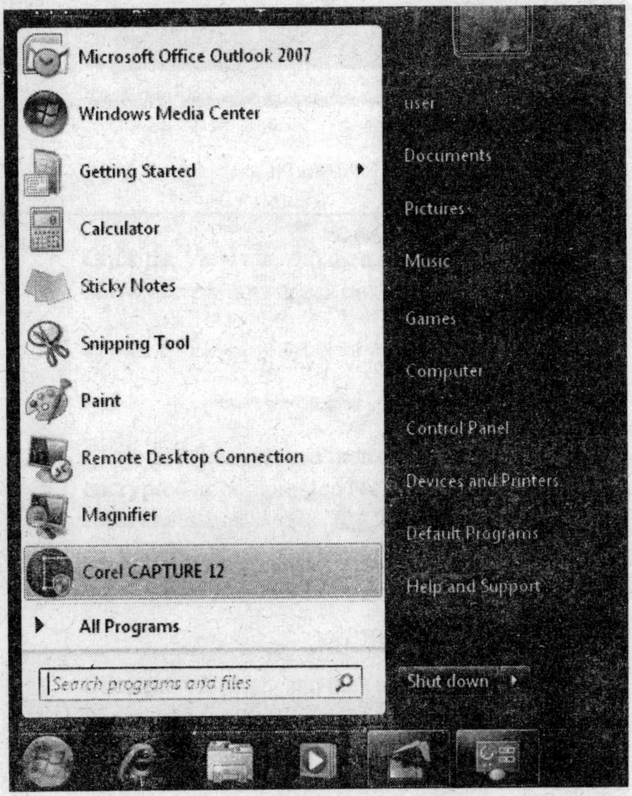

Hiding desktop icons

If you want to temporarily hide all of your desktop icons without actually removing them, right-click an empty part of the desktop, click View, and then click Show desktop icons to clear the check mark from that option. Now no icons are displayed on the desktop. You can get them back by clicking Show desktop icons again.

Icons on the Desktop

On pressing the Start button, as usual you would see the various programs which can be used by just clicking at them. It gives the recently used programs. On the right hand side are the programs which are always there and can be used anytime. These are: User, Documents, Pictures, Music, Games, Computer, Control Panel, Devices and Printers, Default Programs, and Help and Support.

Let us explore computer among them.

Computer

It helps you browse the contents of your computer, open folders, open documents and run your favourite applications. As shown here, it is divided into 2 sections, Favorite Links and Details. You click at any icon on the right hand side of the dialog box and then choose the option on the left hand side.

Details will give you the detail of the item selected. You can access other places by clicking at any one of them.

On the right hand side, you have the options of the followings:

Name: It gives you the option of sorting the icons by Name or by from A to H and I to Z.

Type: You can choose the type from CD Drive, Local Disk and System Folder and then Stack by Type.

Total Size: You can set the drives according to their size.

Free Space: You can set the drive to show how much space is available in them and list them according to the size, as shown below.

On the top there are buttons like this:

Organize: This allows you to organize the folders and files according to your liking. Like creating a New Folder, Cutting, copying, pasting of folders/files. Other options are shown here.

Views: It gives the option of viewing the folders/files in different views.

System properties: Shows information about your computer, such as the processor speed and the amount of installed memory.

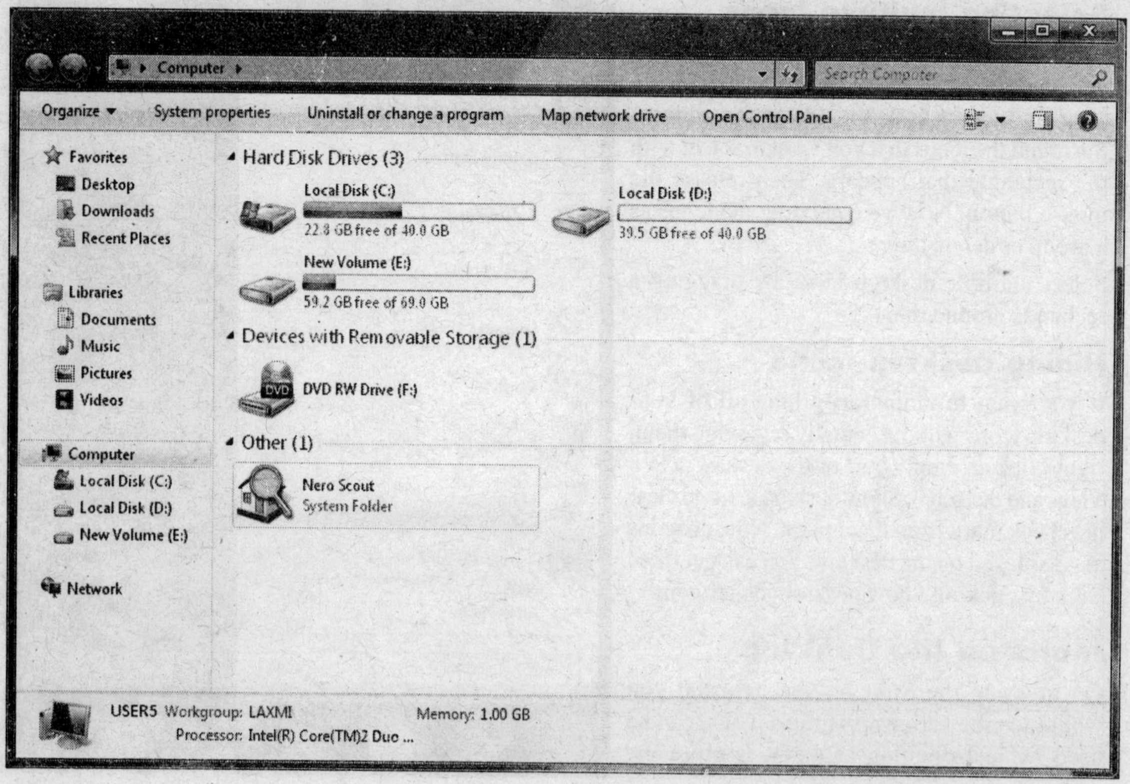

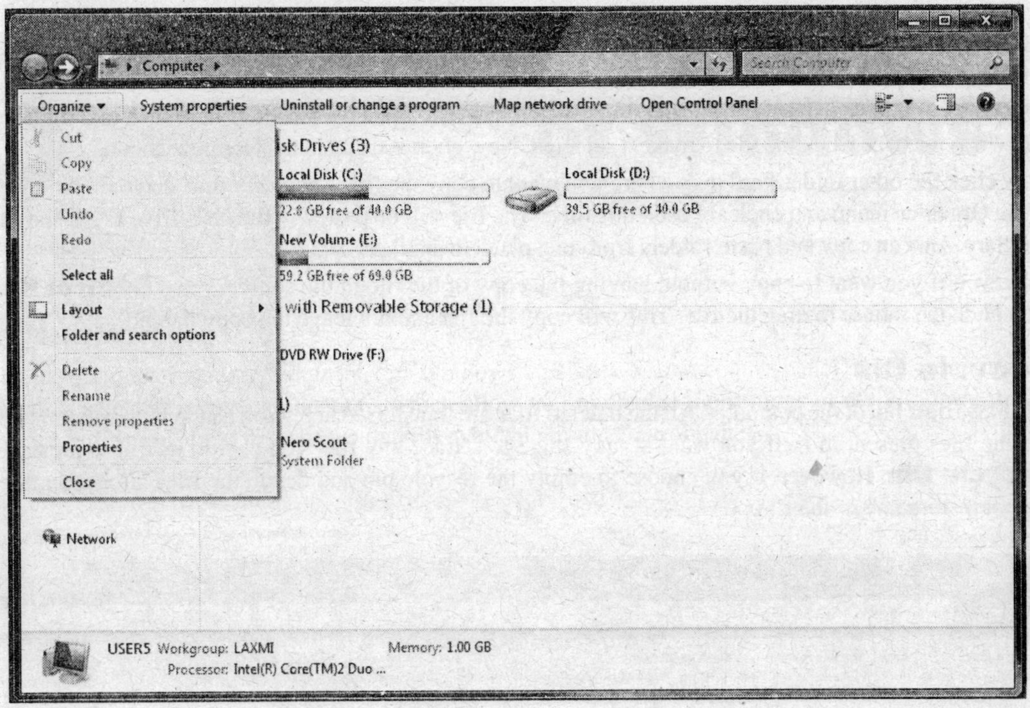

Uninstall or change a program: Allows you to uninstall or change any program in the fixed drive.

Map network drive: It allows you to map a network drive.

Details of the folders available in the hard disk drive C: are shown here.

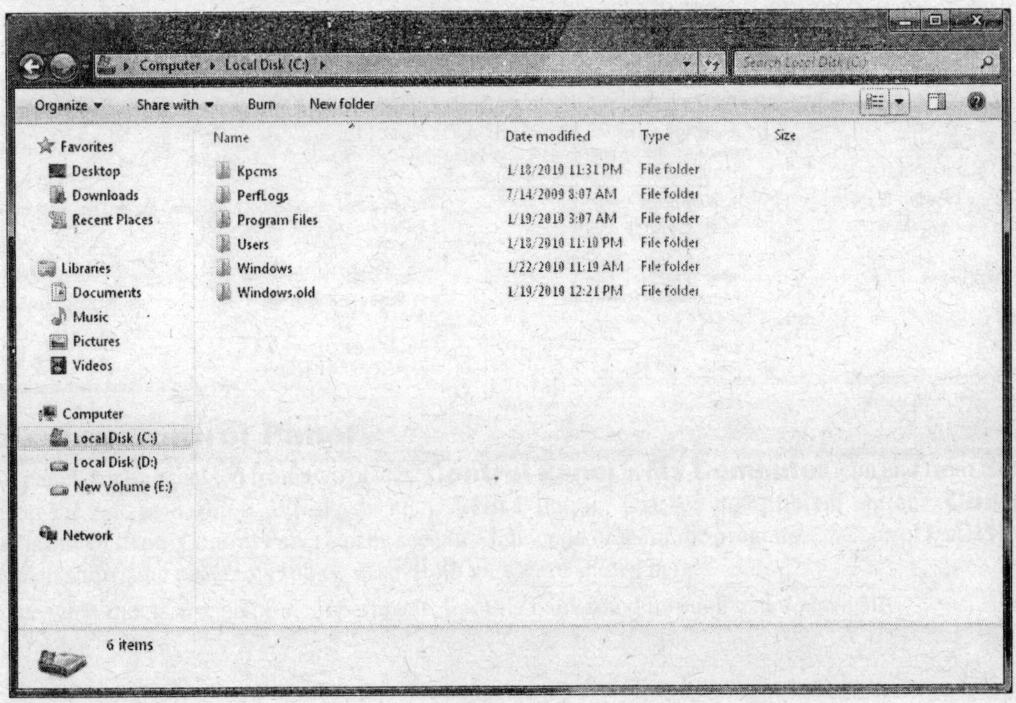

Now let us see how **Computer** is used for working with files.

Copying of Files

Supposing you have to copy a file from one drive to another. Open the folder of hard disk and the particular file where it exists. Click the file to make it selected. Now click at Copy in the Organize menu.

Now click the other folder/hard disk where you want to copy the file. Let us say disk drive F:. Now again go to the Organize menu and click at Paste, this time. The file will be pasted in the disk drive F:, as shown next. Similary you can copy and paste folders from one place to another.

However, if you want to copy without leaving the copy of the file in the source, press **Control Key** and then click the mouse to drag the file. This will copy the file and not leave the copy behind.

Recycle Bin

It is like a dust bin of the computer. All the deleted files are transferred here. You can in fact open this folder to see the files present in it. If you want at any stage to retrace any file, you can do it, if it is present in the **Recycle Bin**. However, if you choose to empty the recycle bin and delete the files altogether, then you cannot restore any of the file.

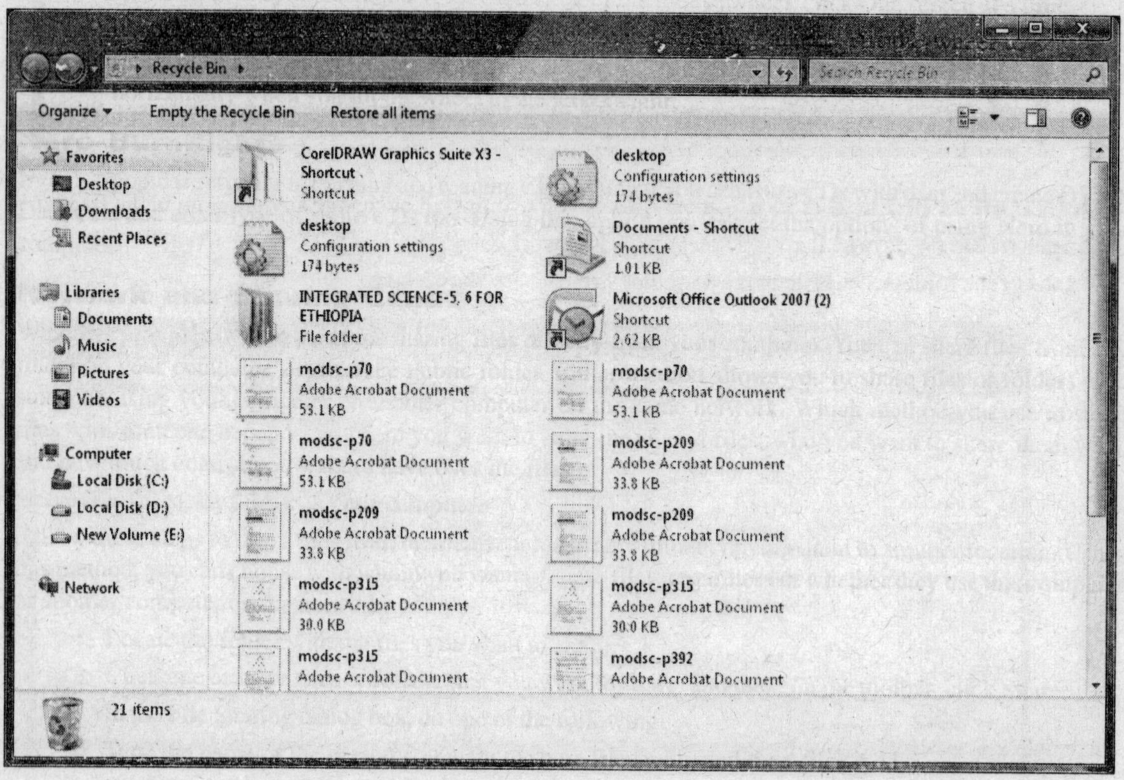

3 Control Panel of Windows 7

Introduction

Like all the earlier versions of Windows, this Windows version too has a control panel. It is a group of icons which when selected invoke applications which allow you to change the settings of the Windows. In this chapter we will study about the various options available in the control panel.

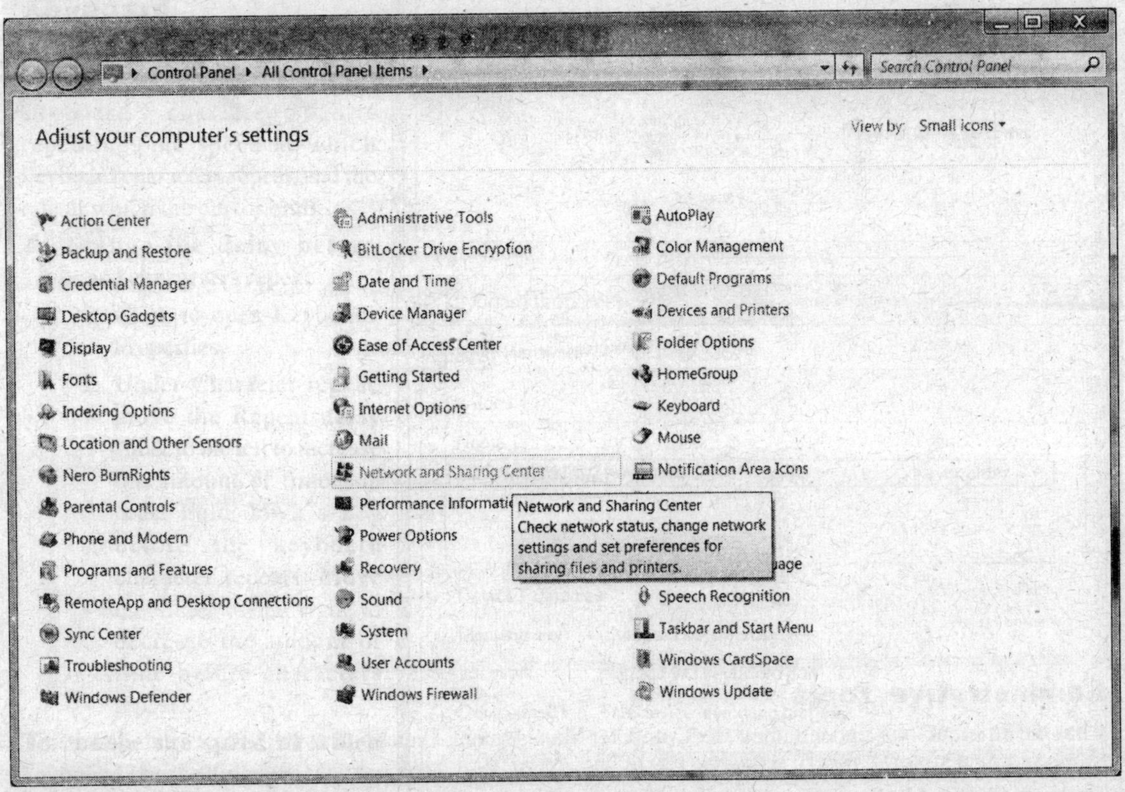

Accessing Control Panel

Control panel can be accessed from two places: **Control Panel** in **My Computer** icon and from **Start** button on the on the desktop. When you click **Start** button, you see the different options. **Control Panel** is one of them. Control Panel can be seen in Alphabetic order of the programs or Control Panel Home view which shows the programs subjec wise. Both views are shown here.

Let us see what function each of them performs. For this I am going through it alphabetically.

Action Center

Windows 7 has a redesigned desktop with many additional customization options. By default, when you log on, the operating sysem displays an Action Center summary Icon in the notification area. This icon has a flag with a red circle with an X in it. Action Center is a program that monitors the status of important security and maintenance areas. If the status of a monitored item changes, Action Center updates the notification icon as appropriate for the severity of the alert.

If you move the mouse pointer over this icon, you see a summary of all alerts. If you click this icon, Windows displays a dialog box with a summary listing of earch alert or action item that needs your attention. Click an alert or action item link to open your default Web browser and display a possible solution. Click the Open Action Center link to display the Action Center..

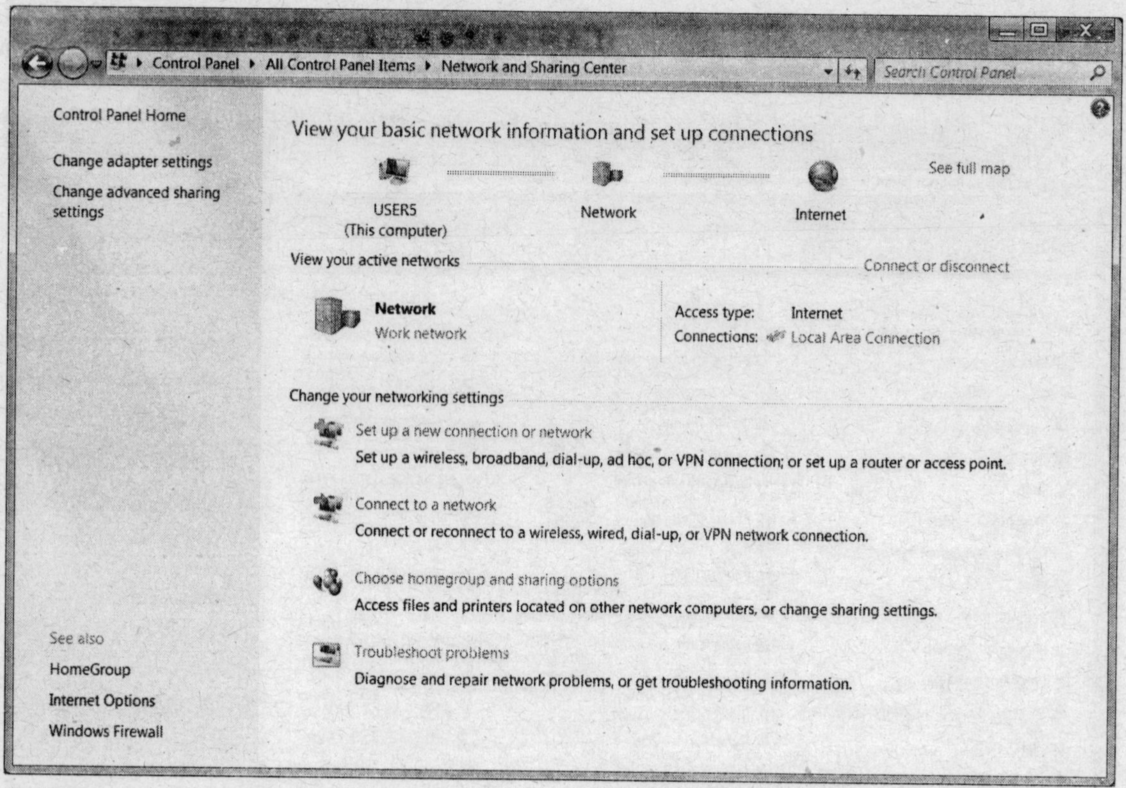

Adminstrative Tools

It has the different tools under it, they are: Computer Management, Data Sources (ODBC), Event Viewer, iSCSI Initiator, Local Security Policy, Memory Diagnostics Tool, Print Management, Reliability and Performance, Services, System Configuration, Task Scheduler and Windows Firewall with Advanced Security. Microsoft Management Console (MMC) hosts and displays administrative tools created by Microsoft and other software vendors. These tools are called snap-ins, and they are used for managing the hardware, software, and network components of Windows. Several of the tools in the Administrative Tools folder, such as Computer Management, are MMC snap-ins.

AutoPlay

AutoPlay, gives you a single place to configure how you would like your CDs and DVDs (and memory cards, flash drives, and cameras) to be run. And you can specify how audio CDs are handled, versus enhanced audio CDs.

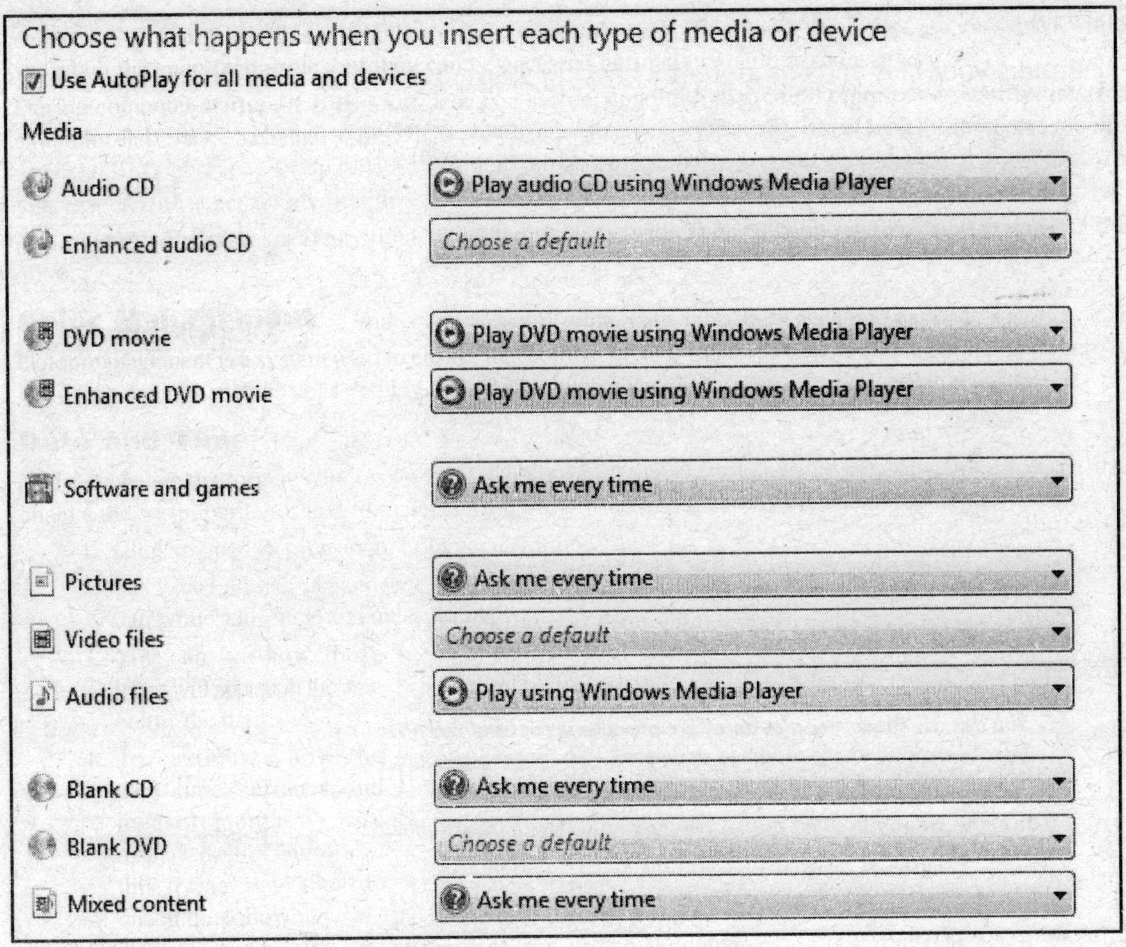

Backup and Restore Centre

Windows 7 provides Backup and Restore Center as a central console for backing up and reovering a computer. You can acces this console by clicking Start, clicking Control Panel and then clicking the Back Up Your Computer link under the System And Security heading. Other tools for backing up and recovering a computer's data include Previous Versions, the Startup Repair tool, Windows Resume Loader, System Restore, and Backup..

BitLocker Drive Encryption

Turning on BitLocker Drive Encryption (BitLocker) protects all files stored on the drive Windows is installed on. Unlike Encrypting File System (EFS), which enables you to encrypt individual files, BitLocker encrypts the entire system drive, including the Windows system files necessary for startup and logon. You can log on and work with your files normally, but BitLocker can help block hackers from accessing the system files they rely on to discover your password, or access your hard disk by removing it from your computer and installing it in a different computer. BitLocker can only help protect files that are stored on the drive that Windows is installed on. If you store files on other drives, you can help protect those files with EFS.

When you add new files to the drive with BitLocker, BitLocker encrypts them automatically. Files remain encrypted only while they are stored in the encrypted drive. Files copied to another drive or computer are

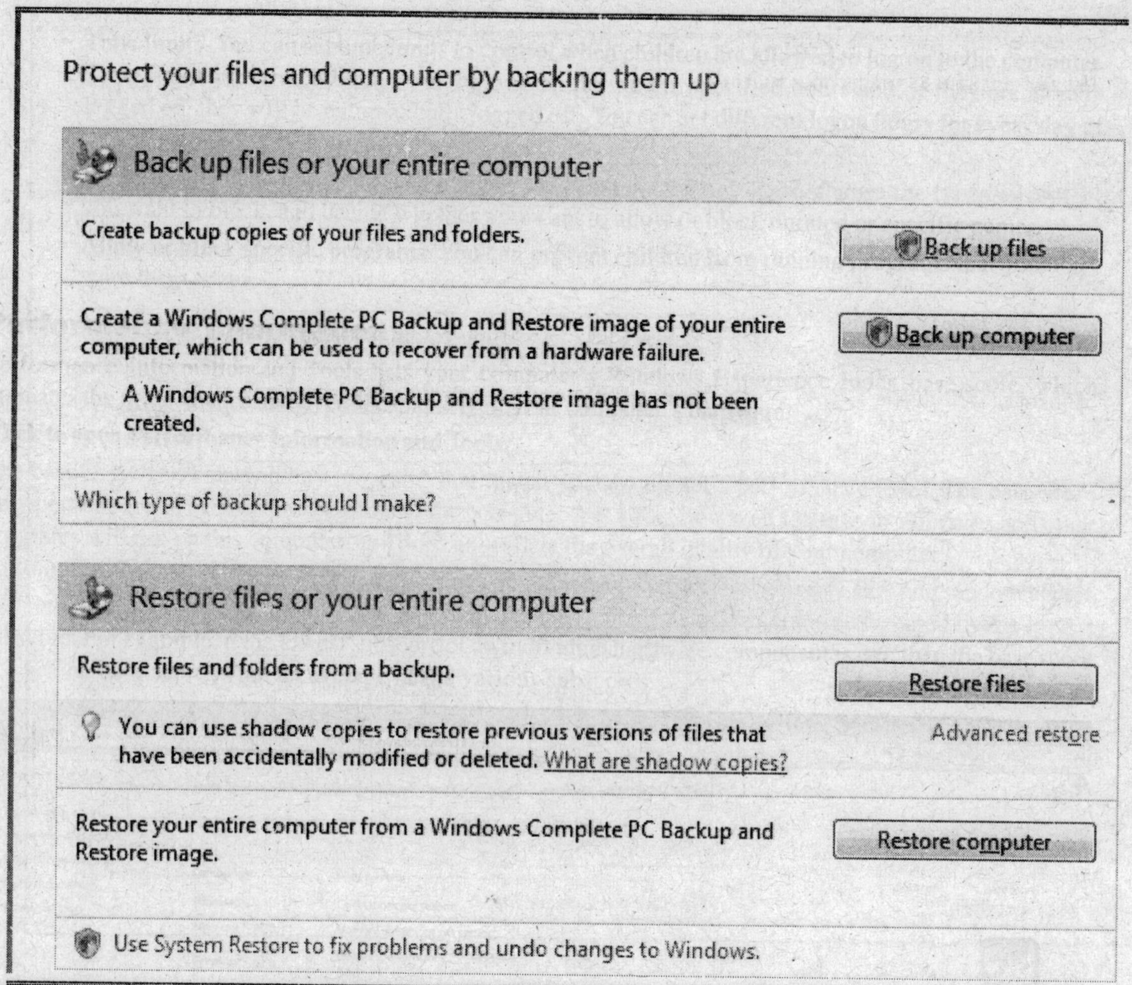

Protect your files and computer by backing them up
Back up files or your entire computer
Create backup copies of your files and folders.
Back up files
Create a Windows Complete PC Backup and Restore image of your entire computer, which can be used to recover from a hardware failure.
Back up computer
A Windows Complete PC Backup and Restore image has not been created.
Which type of backup should I make?
Restore files or your entire computer
Restore files and folders from a backup.
Restore files
You can use shadow copies to restore previous versions of files that have been accidentally modified or deleted. What are shadow copies?
Advanced restore
Restore your entire computer from a Windows Complete PC Backup and Restore image.
Restore computer
Use System Restore to fix problems and undo changes to Windows.

BitLocker Drive Encryption encrypts and protects your data.
BitLocker Drive Encryption helps prevent unauthorized access to any files stored on the volume shown below. You are able to use the computer normally, but unauthorized users cannot read or use your files.
What should I know about BitLocker Drive Encryption before I turn it on?
The drive configuration is unsuitable for BitLocker Drive Encryption. To use BitLocker, please re-partition your hard drive according to the BitLocker requirements.
Set up your hard disk for BitLocker Drive Encryption
A TPM was not found. A TPM is required to turn on BitLocker. If your computer has a TPM, then contact the computer manufacturer for BitLocker-compatible BIOS.
Volumes

decrypted. If you share files with other users, such as through a network, these files are encrypted while stored on the encrypted drive, but they can be accessed normally by authorized users.

During computer startup, if BitLocker detects a system condition that could represent a security risk (for example, disk errors, a change to the BIOS , or changes to any startup files), it will lock the drive and require a special BitLocker recovery password to unlock it. Make sure that you create this recovery password when you turn on BitLocker for the first time; otherwise, you could permanently lose access to your files.

You can turn off BitLocker at any time, either temporarily by disabling it, or permanently by decrypting the drive.

Color Management

Color management is a system used to ensure that color content is rendered to your satisfaction everywhere—including devices such as your display and your printer.

Date and Time

You can change the format Windows uses to display dates, times, currency, and measurements. You can also change the sorting order of text to match sorting rules used in a specific country or region.

1. Click to open Regional and Language Options.
2. Click the Formats tab, and then, in the Current format list, select the locale to use for the display of the date, time, currency, and measurements.
3. You can see how these items will appear in the area below the list.
4. To customize how the date, time, currency, and measurements are displayed, click Customize this format, and then do one of the following:

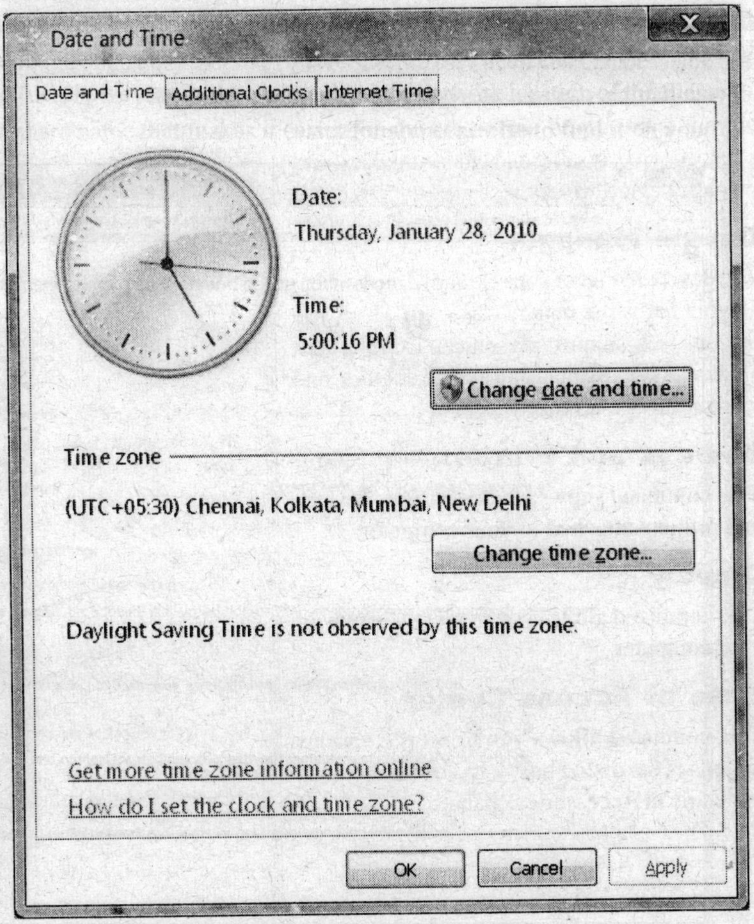

- To change the way your computer displays numbers, click the Numbers tab. Items you might want to change based on the format language you chose are the decimal symbol and list separator, the format used for negative numbers and leading zeros, and the measurement system used (U.S. or metric).
- To change the way your computer displays currency values, click the Currency tab. Items you might want to change based on the format

language you chose are the currency symbol, the formats used for positive or negative amounts, and the punctuation used to separate numbers.

- To change the way your computer displays the time, click the Time tab.
- To change the way your computer displays the date, click the Date tab.

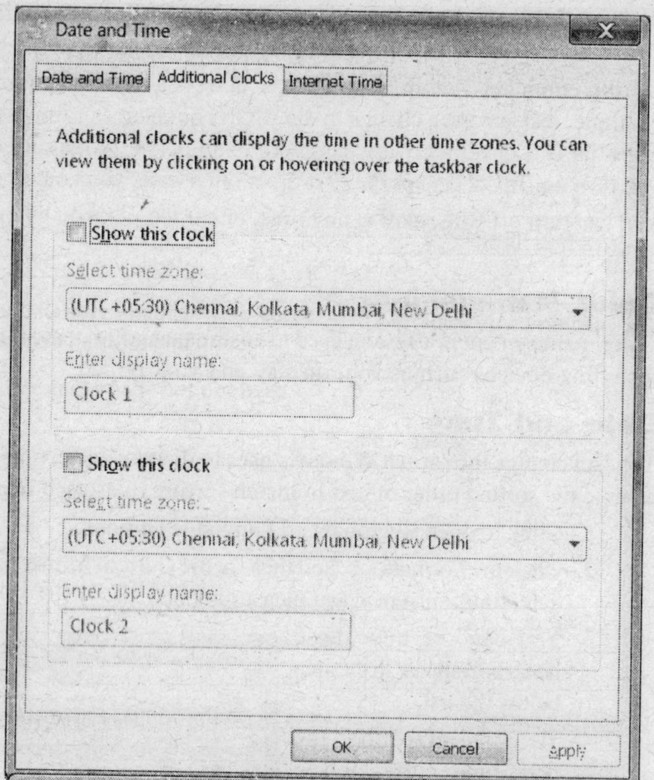

Default Programs

Set Program Access and Computer Defaults makes it easy for you to change the default program used for certain activities, such as web browsing, sending e mail, playing audio and video files, and using instant messaging. You can also specify which of these default programs are displayed on the Start menu, on the desktop, and in other locations.

Desktop Gadgets

The device manager console shows you where all your hardware money was spent. Here, you or your tech-support person can troubleshoot a flaky device, disable and enable devices, and manage device drivers.

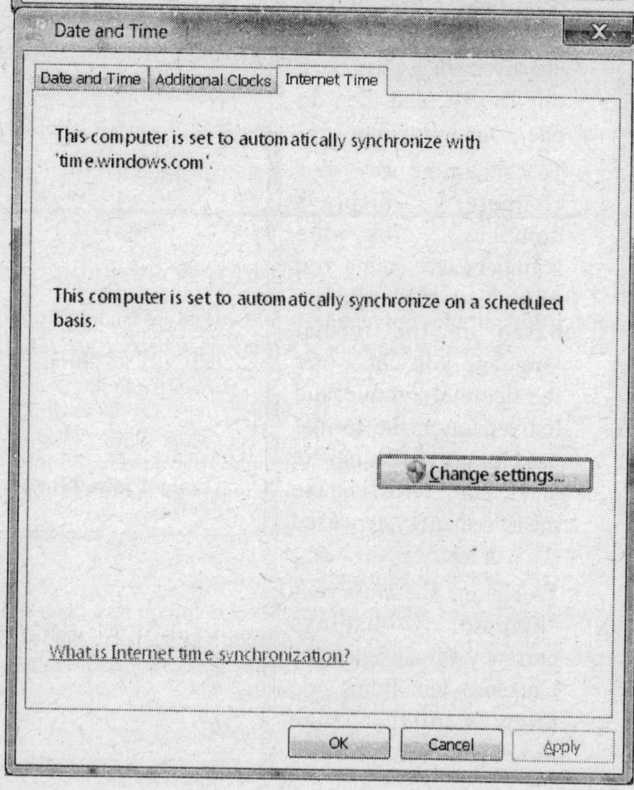

Device Manager

The device manager console shows you where all your hardware money was spent. Here, you or your tech-support person can troubleshoot a flaky device, disable and enable devices, and manage device drivers.

Devices and Printers

This command shows you the various devices and printers attached to your computer.

Display

This command allows you to set the display of your computer.

Ease of Access Center

This command allows you to set the various options of the dialog box. It has been discussed in details in Accessories chapter.

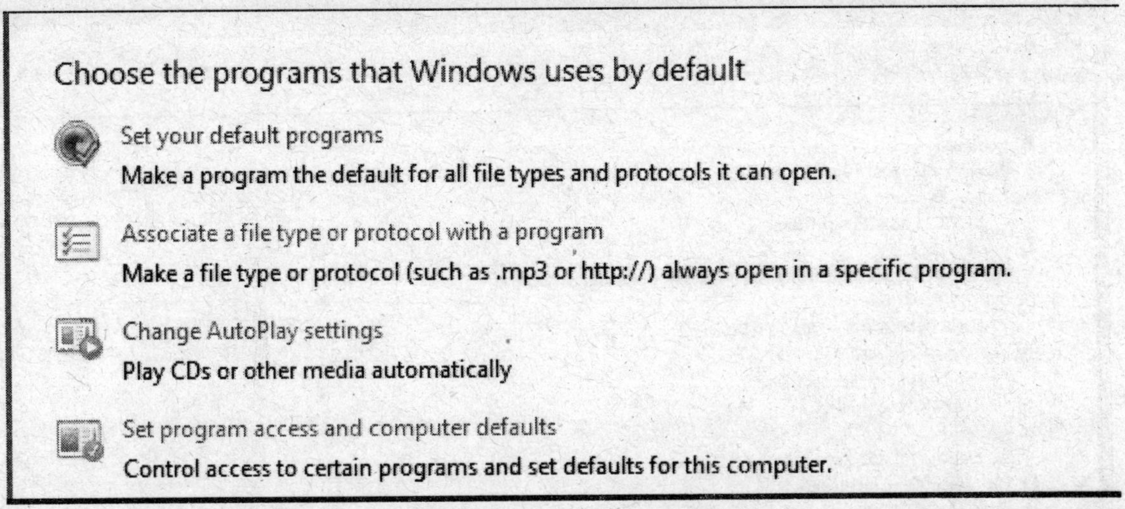

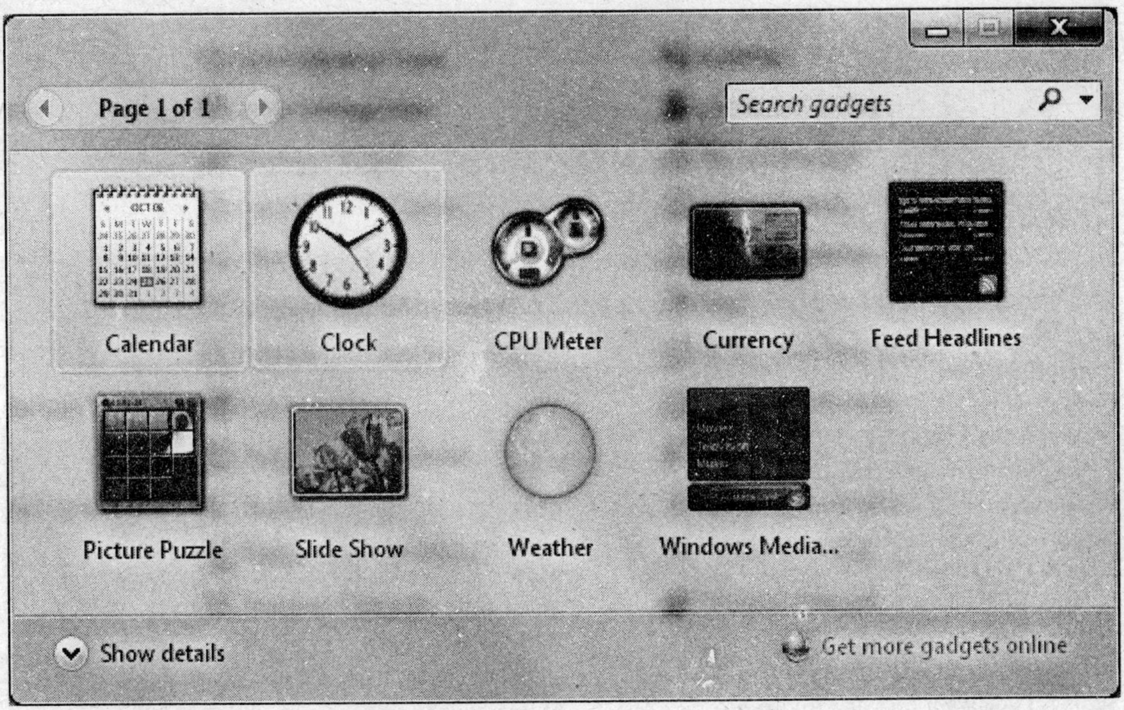

Folder Options

Using Folder Options in Control Panel, you can change the way your files and folders function, as well as how the content in your folders is displayed.

Click to open Folder Options.

Change the way folders are displayed

You can change the way your folders look and work to suit your needs. For example, you can open all files and folders with one click (like links in a webpage) instead of the usual double-click. Here is an overview of the settings you can change:

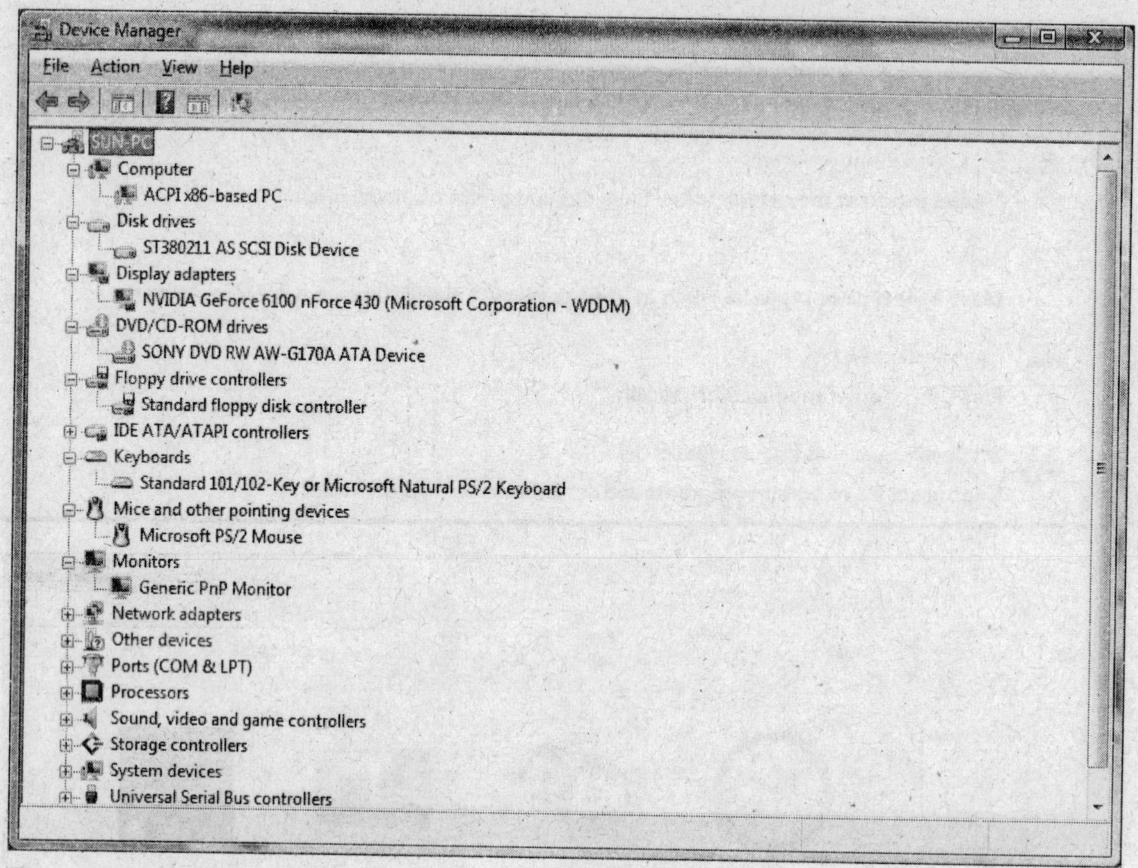

To	*Do this*
Turn off the Details pane and the Preview pane in all folders. This setting gives you more room to display files by hiding panes you might not need.	Click the General tab, and then click Use Windows classic folders. (To turn the panes back on, click Show preview and filters.)
Open every new folder in its own folder window. This can be convenient if you want to keep all the folders you are working with on the screen at the same time.	Click the General tab, and then click Open each folder in its own window. (To make each new folder replace the previous folder window, click Open each folder in the same window.)
Open an item with a single click. Use this setting if you want files and folders to open with one click, just like links in a webpage.	Click the General tab, and then click Single-click to open an item. (To switch back to the standard double-click, click Double-click to open an item.)

Change advanced file and folder settings

You can make additional changes to the appearance and behavior of your files and folders by using the advanced settings of Folder Options in Control Panel. Here is an overview of the advanced settings that you can change:

To	*Do this*
Always show static icons of files and	Click the View tab, and then select the

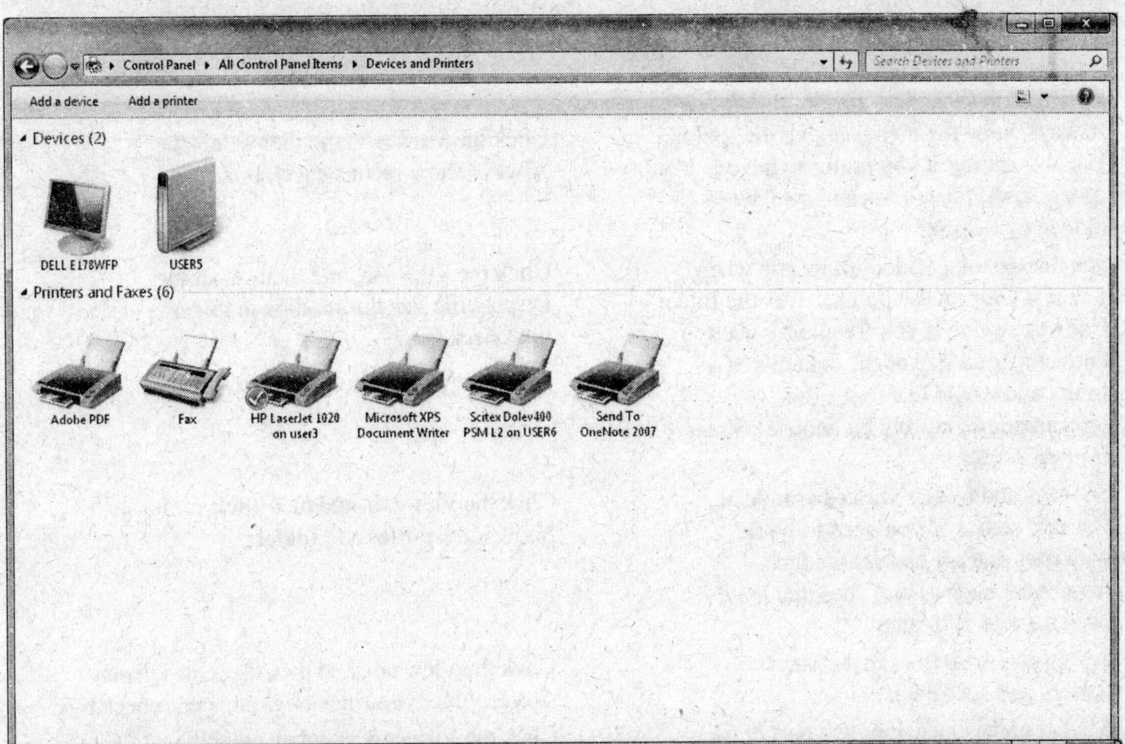
Control Panel ▸ All Control Panel Items ▸ Devices and Printers
Search Devices and Printers
Add a device
Add a printer
Devices (2)
DELL E178WFP
USER5
Printers and Faxes (6)
Adobe PDF
Fax
HP LaserJet 1020 on user3
Microsoft XPS Document Writer
Scitex Dolev400 PSM L2 on USER6
Send To OneNote 2007

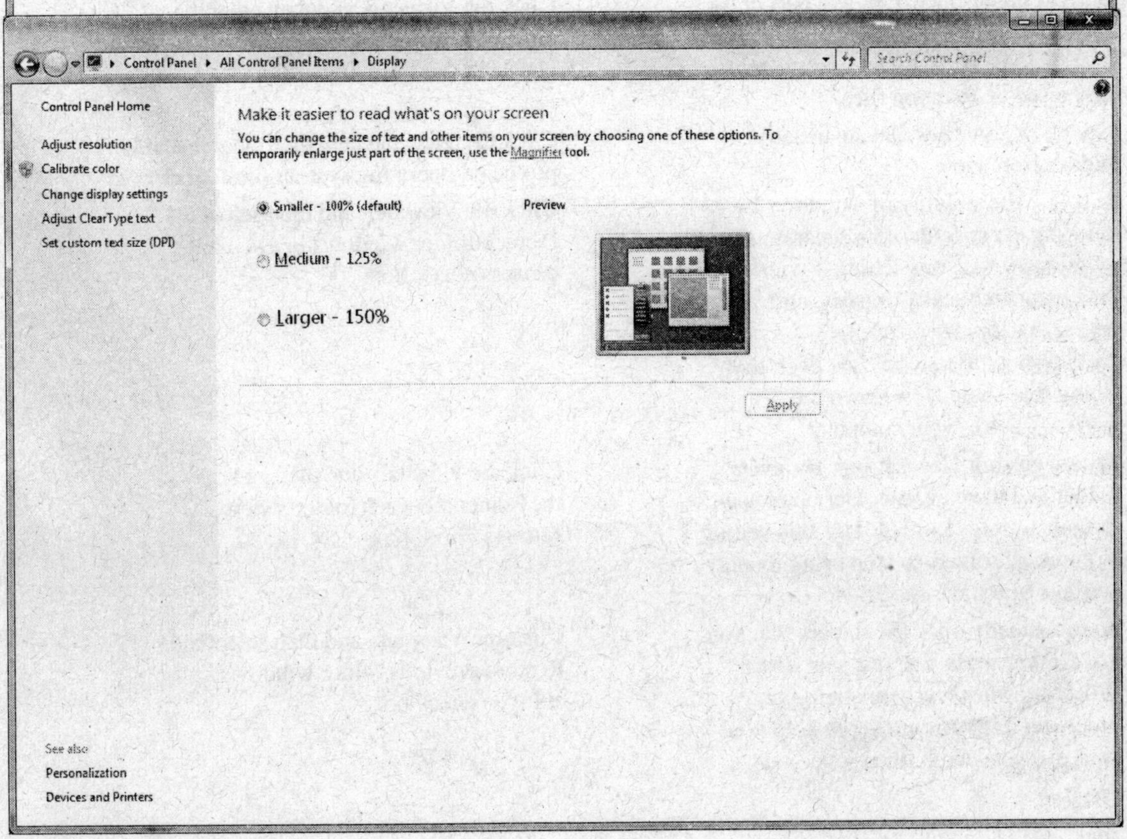
Control Panel ▸ All Control Panel Items ▸ Display
Search Control Panel
Control Panel Home
Adjust resolution
Calibrate color
Change display settings
Adjust ClearType text
Set custom text size (DPI)
Make it easier to read what's on your screen
You can change the size of text and other items on your screen by choosing one of these options. To temporarily enlarge just part of the screen, use the Magnifier tool.
Smaller - 100% (default)
Preview
Medium - 125%
Larger - 150%
Apply
See also
Personalization
Devices and Printers

never show thumbnail previews of files. Use this setting if the thumbnail previews are slowing down your computer. You'll get better performance by using static icons.	Always show icons, never thumbnails check box.
Always show the menus above the toolbar. Use this setting if you prefer to have access to the Classic menus, which are hidden by default.	Click the View tab, and then select the Always show menus check box.
See the size of a folder in a tooltip when you rest your mouse pointer over the folder. Use this setting if you frequently need to know the total size of the contents of a folder and would like to see this information by resting the mouse pointer over the folder.	Click the View tab, and then select the Display file size information in folder tips check box.
See files and folders marked as hidden. Use this setting if you need to work with files that are usually hidden from view, such as user files that have been marked as hidden.	Click the View tab, and then click Show hidden files and folders.
See folders with lines that connect folders and subfolders.	Click the View tab, and then clear the Display simple folder view in Navigation pane check box.
See file name extensions as a part of file names. This is a good way to ensure that files are not malicious software disguised as common files.	Click the View tab, and then clear the Hide extensions for known file types check box.
See all system files that are usually hidden from view.	Click the View tab, and then clear the Hide protected operating system files check box.
Increase the stability of Windows by opening every folder in a separate part of memory. Use this setting if your computer frequently crashes, and you are trying to minimize problems or troubleshoot. Be aware, however, that doing this could slow down the performance of your computer.	Click the View tab, and then select the Launch folder windows in a separate process check box.
Ignore custom view settings for every folder and have every folder open using default settings instead. Use this setting to force all folders to stop using display settings you have specified.	Click the View tab, and then clear the Remember each folder's view settings check box.
Automatically open the folders that you were using when you last shut down Windows whenever you start your computer. Use this setting to help you preserve your work from session to session.	Click the View tab, and then select the Restore previous folder windows at logon check box.

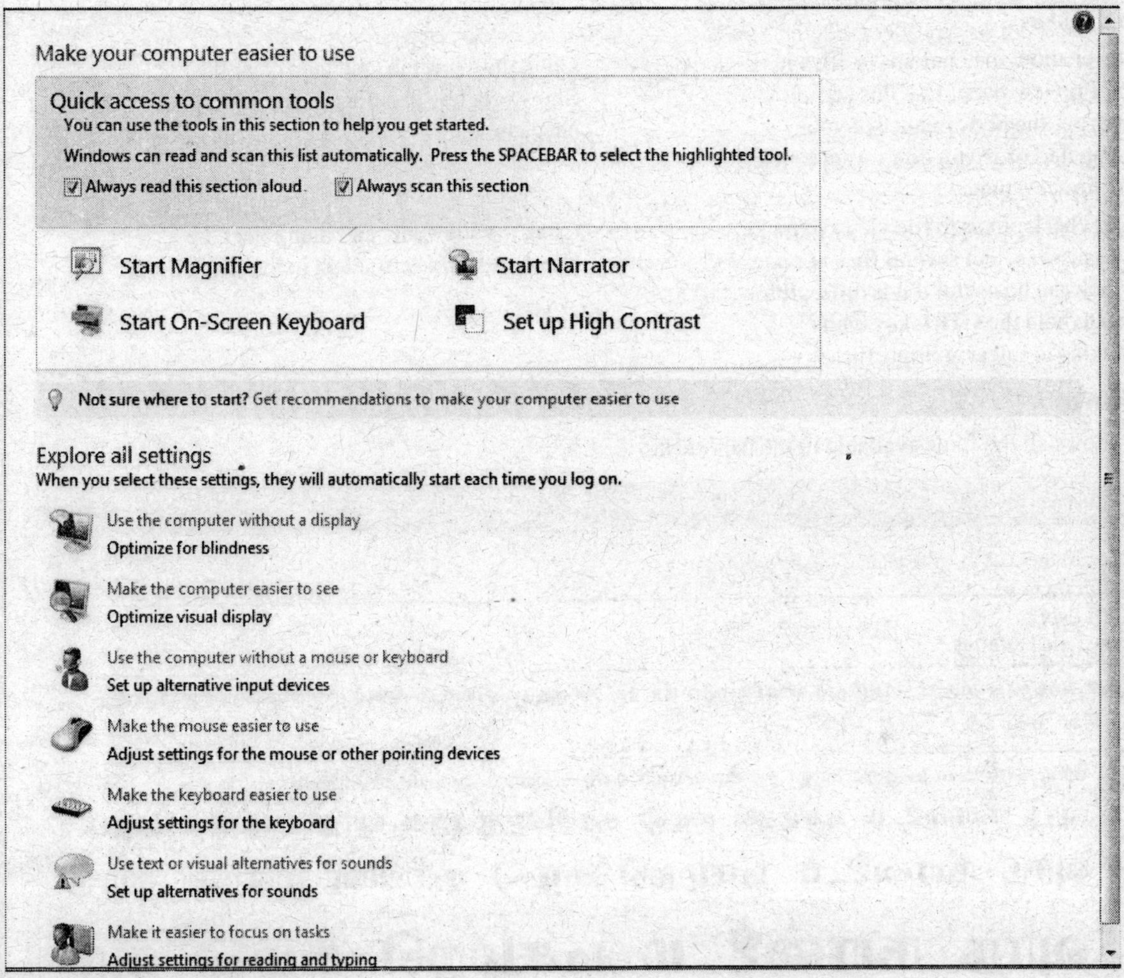

Hide the drive letter of each drive or device in the Computer folder. Use this setting if you don't want to see drive letters displayed on your computer and prefer to see only the friendly name of each drive.	Click the View tab, and then clear the Show drive letters check box.
Display encrypted or compressed NTFS files as ordinary files, without any unique color coding to identify them. Use this setting if you have encrypted or compressed NTFS files and do not want to see them represented differently than other files on your computer.	Click the View tab, and then clear the Show encrypted or compressed NTFS files in color check box.
Turn off the tooltips that appear when you rest your mouse pointer over files. Use this setting if you don't want to see the file information that appears in tooltips	Click the View tab, and then clear the Show pop-up descriptions for folder and desktop items check box.

when you rest the pointer over files and folders.	
Never show the contents of files in the Preview pane. Use this setting to improve the performance of your computer, or if you don't want to use the Preview pane.	Click the View tab, and then clear the Show preview handlers in preview pane check box.
Add check boxes to file views to make it easier to select several files at once, which can be useful if it is difficult for you to hold the CTRL key while clicking to select multiple files.	Click the View tab, and then select the Use check boxes to select items check box.

Fonts

It shows all the fonts available in the hard disk.

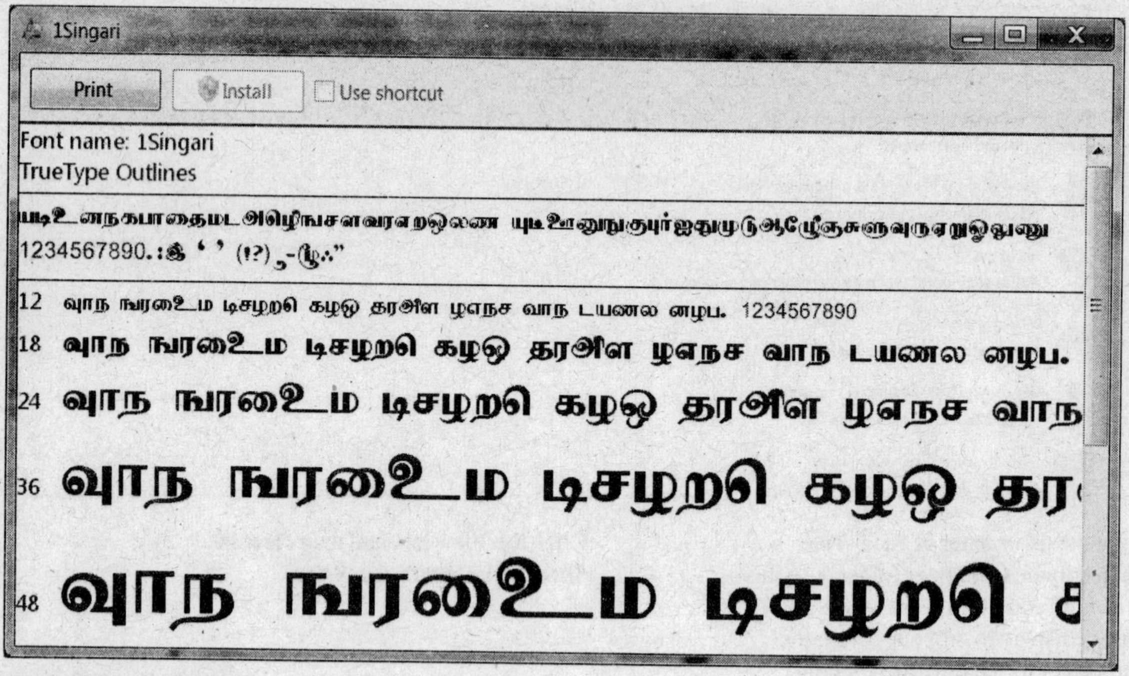

Getting Started

If you are new to Windows, then this is for you. From here you can work your way out to the various features of the software.

HomeGroup

Using this command you can share with other home computers running Windows 7. With homegroup, you can share files and printers with other computers running Windows 7. You can also stream media to devices. The homegroup is protected with a password, and you will always be able to choose what you share with the group.

Indexing Options

Similar to the way the index in a book helps you to keep track of its contents, the index in Windows keeps track

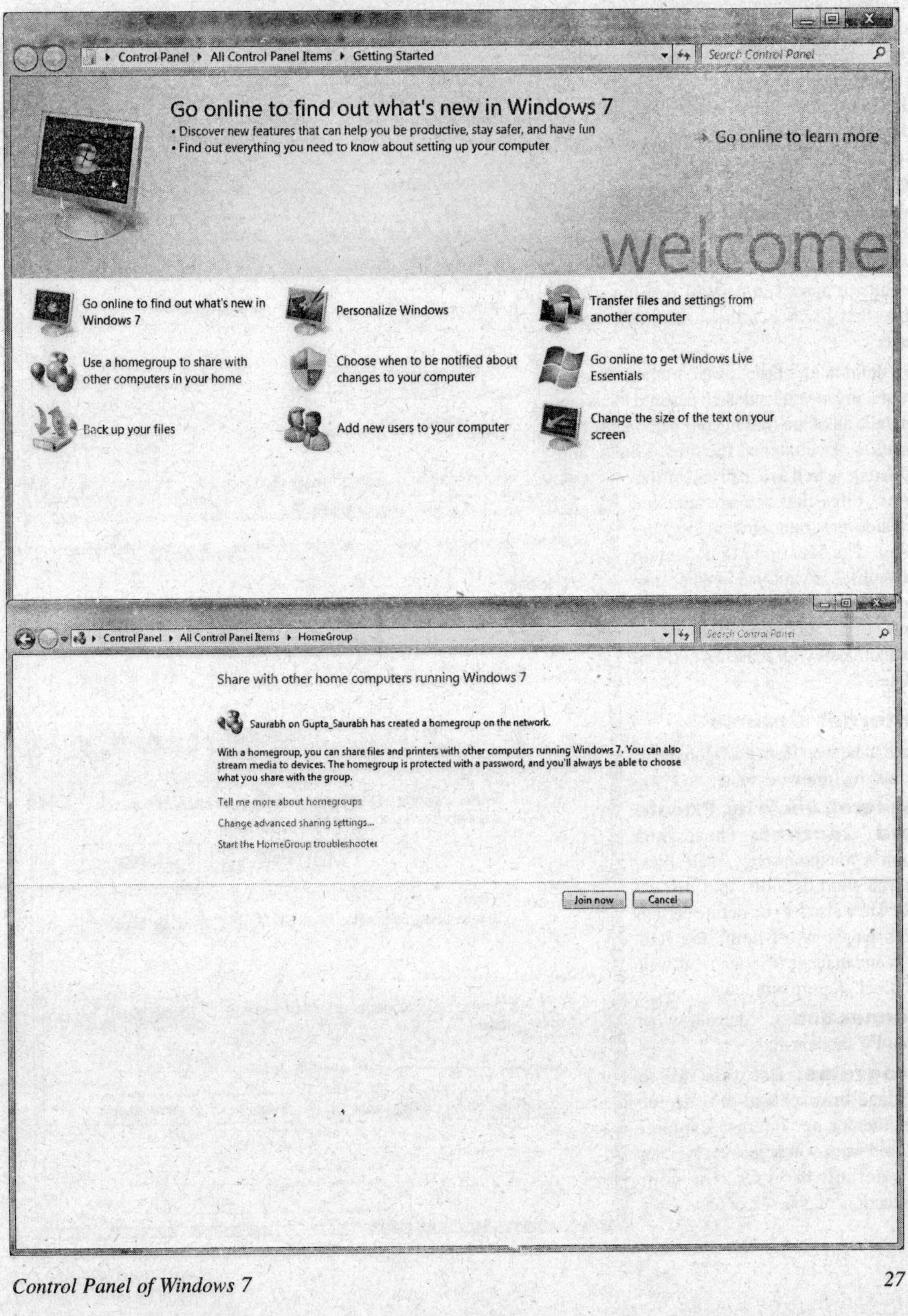

Control Panel of Windows 7

of the files on your computer. The index stores information about files, including the file name, date modified, and properties like author, tags, and rating. You will never see the index, but it is used by Windows to perform very fast searches of the most common files on your computer.

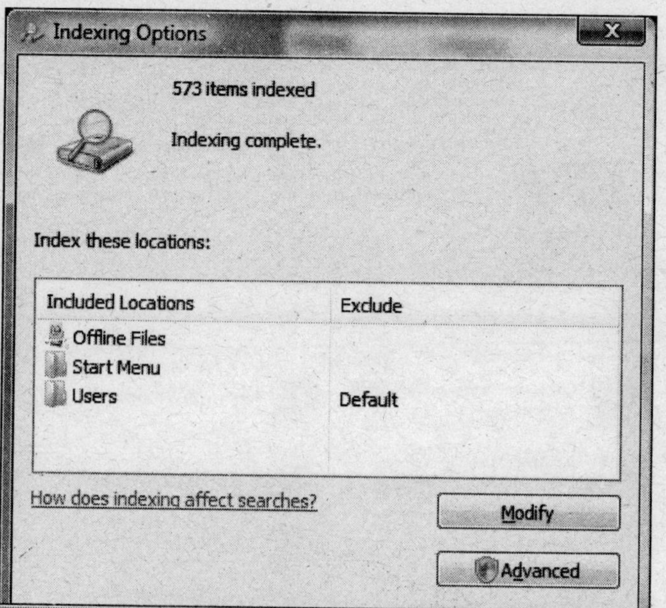

The index is used to make searching for files much faster. Instead of looking through your entire hard disk for a file name or file property, Windows scans the index, which allows most results to appear in a small fraction of the time that a search without the index would take.

By default, all of the most common files on your computer are indexed. Indexed locations include all of the files in your personal folder (such as Documents, Pictures, Music, and Videos), as well as e mail and offline files. Files that are not indexed include program files and system files. The locations that contain those files are not indexed because you rarely need to search those files, and so not including them in the index makes your searches perform faster.

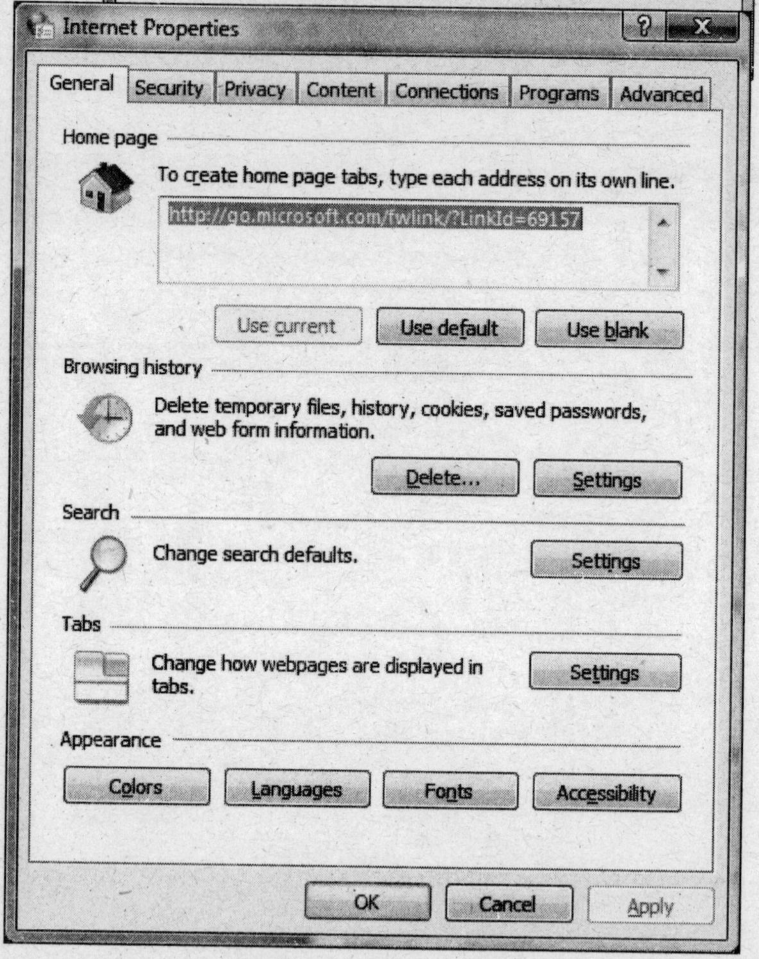

Internet Options

As can be seen from the figure here, it has the following tabs:

General, Security, Private and Content: These tabs control your home page, cache files, search field defaults, and history list. They also let you define certain Web pages as off-limits for your kids and manage RSS feeds, as well as block pop-up windows.

Connections: Controls when your PC modem dials.

Programs: Use this tab to manage browser add-ons, decide whether or not Internet Explorer should warn you whenever it is not the default browser (for your protection, of course), or choose the default programs that open, should you click a link to email someone, open a media file, or view the HTML source of a Web page.

Advanced: On this tab, you will find dozens of checkboxes, most of which are useful only in rare circumstances and affect your Web experience only in mirror ways. For example, "Enable personalized favorites menu" shortens your list of bookmarks over time, as Internet Explorer hides the names of Web sites you haven't visited in a while.

Keyboard

You can customize how long you must press a key before the keyboard character starts repeating, the speed at which keyboard characters repeat, and the rate at which the cursor blinks.

To change the delay before keyboard characters repeat

1. Click to open Keyboard Properties.
2. Under Character repeat, move the Repeat delay slider to the left to increase the amount of time you must hold down a key before the keyboard character repeats. Move the slider to the right to decrease the amount of time before characters repeat..

To change the speed at which keyboard characters repeat

1. Click to open Keyboard Properties.
2. Under Character repeat, move the Repeat rate slider to the left to make keyboard characters repeat more slowly, or to the right to make them repeat faster.

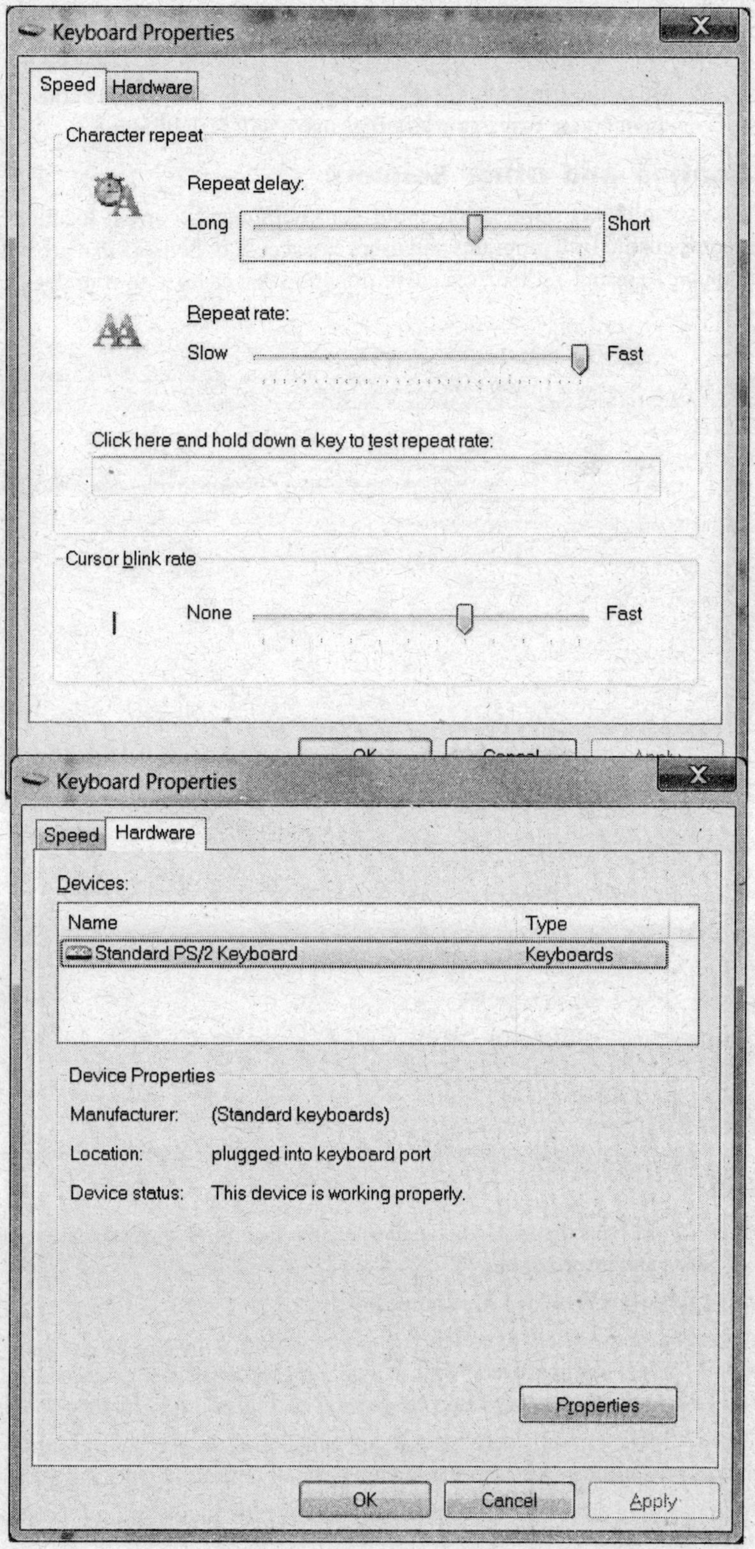

To change the cursor blink rate

1. Click to open Keyboard Properties.
2. Move the Cursor blink rate slider to the right to increase the cursor blink speed. If you move the slider all the way to the left, the cursor will stop blinking.

Location and Other Sensors

Sensors can detect information about your computer's current location, surroundings, and more. Once a sensor is enabled, all programs and users can access it. Sensors that are not enabled are still installed on your computer To install a sensor, see the information that came with your device or go to the device manufacturer's website.

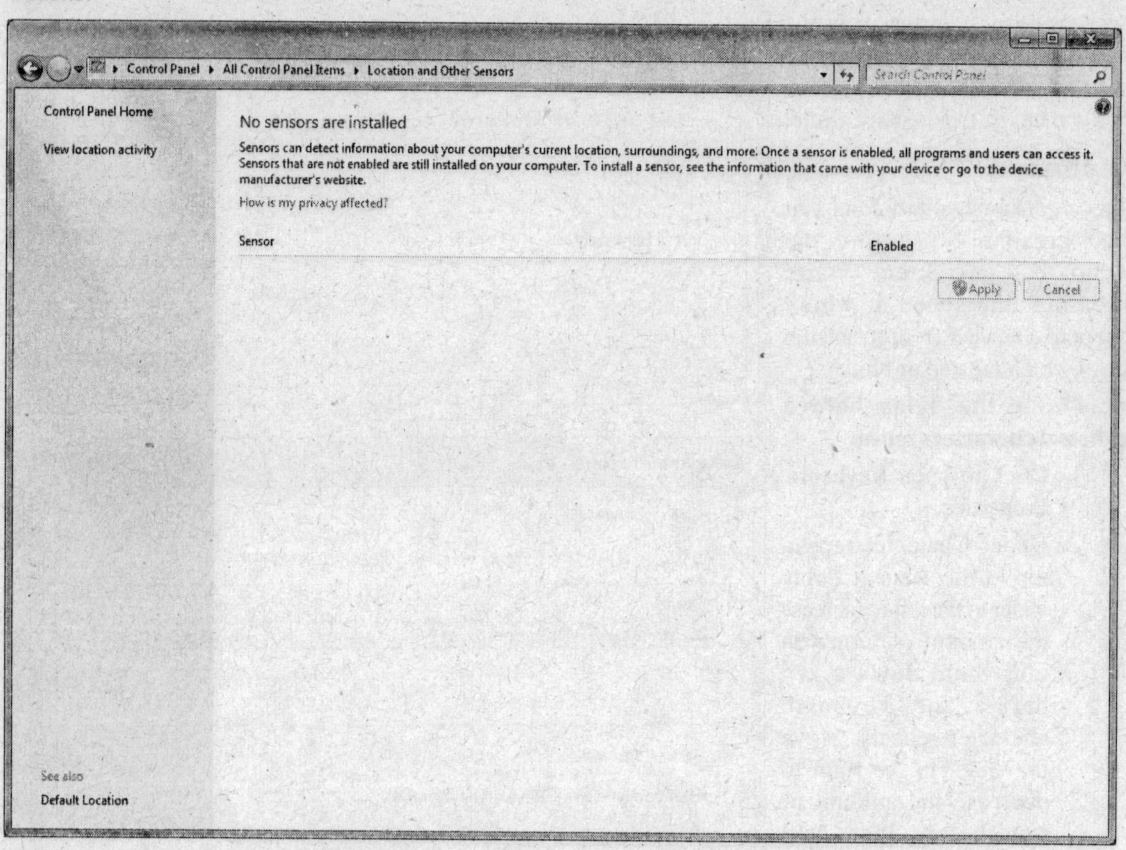

Mail

Windows Mail has the tools you need to exchange e mail with colleagues and friends, or join newsgroups to trade ideas and information.

Add or remove a Windows Mail account

You can set up a variety of different accounts using Windows Mail. You can set up a single personal e mail account, or you might also add your work e mail account and some newsgroups as well. Windows Mail makes managing multiple accounts easy by putting each account in its own folder.

Windows Mail supports three types of accounts: mail, news (newsgroups), and directory services. Directory services are online address books that are typically offered by organizations such as colleges and businesses.

Before you add an account, be sure that you have the logon and server information for your e mail account.

Mouse

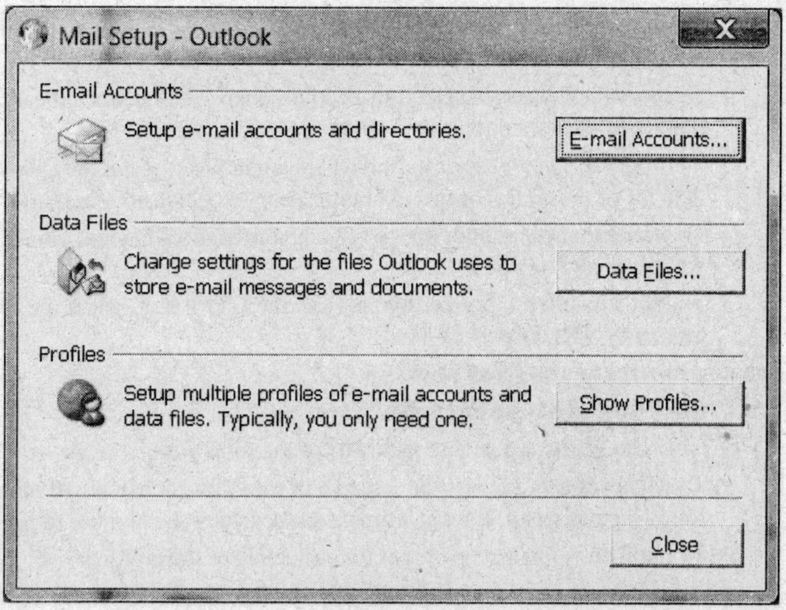

You can customize your mouse in a variety of ways, such as swapping the functions of your mouse buttons, making the mouse pointer more visible, and altering the scroll wheel speed.

To change how the mouse buttons work

1. Click to open Mouse Properties.
2. Click the Buttons tab, and then do any of the following:

- To swap the functions of the right and left mouse buttons, select the Switch primary and secondary buttons check box.
- To change how quickly you must click the buttons to perform a double-click, move the Double-click speed slider towards Slow or Fast.
- To turn on ClickLock, which enables you to highlight or drag without holding down the mouse button, select the Turn on ClickLock check box.

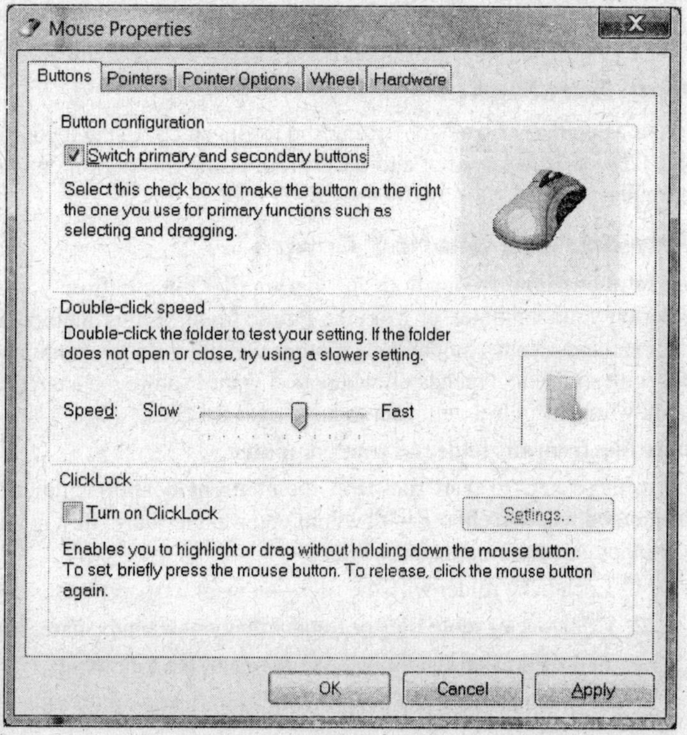

To change how the mouse pointer looks

1. Click to open Mouse Properties.
2. Click the Pointers tab, and then do one of the following:

- To give all of your pointers a new look, click the Scheme list, and then click a new mouse pointer scheme.
- To change an individual pointer, click the pointer you want to change in the Customize list, click Browse, click the pointer you want to use, and then click Open.

To change how the mouse pointer works

1. Click to open Mouse Properties.
2. Click the Pointer Options tab, and then do any of the following:

- To change the speed at which the mouse pointer moves, move the Select a pointer speed slider towards Slow or Fast.

- To make the pointer work more accurately when you're moving the mouse slowly, select the Enhance pointer precision check box.
- To speed the process of selecting a choice when a dialog box appears, select the Automatically move pointer to the default button in a dialog box check box .
- To make the pointer easier to find when you move it, select the Display pointer trails check box, and then move the slider towards Short or Long to decrease or increase the length of the pointer trail.
- To ensure that the pointer doesn't block your view of the text you're typing, select the Hide pointer while typing check box.
- To find a misplaced pointer by pressing the CTRL key, select the Show location of pointer when I press the CTRL key check box.

To change how the mouse wheel works

1. Click to open Mouse Properties.
2. Click the Wheel tab, and then do one of the following:

- To set the number of lines the screen will scroll for each notch of mouse wheel movement, click The following number of lines at a time, and then enter the number of lines you want to scroll in the box.
- To scroll an entire screen of text for each click of the mouse wheel, click One screen at a time.
- If your mouse has a wheel that supports horizontal scrolling, in the Tilt the wheel to scroll the following number of characters at a time box, enter the number of characters you want to scroll horizontally when you tilt the wheel to the left or right.

Nero BurnRights

Nero is a popular software for writing and reading CDs. Using it you can Burn CDs with data and create DVDs/ Data CDs and other type of audio CDs too. Using this option you can set the options of using Nero in your computer.

Network and Sharing Centre

Windows provides two methods for sharing files directly from your computer. You can share files from any folder on your computer, or from the Public folder. Either method allows you to share files or folders with someone using your computer or another computer on the same network. Which method you use to share files with someone depends on where you want to store the shared files, who you want to share them with, and how much control you want to have over the files.

Share files from any folder on your computer

Follow these steps to share files from their current location without copying them to another location. Using this method, you can choose with whom you want to share files, regardless of whether they use this computer or another computer on the network.

1. Locate the folder with the files you want to share.
2. Click one or more files or folders that you want to share, and then, on the toolbar, click Share.
3. In the File Sharing dialog box, do one of the following:

- Type the name of the person you want to share files with, and then click Add.
- Click the arrow to the right of the text box, click the person's name in the list, and then click Add.
- If you don't see the name of the person you want to share files with in the list, click the arrow to the right of the text box, and then click Create a new user to create a new user account so that you can share files with the person using this account.

4. The name of the person or group that you selected appears in the list of people you want to share files with.

5. Under Permission Level, click the arrow next to the permission level for that person or group, and then do one of the following to set sharing permissions:
   - Click Reader to restrict the person or group to viewing files in the shared folder.
   - Click Contributor to allow the person or group to view all files, add files, and change or delete the files that they add.
   - Click Co-owner to allow the person or group to view, change, add, and delete files in the shared folder.
   - If you are sharing a file instead of a folder, there is no option to set the permission level to Contributor.
6. When you are finished choosing the people or groups you want to share files with, click Share. If you are prompted for an administrator password or confirmation, type the password or provide confirmation.
7. After you receive confirmation that your folder is shared, you should send a link to your shared files to the people you are sharing them with, so they know the files are shared and how to access them. Do one of the following:
   - Click E mail Link to automatically open a Windows Mail e mail message with the link to your shared files.
   - Manually copy and paste the link displayed on this screen into an e mail message. Right-click the link and click Copy Link. Then open a new e mail message and paste in the link. You might want to do this if you don't use Windows Mail as your e mail program.
8. If you don't want to send an e mail message to the person you are sharing files with, click Done. They won't be able to find the shared files, however, until you give them the network location of the files.
   - You can give a shared folder a share name that makes it easier for someone else to find it on your

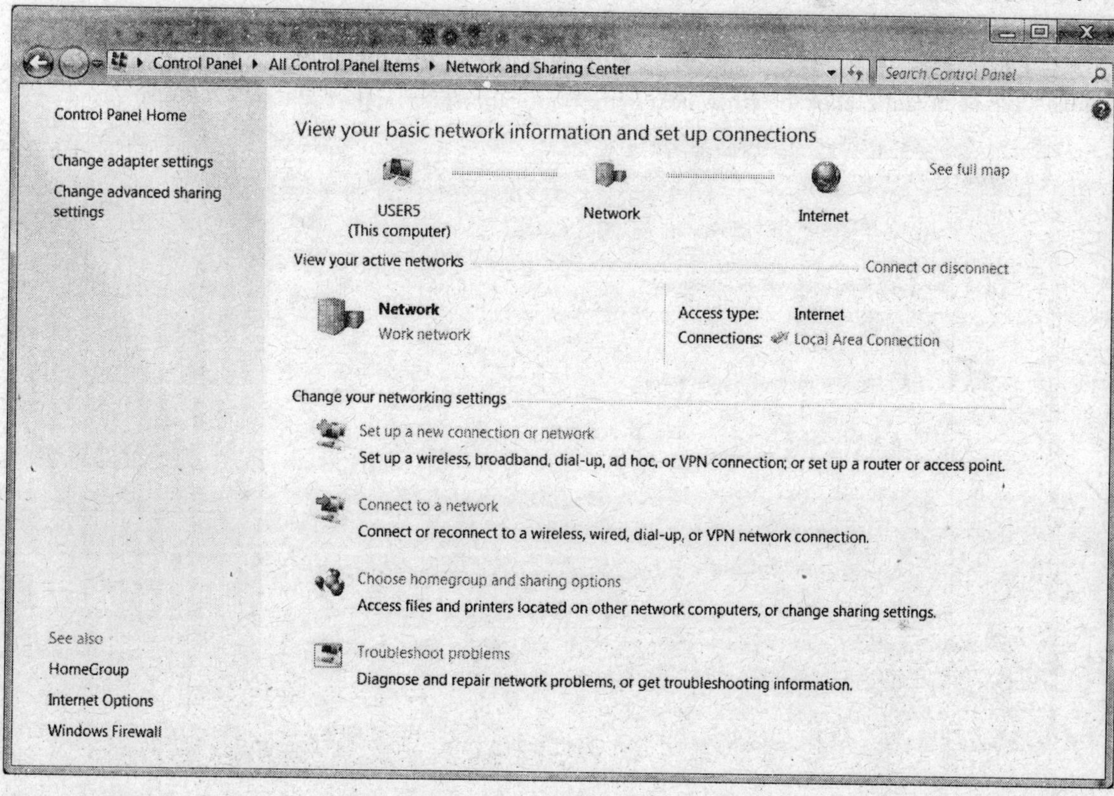

computer. You can do this by using the Advanced Sharing dialog box for the folder. To access this dialog box, right-click a folder you have already shared, click Properties, click the Sharing tab, and then click Advanced Sharing. If you are prompted for an administrator password or confirmation, type the password or provide confirmation.

Share files from the Public folder

When you share files from the Public folder, you don't share them with specific people. Anyone with a user account on this computer can access the Public folder, but you decide whether to allow access to people on your network. You can only grant access to everyone or no one on the network.

You can also turn on password-protected sharing. This limits network access to the Public folder to only those people with a user account and password on your computer. By default, network access to the Public folder is turned off unless you enable it.

To share files from the public folder:

1. Copy or move whichever files you want to share to the Public folder or one of its subfolders, such as Public Documents or Public Music.
2. Your files in the Public folder are now shared with anyone who has access to the Public folder.

- You can't restrict access to some individual files and folders within the Public Folder but allow access to other files and folders there. If users have access to the Public folder, they will have access to everything in it.
- When you share files and folders with people using other computers, they can open and view those files and folders just as if they were stored on their own computers. Any changes you allow them to make to a shared file or folder will change the file or folder on your computer. However, you can restrict people to just viewing your shared files, without the ability to change them.

Notification Area Icons

If you choose to hide icons and notifications, you won't be notified about changes or updates. To view hidden icons at any time, click the arrow next to the notification area on the taskbar.

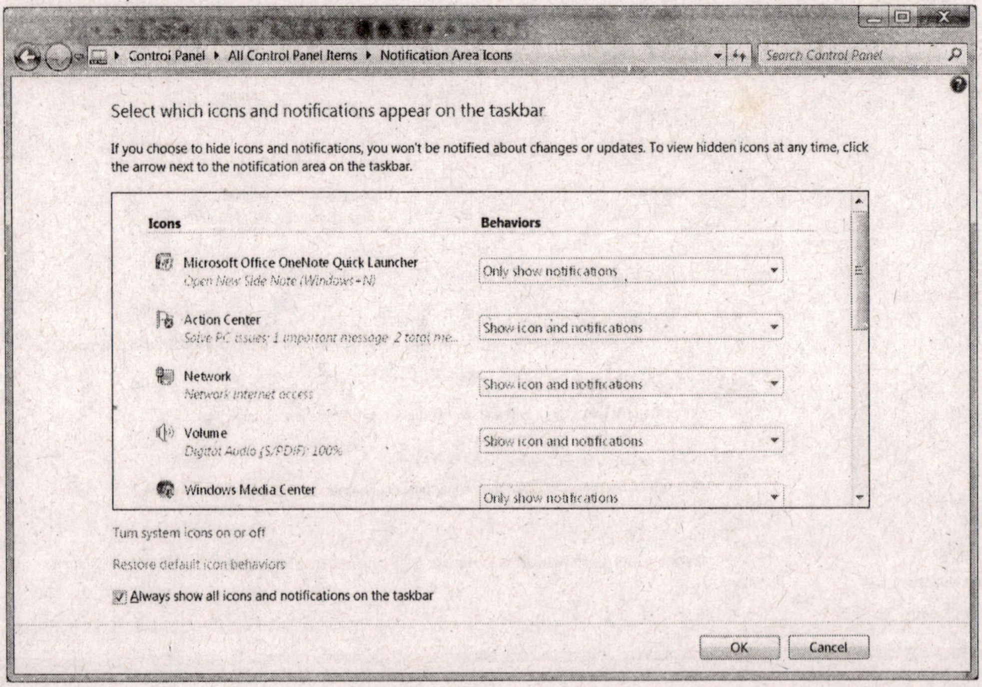

Parental Controls

You can use Parental Controls to help manage how your children use the computer. For example, you can set limits on your children's access to the web, the hours that they can log on to the computer, and which games they can play and programs they can run.

When Parental Controls blocks access to a webpage or game, a notification is displayed that the webpage or program has been blocked. Your child can click a link in the notification to request permission for access to that webpage or program. You can allow access by entering your account information.

Before you get started, make sure that each child that you want to set up Parental Controls for has a standard user account because Parental Controls can only be applied to standard user accounts. To set up Parental Controls for your child, you'll need an Administrator user account. Parental Controls cannot be applied to an Administrator user account.

To turn on Parental Controls for a standard user account

1. Click to open Parental Controls. If you are prompted for an administrator password or confirmation, type the password or provide confirmation.
2. Click the standard user account for which you want to set Parental Controls.
3. Under Parental Controls, click On.
4. Once you've turned on Parental Controls for your child's standard user account, you can adjust the individual settings that you want to control. You can control the following areas:

- Web restrictions. You can restrict the websites that children can visit, make sure children only visit age-appropriate websites, indicate whether you want to allow file downloads, and set up which content you want the content filters to block and allow. You can also block or allow specific websites.

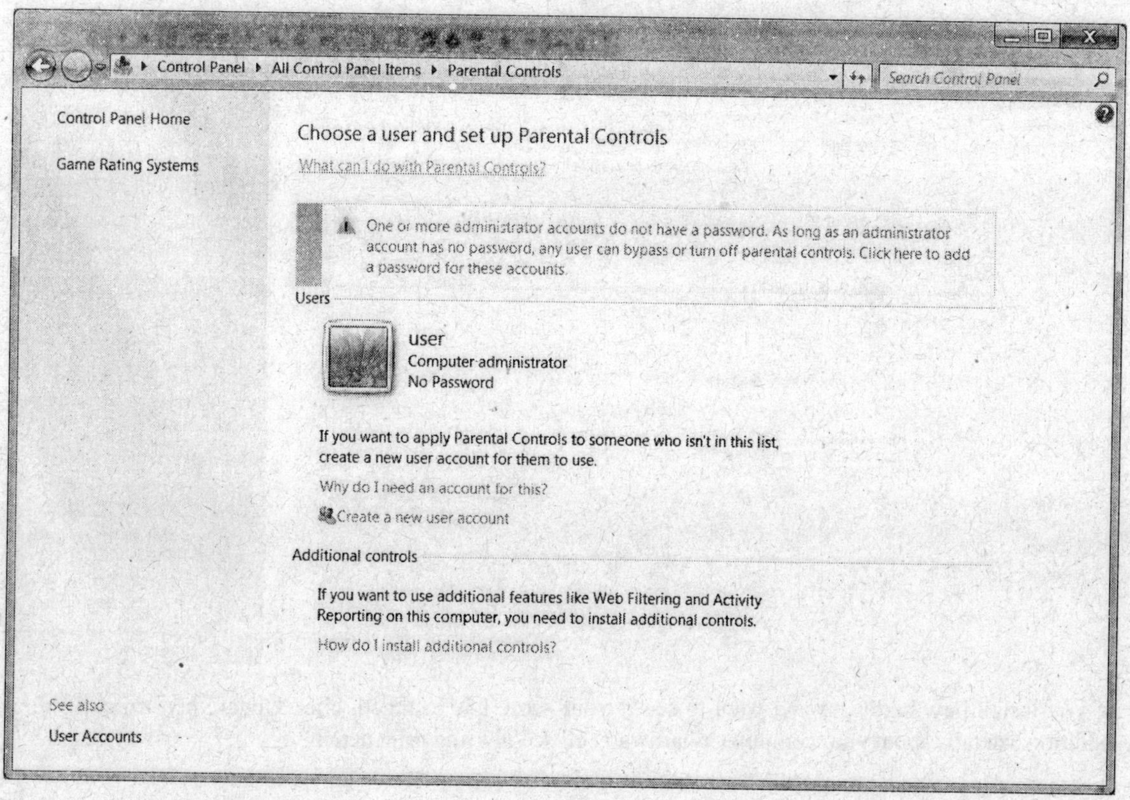

- Time limits. You can set time limits to control when children are allowed to log on to the computer. Time limits prevent children from logging on during the specified hours and, if they are already logged on, they will be automatically logged off. You can set different logon hours for every day of the week.
- Games. You can control access to games, choose an age rating level, choose the types of content you want to block, and decide whether you want to allow or block unrated or specific games.
- Allow or block specific programs. You can prevent children from running programs that you don't want them to run.

Performance Information

Performance Information and Tools lists your computer's Windows Experience Index base score, which indicates the performance and overall capability of your computer's hardware.

Click to open Performance Information and Tools.

The base score can help you buy programs that match your computer's performance level. The base score only pertains to the performance aspects of the computer that affect how well features in Windows and other programs will run on this computer, and does not reflect the overall quality of your computer.

Individual hardware components, such as your computer's central processing unit (CPU) and random access memory (RAM), are tested and receive a subscore. Your computer's base score is determined by the lowest subscore. For example, if the lowest subscore of an individual hardware component is 2.6, then the base score is 2.6. The base score is not an average of the various subscores.

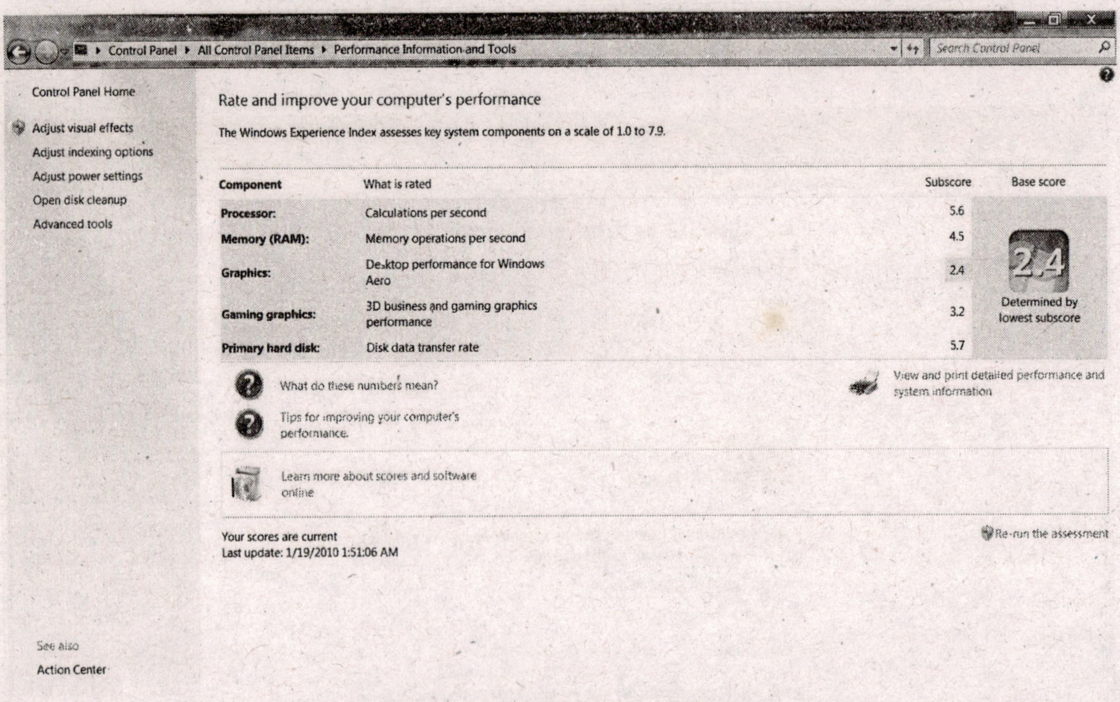

If you install new hardware and want to see if your score has changed, click Update my score. To view additional details about your computer's hardware, click View and print details.

Personalize

You can add a personal touch to your computer by using themes, changing the computer's colors and sounds, and choosing your own desktop background, screen saver, and user account picture.

Themes

A theme is a collection of visual elements that can affect the style of windows, icons, fonts, colors, and sometime sounds. For example, a nature-based theme might include a desktop background with plants, a pointer that looks like a leaf, and system sounds that mimic bird chirps.

Color

Windows Aero is the premium visual experience of this version of Windows. It features a transparent glass design with subtle window animations and new window colors. Click the Start button, click Control Panel, click Appearance and Personalization, click Personalization, and then click Window Color and Appearance.

- If you see the Appearance Settings dialog box instead of the Window Color and Appearance window, the theme might not be set to Windows Vista, the color scheme might not be set to Windows Aero, or the computer might not meet the minimum hardware requirements for running Windows Aero.

Sound

You can change the sound your computer makes when you receive e mail, start Windows, or shut down your computer.

Desktop background

The desktop background, also called wallpaper, is a picture or design on the desktop. It provides a backdrop to your open windows.

Screen saver

A screen saver is a picture or animation that appears on the screen when you haven't used the mouse or keyboard for a set period of time. Windows includes a variety of screen savers to choose from. You can create a personalized screen saver by displaying selected pictures and videos as a slide show.

To use pictures as a slide show

1. Click to open Screen Saver Settings.
2. Click the Screen saver list, and then click Photos.
3. If you want to specify a location for the pictures you want to use in your screen saver, modify the slide show speed, or configure any other screen saver settings, click Settings. After you make your changes, click Save.
4. Click OK.

User account picture

A user account picture helps identify your account on a computer. The picture is displayed on the Welcome screen and on the Start menu. You can change your user account picture to one of the pictures included with Windows, or you can use your own picture.

Windows Sidebar

Windows Sidebar provides a way to organize the information, games, and tasks that you want to access quickly without cluttering your workspace. It's made up of gadgets, which are customizable mini-programs that can display continuously updated headlines, a picture slide show, contacts, and more, without having to open a new window.

Phone and Modem Options

The following are descriptions of the settings on the Dialing Rules, Modems, and Advanced tabs in Phone and Modem Options.

Click to open Phone and Modem Options.

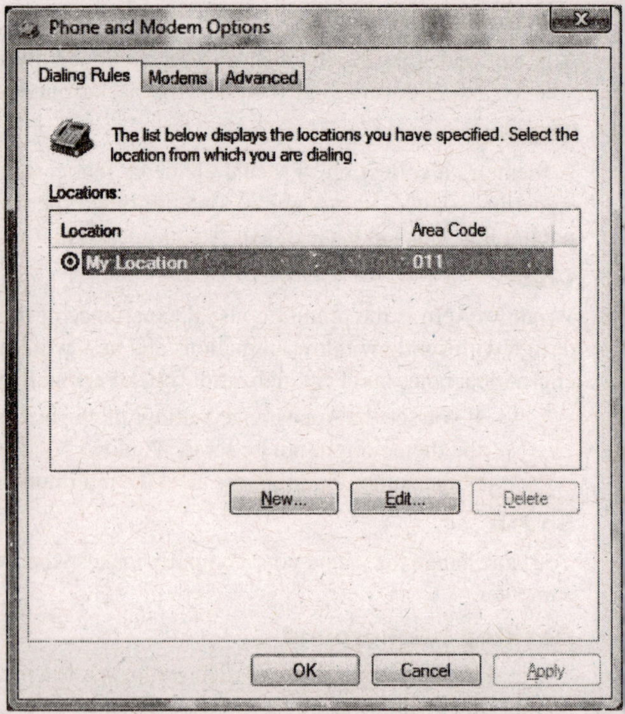

If you haven't opened Phone and Modem Options before, a dialog box will be displayed, prompting you to type your area code and other access codes.

Dialing Rules tab

The Dialing Rules tab lists all currently defined dialing locations (sets of rules applied to outgoing phone calls from your computer's modem). Use this tab to add, delete, or configure dialing locations. When you specify the destination phone number, the rules associated with the dialing location determine whether the area code must be included, whether a calling card should be used, and so on.

The following table describes the options on the Dialing Rules tab.

Control	***Description***
Locations	Lists all of the currently defined locations on your computer. The currently selected location appears in bold text, and its rules apply to any phone calls made from your computer. Double-clicking a location opens the Edit dialog box, where you can make changes to the rules associated with that location.
New	Allows you to create a new location and specify the rules associated with that location.
Edit	Allows you to edit the rules for the currently selected location.
Delete	Removes the currently selected location and all rules associated with it. It does not remove any existing calling card definitions.

Modems tab

The Modems tab lists all modems currently installed on your computer. Use this tab to add, remove, and configure modems.

The following table describes the options on the Modems tab.

Control	***Description***
The following modems are installed	Lists the modems currently installed on your computer, and the communications port your computer uses to communicate with each modem.
Add	Allows you to install a new modem on your computer. If the drivers for your new modem are not already installed on your computer, you will be asked to install the drivers provided by the modem manufacturer.
Remove	Uninstalls the currently selected modem from your computer. You should unplug or remove the modem from your computer after uninstalling it, or it could be detected and reinstalled the next time you start your computer.
Properties	Allows you to view or change the configuration of the currently selected modem. The options available depend on the make and model of the modem.

Advanced tab

The Advanced tab lists the telephony providers (software used to communicate with telephony hardware, such as modems) currently installed on your computer. Use this tab to add, remove, and configure providers.

The following table describes the options on the Advanced tab.

Control	*Description*
Providers	Lists the telephony providers currently installed on your computer.
Add	Allows you to add a Telephony Application Programming Interface (TAPI) service provider to the list and make it available to telephony programs. To do this, you must have the drivers for the TAPI-supported telephony hardware already installed on your computer.
Remove	Removes the selected TAPI service provider from the list. Removing a TAPI service provider makes it unavailable to telephony programs. It does not delete any files from your computer.
Configure	Allows you to view or change the properties of the selected TAPI service provider. If this is unavailable, there are no configurable properties for the service provider.

Power Options

The Power Options program manages the power consumption of your computer. That's a big deal when you are running off a laptop's battery, of course, but it's also important if you'd like to save money (and the environment) by cutting down on the juice consumed by your desktop PC. In Windows 7, Microsoft has tried to simplify the business of managing the electricity/speed tradeoff in two ways. First, it has abandoned the old name power scheme and adopted a new one: power plan.

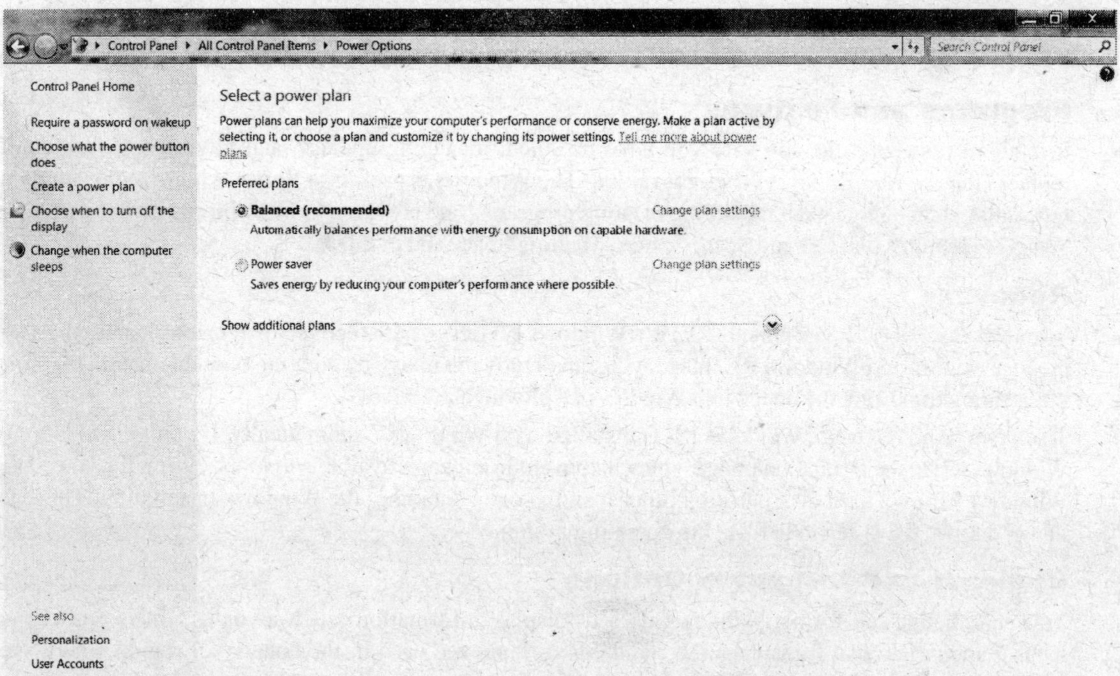

Program Updates

This option allows you to check the various updates available for the installed programs of your computer

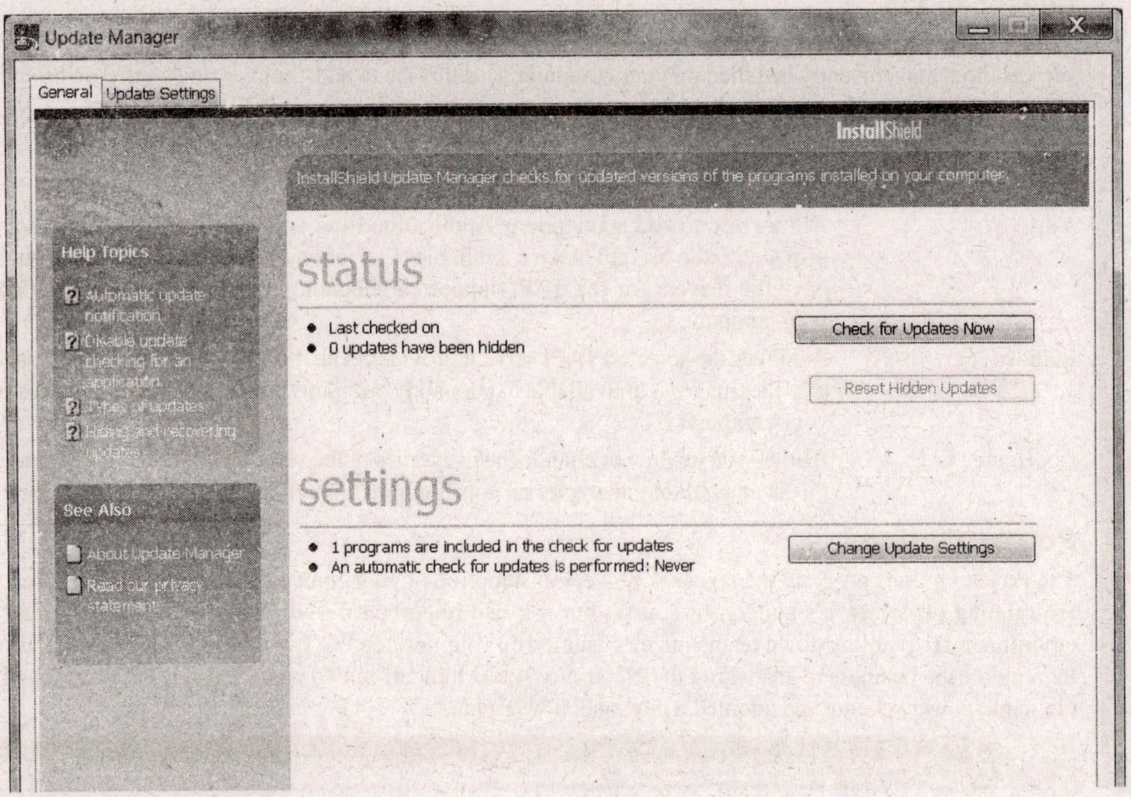

Programs and Features

It is about managing the software you have installed, managing updates, and buying software online. It replaces the old Add/Remove Programs option. The Windows is useful for fixing, which might simply mean reinstalling, changing, and uninstalling existing programs, and is the only place you can go to turn on, or off, Windows features like Fax and Scan, Games, Meeting Space and more.

Recovery

Windows Recovery Environment (RE) is a Windows PE image with recovery extensions installed. After you create a customized Windows RE image, you can deploy the image by creating bootable media that uses the image or by importing the image into Windows Deployment Services.

To enable rapid recovery, Windows RE is installed with Windows 7 auomatically. If you've added a custom Windows RE to the instalation image, your custom environment is available to users. Normally, you configure Windows RE on a hard disk partition other than the one containing the Windows installation. This ensures that Windows RE is separate from the operating system.

Regional and Language Options

You can change the format Windows uses to display information (such as dates, times, currency, and measurements) so that it matches the standards or language used in the country or region where you are located. For example, if you work on documents in both French and English, you can change the format to French so that you can display currency in Euros or display dates in the day/month/year format.

If you need to type and edit documents in more than one language, you can add input languages. Many input languages support a variety of keyboard layouts, input method editors (IMEs), and speech and handwriting recognition programs. Deciding which of these options to use is usually a matter of personal preference.

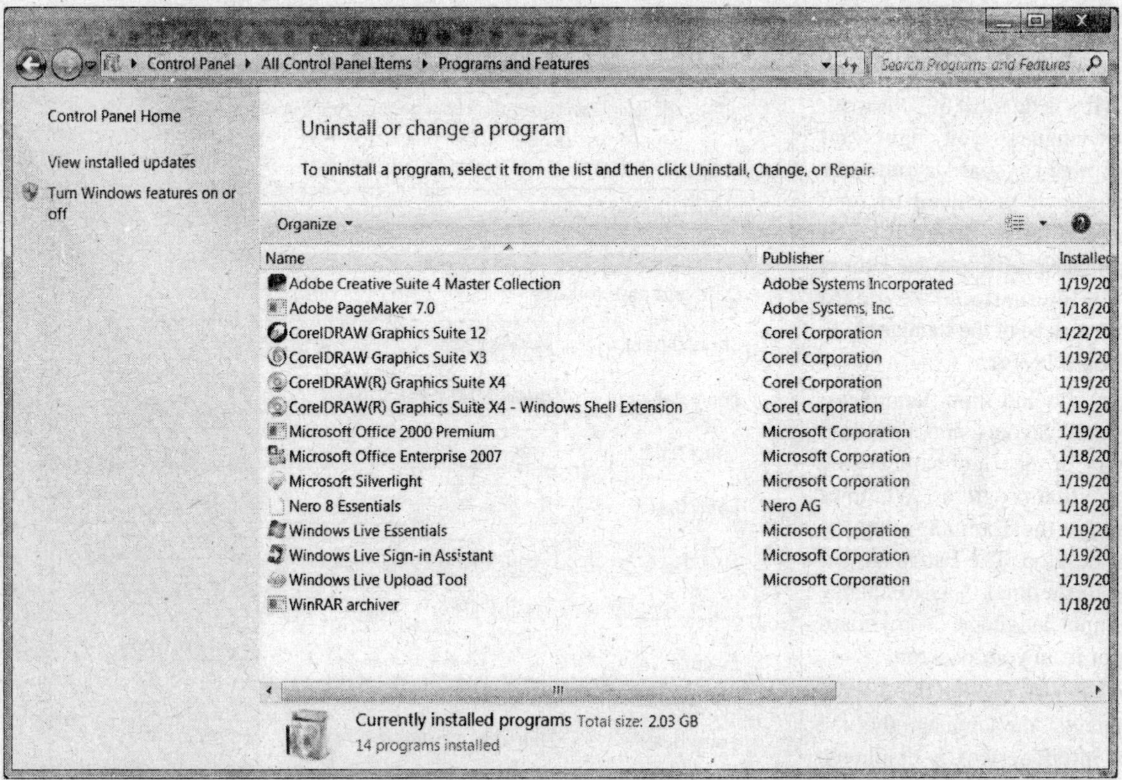
Control Panel ▸ All Control Panel Items ▸ Programs and Features
Search Programs and Features
Control Panel Home
View installed updates
Turn Windows features on or off
Uninstall or change a program
To uninstall a program, select it from the list and then click Uninstall, Change, or Repair.
Organize
Name
Publisher
Installed
Adobe Creative Suite 4 Master Collection
Adobe Systems Incorporated
Adobe PageMaker 7.0
Adobe Systems, Inc.
CorelDRAW Graphics Suite 12
Corel Corporation
CorelDRAW Graphics Suite X3
CorelDRAW(R) Graphics Suite X4
CorelDRAW(R) Graphics Suite X4 - Windows Shell Extension
Microsoft Office 2000 Premium
Microsoft Corporation
Microsoft Office Enterprise 2007
Microsoft Silverlight
Nero 8 Essentials
Nero AG
Windows Live Essentials
Windows Live Sign-in Assistant
Windows Live Upload Tool
WinRAR archiver
Currently installed programs Total size: 2.03 GB
14 programs installed

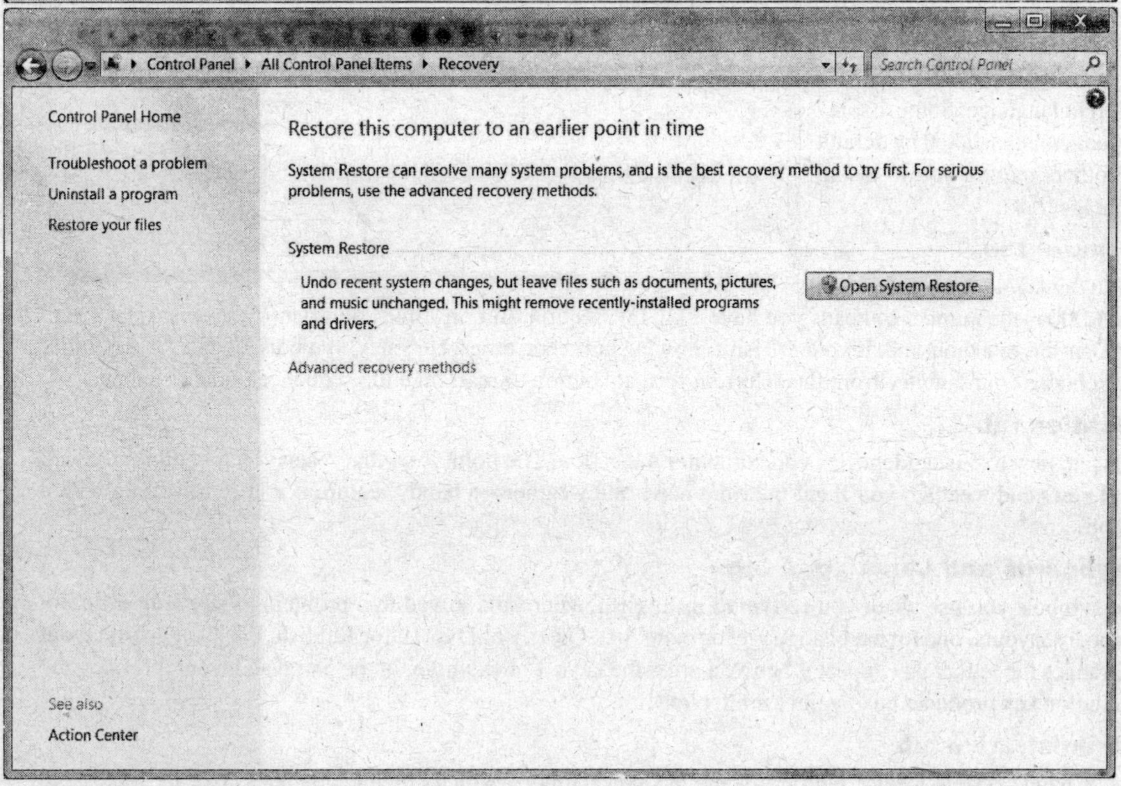
Control Panel ▸ All Control Panel Items ▸ Recovery
Search Control Panel
Control Panel Home
Troubleshoot a problem
Uninstall a program
Restore your files
Restore this computer to an earlier point in time
System Restore can resolve many system problems, and is the best recovery method to try first. For serious problems, use the advanced recovery methods.
System Restore
Undo recent system changes, but leave files such as documents, pictures, and music unchanged. This might remove recently-installed programs and drivers.
Open System Restore
Advanced recovery methods
See also
Action Center

Experiment with the options to discover which work best for you. Even if you do most of your work in one language, you might want to try other keyboard layouts. For example, if you need to type accented letters in English, it might be easier to use the United States-International keyboard layout instead of the standard U.S. keyboard layout.

When you add input languages, keyboard layouts, input method editors, or speech or handwriting recognition programs, Windows displays the Language bar on your desktop. The Language bar provides a quick way to change the input language or keyboard layout from your desktop.

You can also change the display language—the language that the user interface text is displayed in—so that you can view wizards, dialog boxes, menus, and other items in the user interface in a different language. Some display languages are installed by default and others require you to install language files.

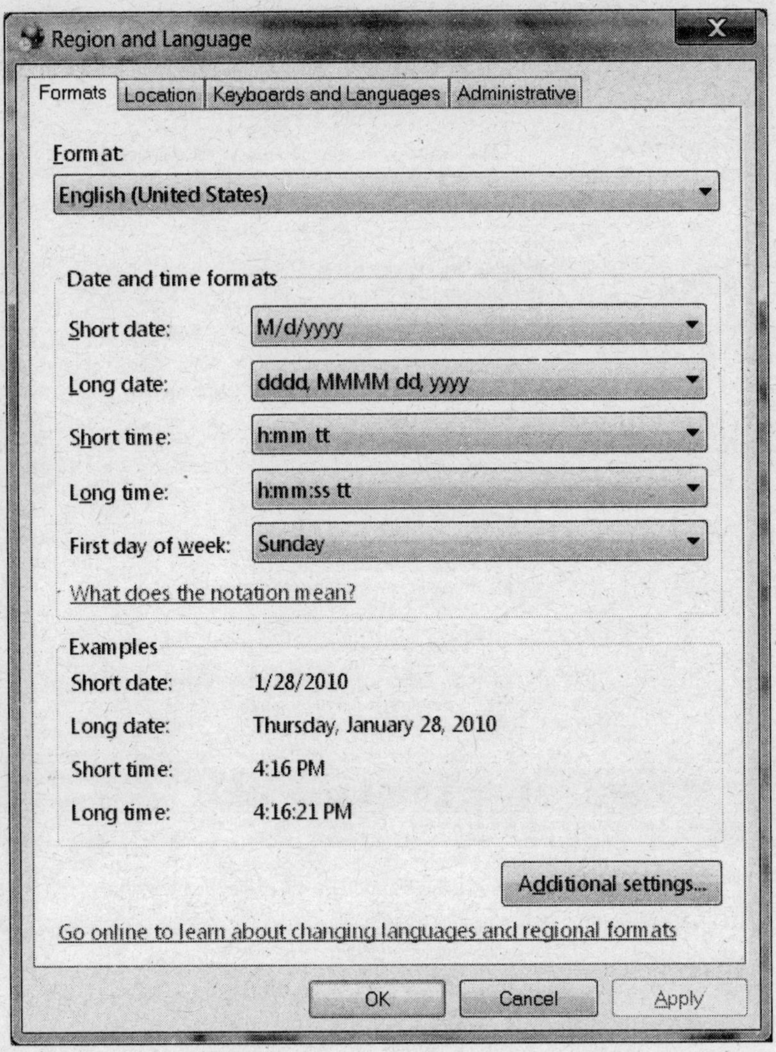

Formats tab

If you think 7/4 means July 4 and that 1,000 is the number of heads you have, skip this section. But, in some countries 7/4 means April 7, and 1,000 means one thousand. If your PC isn't showing numbers, times, currency, symbols, or dates in a familiar way, choose your country from the "Current format" button to rearrange the sequence of date elements.

Location tab

This tab, new to Vista, identifies you computer's location. The point is so that when you go online to check local news and weather, you'll get the right news and weather—a handy feature if you're travelling with a laptop.

Keyboards and Languages tabs

The symbols you use when you're typing in English. Microsoft solved this problem by creating different keyboard layouts, one for each language, or more, like Qwerty or Dvorak for English. Each keyboard layout rearranges the letters that appear when you press the keys. For example, in the Swedish layout, pressing the semicolon key produces an Ö—not a simicolon(;).

Administrative tab

The "Change system locale" button this tab lets you specify—which language handles error messages and the occasional dialog box. The "Copy to reserved account" button lets the newly configured language settings apply to new user accounts, so anyone who gets a new account on this computer will have your language, format, and keyboard settings conveniently available to them.

Remote App and Desktop Connections

Windows 7 has several remote connectivity features. With Remote Assistance, users can send invitations to support technicians, enabling the technicians to service a computer remotely. With Remote Desktop, users can connect remotely to a computer and access it resources. Remote Assistance and Remote Desktop can function throught Network Address Translation (NAT) firewalls. Remote Assistance also has built-in diagnostic tools. To allow for easier troubleshooting and escalation of support issues, two different support staff can connect to a remote computer simultaneously. When troubleshooting requires restarting the computer, Remote Assistance sessions are reestablished automatically after the computer being diagnosed reboots.

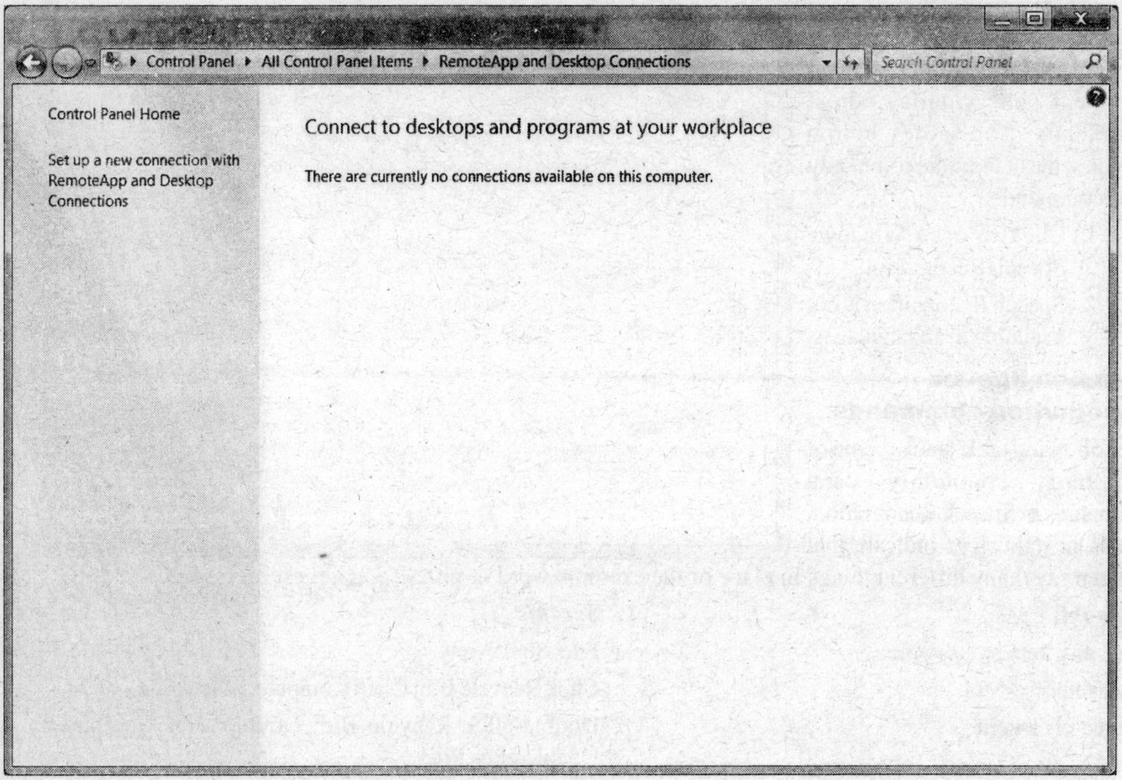

Sound

In Windows, the Sound dialog box has been simplified. It now contains only four tabs that control every aspect of your microphone and speakers: Playback, Recording, Sounds and Communications.

Playback and Recording tabs

These tabs simply contain the icon for each attached sound device. To change a device's settings, select it, and then click Configure.

Sounds tab

Windows comes with a new, freshly composed suite of little sound effects—beeps, musical ripples, and chords—that play when you turn on the PC, trigger an error message, empty the Recycle Bin, and so on. And if you like, you can hear them on many other occasions, such as when you open or exit a program, open a menu, restore a window, and so on. The tab lets you specify which sound effect plays for which situation.

Speech Recognition

To use Speech Recognition, the first thing you need to do is set it up on your computer. To learn how to do that, see Set up Speech Recognition. When you're ready to use Speech Recognition, you need to speak in simple, short commands. The tables below include some of the more commonly used commands.

1. Click to open Windows Speech Recognition.
2. Speech Recognition is not available in all languages.

Common Speech Recognition commands

The following table shows some of the most commonly used commands in Speech Recognition. Words in italic font indicate that you can say many different things in place of the example word or phrase and get useful results.

To do this	*Say this*
Click any item by its name	File; Start; View
Click item	Click Recycle Bin; Click Computer; Click File
Double-click item	Double-click Recycle Bin; Double-click Computer; Double-click File
Switch to an open program	Switch to Paint; Switch to WordPad; Switch to program name; Switch application
Scroll direction	Scroll up; Scroll down; Scroll left; Scroll right
Insert a new paragraph or new line in a document	New paragraph; New line
Select a word in a document	Select word
Select a word and start to correct it	Correct word
Select and delete specific words	Delete word
Show a list of applicable commands	What can I say?
Update the list of speech commands that are currently available	Refresh speech commands
Make the computer listen to you	Start listening

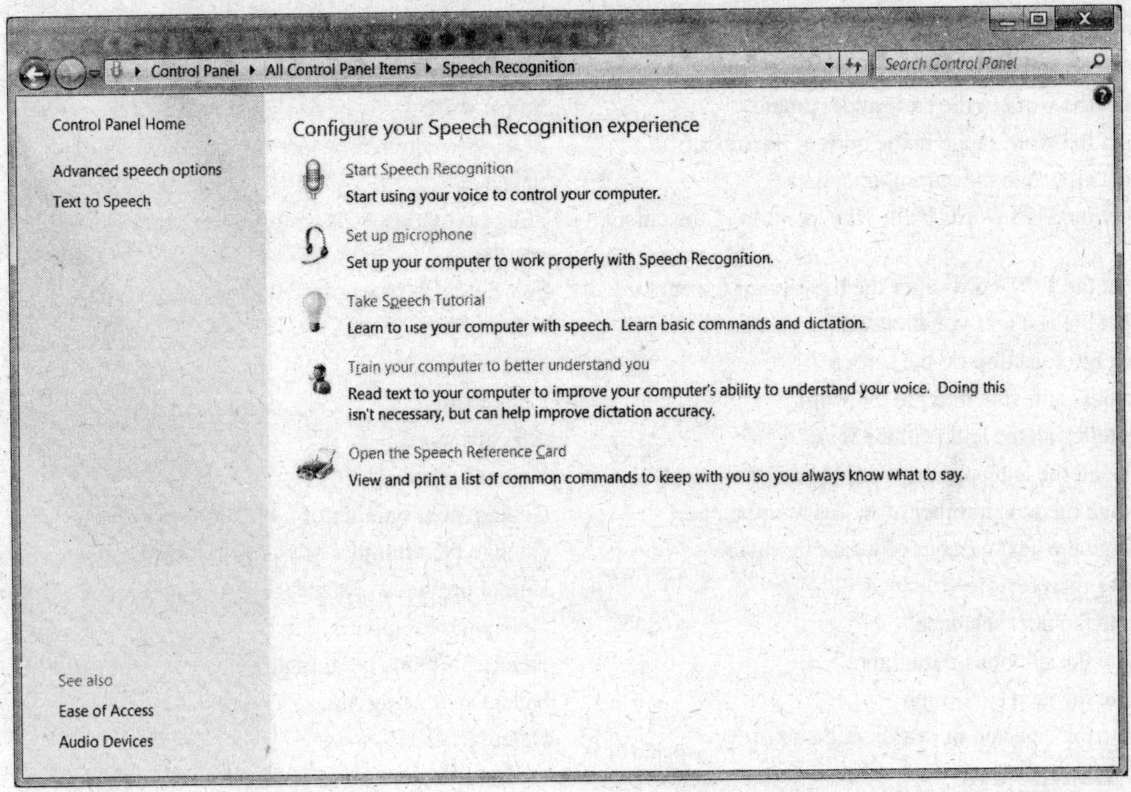

Make the computer stop listening	Stop listening
Move the Speech Recognition microphone out of the way	Move speech recognition
Minimize the microphone bar	Minimize speech recognition

Dictation

The following table shows commands for using Speech Recognition to work with text. Words in italic font indicate that you can say many different things in place of the example word or phrase and get useful results.

To do this	***Say this***
Insert a new line in the document	New line
Insert a new paragraph in the document	New paragraph
Insert a tab	Tab
Insert the literal word for the next command; for example, you can insert the word "comma" instead of the punctuation mark	Literal word
Insert the numeral form of a number	Numeral number
Put the cursor before a specific word	Go to word
Put the cursor after a specific word	Go after word
Do not insert a space before the next word	No space
Go to the start of the sentence that the cursor is in	Go to start of sentence
Go to the start of the paragraph the cursor is in	Go to start of paragraph
Go to the start of the document	Go to start of document
Go to the end of the sentence that the cursor is in	Go to end of sentence

Go to the end of the paragraph the cursor is in	Go to end of paragraph
Go to the end of the current document	Go to end of document
Select the word in the current document	Select word
Select the word range in the current document	Select word range; Select word through word
Select all text in the current document	Select all
Select the 1-20 words before the location of the cursor	Select previous 1-20 words; Select previous 10 words
Select the 1-20 words after the location of the cursor	Select next 1-20 words; Select next 10 words
Select the last text you dictated	Select that
Clear the selection on the screen	Clear selection
Capitalize the first letter of the word	Caps word
Capitalize all the letters of the word	All caps word
Make all the letters in the word lowercase	No caps word
Change the next number of words to uppercase	Change next number of words to uppercase
Change the next number of words to lowercase	Change next number of words to lowercase
Delete the previous sentence	Delete previous sentence
Delete the next sentence	Delete next sentence
Delete the previous paragraph	Delete previous paragraph
Delete the next paragraph	Delete next paragraph
Delete the selected or last dictated text	Delete that

Keyboard keys

The following table shows commands for using Speech Recognition to press keyboard keys. Words in italic font indicate that you can say many different things in place of the example word or phrase and get useful results.

To do this	*Say this*
Press any key on the keyboard	Press keyboard key; Press a; Press capital b; Press SHIFT plus a; Press CTRL plus a
Press certain keyboard keys without saying "Press" first	Delete; Backspace; Enter; Page Up; Page down; Home; End; Tab

- You can also use the ICAO\NATO phonetic alphabet to say the keyboard keys to press. For example, you can say "Press alpha" to press "a" or "Press bravo" to press "b."
- Using Speech Recognition to press keyboard keys will only work with Latin alphabets.

Punctuation marks and special characters

The following table shows commands for using Speech Recognition to insert punctuation marks and special characters. Words in italic font indicate that you can say many different things in place of the example word or phrase and get useful results.

To make this appear	*Say this*	*To make this appear*	*Say this*
,	Comma	;	Semicolon
.	Period; Dot; Full stop; Decimal point	:	Colon
"	Open double quote; Open quote; Open inverted commas		
"	Close double quote; Close quote; Close inverted commas		
'	apostrophe	'	Open single quote

’	Close single quote	>	Greater than sign
<	Less than sign	/	Forward slash
\	Backslash	~	Tilde
@	At sign	!	Exclamation mark; Exclamation point
?	Question mark	#	Number sign; Pound sign; Hash sign
$	Dollar sign	%	Percent sign
^	Caret	(	Open parenthesis; Open paren
)	Close parenthesis; Close paren	_	Underscore
-	Hyphen; Minus sign; Dash	–	En dash
—	Em dash; Double dash	=	Equal sign
+	Plus sign	{	Open brace; Open curly bracket
}	Close brace; Close curly bracket	[	Open bracket; Open square bracket
]	Close bracket; Close square bracket	|	Vertical bar
:-)	Press smiley face	:-(	Press frowny face
;-)	Press winky face	™	Trademark sign
¾	Three quarter sign	¼	One quarter sign
½	One half sign	£	Pound sterling sign; pound; pound sign
&	Ampersand; and sign	*	asterisk
//	Double slash	‘	Back quote
<	Open angle bracket	>	Close angle bracket
±	Plus or minus sign	«	Open angle quote
»	Close angle quote	×	Multiplication sign
÷	Division sign	¢	Cent sign
¥	Yen sign	§	Section sign
©	Copyright sign	®	Registered, Registered trademark sign
°	Degree sign	¶	Paragraph sign
…	Ellipsis; Dot dot dot	*f*	Function sign

Controls

The following table shows commands for using Speech Recognition to perform tasks in Windows. Words in italic font indicate that you can say many different things in place of the example word or phrase and get useful results.

To do this	***Say this***
Click any item by saying its name	File; Edit; View; Save; bold
Click any item	Click File; Click bold; Click Save; Click Close
Double-click any item	Double-click Computer; Double-click Recycle Bin; Double-click Folder name
Right-click any item	Right-click Computer; Right-click Recycle Bin; Right-click Folder name
Minimize all windows to show your desktop	Show Desktop
Click something you don’t know the name of	Show numbers (Numbers will appear on the screen for every item in the active window)
Click a numbered item	19 OK; 5 OK

Double-click a numbered item	Double-click 19; Double-click 5
Right-click a numbered item	Right-click 19; Right-click 5

Windows

The following table shows commands for using Speech Recognition to work with windows and programs. Words in italic font indicate that you can say many different things in place of the example word or phrase and get useful results.

To do this	*Say this*
Open a program	Open Paint; Open WordPad; Open program name
Switch to an open program	Switch to Paint; Switch to WordPad; Switch to program name; Switch application
Close a program	Close that; Close Paint; Close Documents; Close Internet Explorer (only works with the active window)
Restore	Restore that; Restore Paint; Restore Internet Explorer (only works with the active window)
Minimize	Minimize that; Minimize Paint; Minimize Internet Explorer (only works with the active window)
Maximize	Maximize that; Maximize Paint; Maximize Internet Explorer (only works with the active window)
Cut	Cut that; Cut
Copy	Copy that; Copy
Paste	Paste
Delete	Delete that; Delete
Undo	Undo that; Scratch that; Undo
Scroll direction	Scroll up; Scroll down; Scroll right; Scroll left
Scroll an exact distance in pages	Scroll down 2 pages; Scroll up 10 pages
Scroll an exact distance in other units	Scroll up 5; Scroll down 7
Go to a field in a form or a program	Go to field name; Go to Subject; Go to Address; Go to Cc

Click anywhere on the screen

The following table shows commands for using Speech Recognition to click anywhere on the screen. Words in italic font indicate that you can say many different things in place of the example word or phrase and get useful results.

To do this	*Say this*
Show the mousegrid	Mousegrid
Move the mouse pointer to the center of any mousegrid square	number—or numbers—of the square; 1; 7; 9; 1, 7, 9
Click any mousegrid square	Click number of the square
Select an item to drag with the mousegrid	number—or numbers—of the square where the item appears; 3, 7, 9 (followed by) mark
Select an area where you want to drag the item with the mousegrid	number—or numbers—of the square where you want to drag; 4, 5, 6 (followed by) click

Sync Center

Sync is short for synchronization. In Windows, sync is the process of keeping two or more versions of the same file stored in different locations matched with each other. If you add, change, or delete a file in one location, Windows can add, change, or delete the same file in the other locations that you choose to sync with, whenever you choose to sync.

Sync Center is a feature of Windows that allows you to keep information in sync between your computer and Mobile devices that you plug in to your computer or to which you connect wirelessly (such as portable music players, digital cameras, and mobile phones).

- Files stored in folders on network servers. (These are called offline files because you can access them even when your computer or the server is not connected to the network.)
- Programs that support Sync Center.

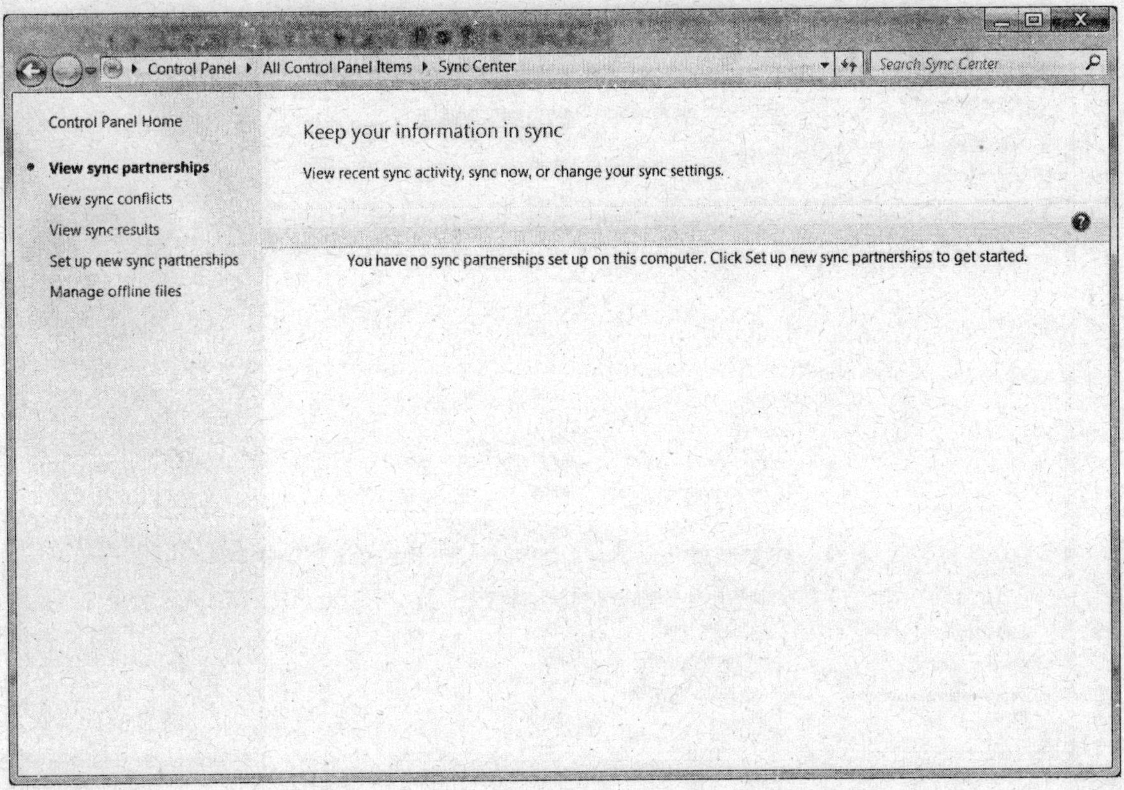

System

The system dialog box has the following information.

What edition of Windows 7 is installed on your computer?

As you know, Windows 7 comes in several editions. Not all editions are made equal; if you're failing to find some feature that you could have sworn is supposed to be in Windows 7, it's good to check here. You might find out that the feature you want is available only on higher-priced versions.

PC's performance in terms of Rating

Ratings are displayed in the Rating column in your library. By default, most items in your library are automatically given an auto rating. The auto rating is controlled by non-Microsoft data providers, such as AMG and some online stores. You can override an auto rating by explicitly choosing a new user rating. You can distinguish between the two types of ratings by the appearance of the stars, which are blue for auto ratings and bright yellow for user ratings.

The model name and speed of your PC's processor chip

Such as Intel Core Duo CPU E7400 @2.80 GHz.

How much memory your PC has?

That's a very helpful number to know, particularly if you need to improve your computer's speed.

Your computer's name, domain or workgroup

Remember, your computer name and description are primarily useful on a network, since that's how other people will identify your computer. Unless you tell it otherwise, Vista names your computer after you login name, somtheing like SUN-PC.

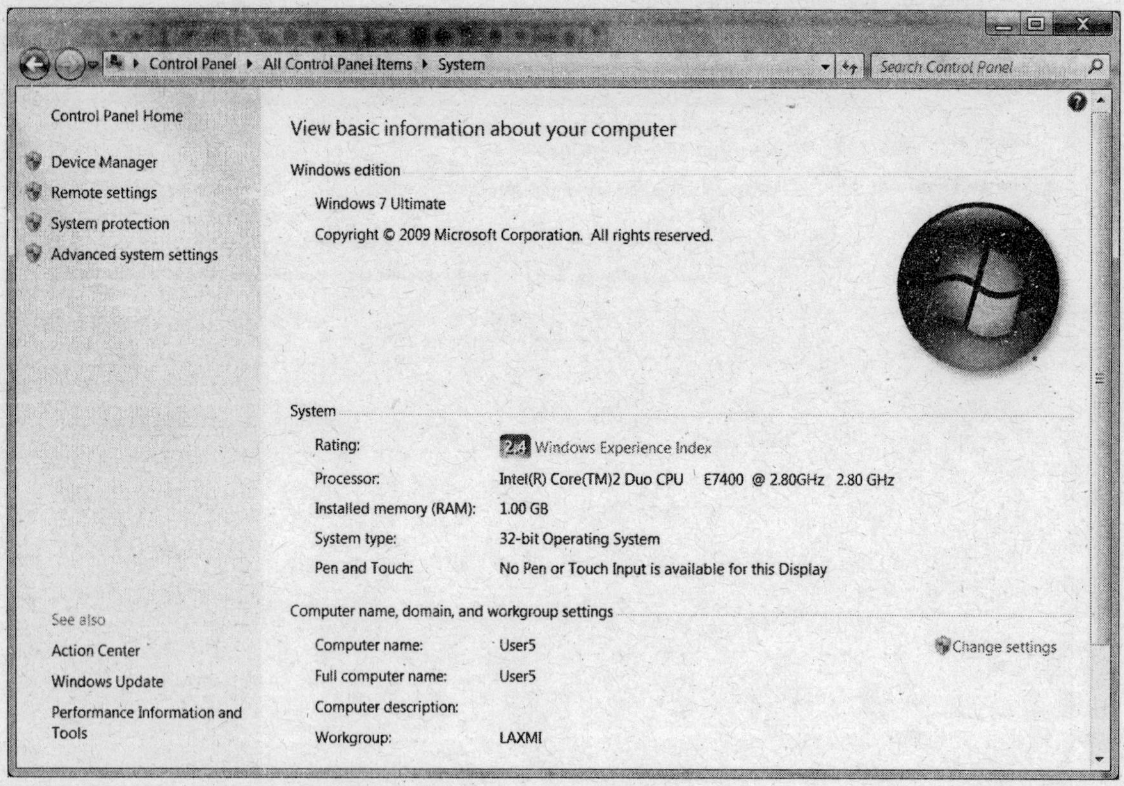

Taskbar and Start Menu

The Start menu is the main gateway to your computer's programs, folders, and settings. It's called a menu because it provides a list of choices, just as a restaurant menu does. And as "Start" implies, it's often the place that you'll go to start or open things.

Use the Start menu to do these common activities:

- Start programs
- Open commonly used folders
- Search for files, folders, and programs
- Adjust computer settings
- Get help with the Windows operating system

- Turn off the computer
- Log off from Windows or switch to a different user account

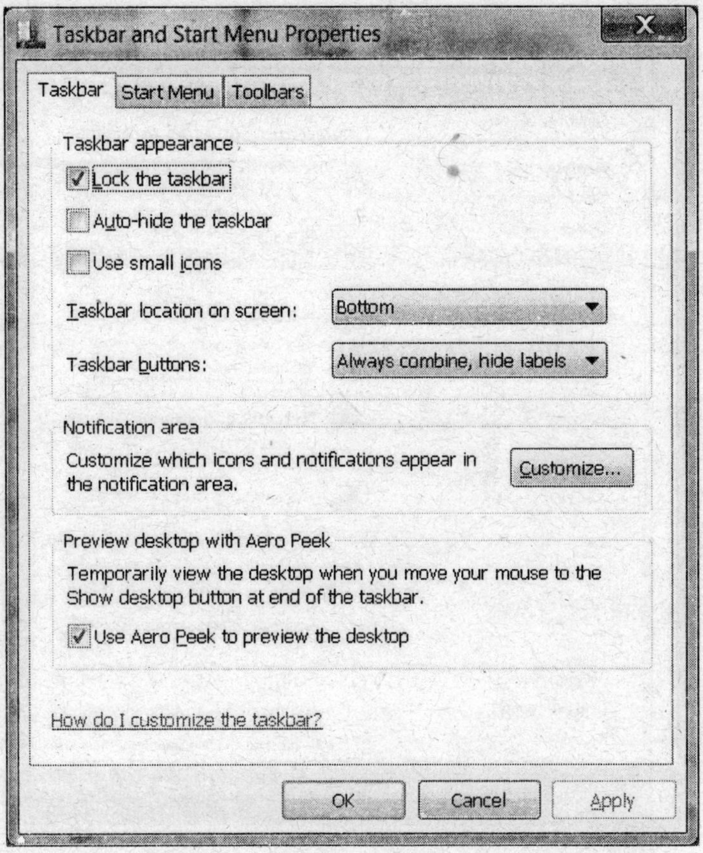

The taskbar is the long horizontal bar at the bottom of your screen. Unlike the desktop, which can get obscured by the windows on top of it, the taskbar is visible almost all the time. It has four main sections:

- The Start button, which opens the Start menu.
- The Quick Launch toolbar, which lets you start programs with one click.
- The middle section, which shows you which programs and documents you have open and allows you to quickly switch between them.
- The notification area, which includes a clock and icons (small pictures) that communicate the status of certain programs and computer settings.

Troubleshooting

It allows you to check your computer for minor problems before you call the engineer, for repairs. You can click on a task to automatically troubleshoot and fix common computer problems. To view more troubleshooters, click on a category or usee the Search box. Various category are: Programs, Hardware and Sound, Network and Internet, Appearance and Personalization, and System and Security.

User Accounts

User Account Control (UAC) is a new set of infrastructure technologies in this version of Windows that helps prevent malicious programs, sometimes called "malware," from damaging a system, while also helping organizations to deploy a better-managed desktop.

With UAC, applications and tasks always run in the security context of a non-administrator account, unless an administrator specifically authorizes administrator-level access to the system. UAC stops the automatic installation of unauthorized applications, and prevents inadvertent changes to system settings.

How does UAC work?

In this version of Windows, there are two levels of users: standard users and administrators. Standard users are members of the Users group and administrators are members of the Administrators group on the computer.

Unlike previous versions of Windows, both standard users and administrators access resources and run applications in the security context of standard users by default. When any user logs on to a computer, the system creates an access token for the user. This access token contains information about the level of access that the user is granted, including specific security identifiers (SIDs) and Windows privileges. When an

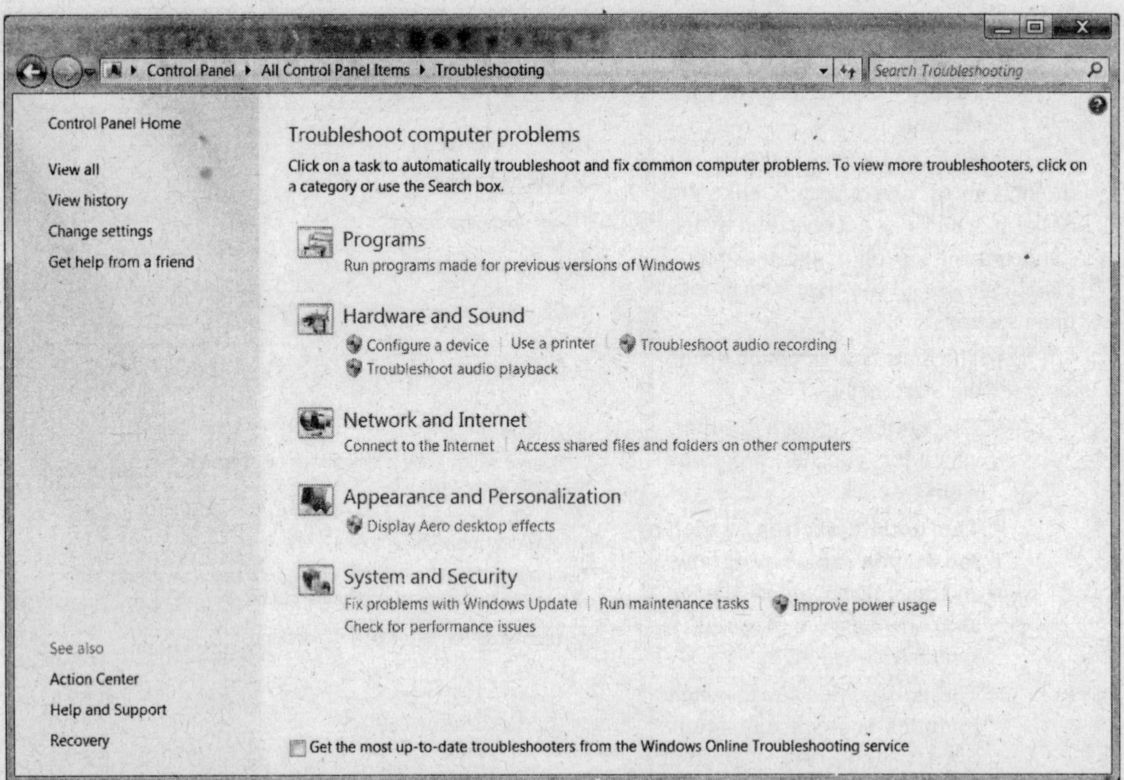
Control Panel ▸ All Control Panel Items ▸ Troubleshooting
Search Troubleshooting
Control Panel Home
View all
View history
Change settings
Get help from a friend
See also
Action Center
Help and Support
Recovery
Troubleshoot computer problems
Click on a task to automatically troubleshoot and fix common computer problems. To view more troubleshooters, click on a category or use the Search box.
Programs
Run programs made for previous versions of Windows
Hardware and Sound
Configure a device
Use a printer
Troubleshoot audio recording
Troubleshoot audio playback
Network and Internet
Connect to the Internet
Access shared files and folders on other computers
Appearance and Personalization
Display Aero desktop effects
System and Security
Fix problems with Windows Update
Run maintenance tasks
Improve power usage
Check for performance issues
Get the most up-to-date troubleshooters from the Windows Online Troubleshooting service

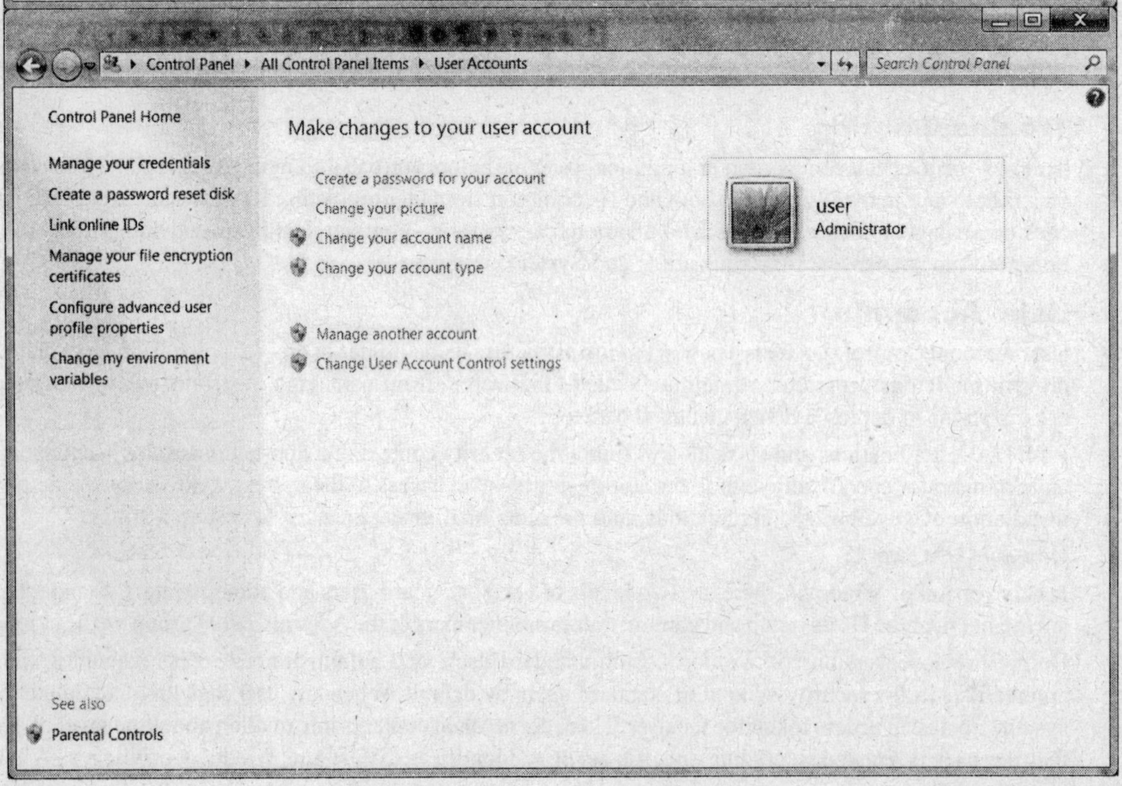
Control Panel ▸ All Control Panel Items ▸ User Accounts
Search Control Panel
Control Panel Home
Manage your credentials
Create a password reset disk
Link online IDs
Manage your file encryption certificates
Configure advanced user profile properties
Change my environment variables
See also
Parental Controls
Make changes to your user account
Create a password for your account
Change your picture
Change your account name
Change your account type
Manage another account
Change User Account Control settings
user
Administrator

administrator logs on, this version of Windows creates two separate access tokens for the user: a standard user access token and an administrator access token. The standard user access token contains the same user-specific information as the administrator access token, but the administrative Windows privileges and SIDs have been removed. The standard user access token is used to start applications that do not perform administrative tasks ("standard user applications").

When the administrator needs to run applications that perform administrative tasks ("administrator applications"), this version of Windows prompts the users to change or "elevate" their security context from a standard user to an administrator. This default administrator user experience is called Admin Approval Mode. In this mode, applications require specific permission to run as an administrator application (an application that has the same access as an administrator).

When an administrator application is starting, by default a User Account Control message appears. If the user is an administrator, the message gives a choice to allow the application to start or to prevent it from starting. If the user is a standard user, the user can enter the user name and password of an account that is a member of the local Administrators group.

Windows CardSpace

Ever have to fill out a form on the Internet—name, address, email address—only to go to a differnt site that requests exactly the same information. CardSpace is Microsoft's attempt to solve that duplication-of-effort problem. You are supposed to create a profile containing this kind of information, like a digital ID card. You show your card at a site, and the site gest your information off the card, saving you all that retyping.

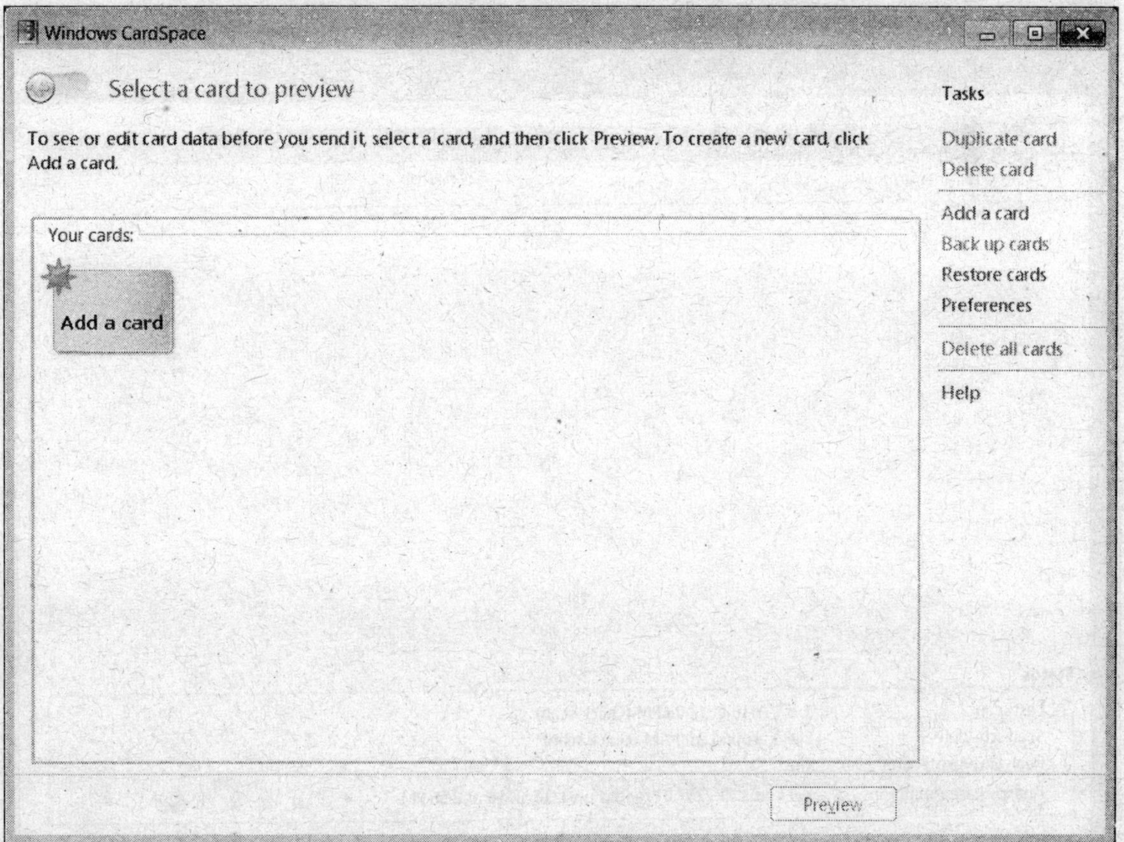

Windows Defender

It's important to run antispyware software whenever you're using your computer. Spyware and other potentially unwanted software can try to install itself on your computer any time you connect to the Internet. It can also infect your computer when you install some programs using a CD, DVD, or other removable media. Potentially unwanted or malicious software can also be programmed to run at unexpected times, not just when it is installed.

Windows Defender offers three ways to help keep spyware and other potentially unwanted software from infecting your computer:

- **Real-time protection. Windows** Defender alerts you when spyware or potentially unwanted software attempts to install itself or to run on your computer. It also alerts you when programs attempt to change important Windows settings.
- **SpyNet community**. The online Microsoft SpyNet community helps you see how other people respond to software that has not yet been classified for risks. Seeing if other members of the community allow software can help you choose whether to allow it on your computer. In turn, if you participate, your choices are added to the community ratings to help other people choose what to do.
- **Scanning options**. You can use Windows Defender to scan for spyware and other potentially unwanted software that might be installed on your computer, to schedule scans on a regular basis, and to automatically remove any malicious software that is detected during a scan.

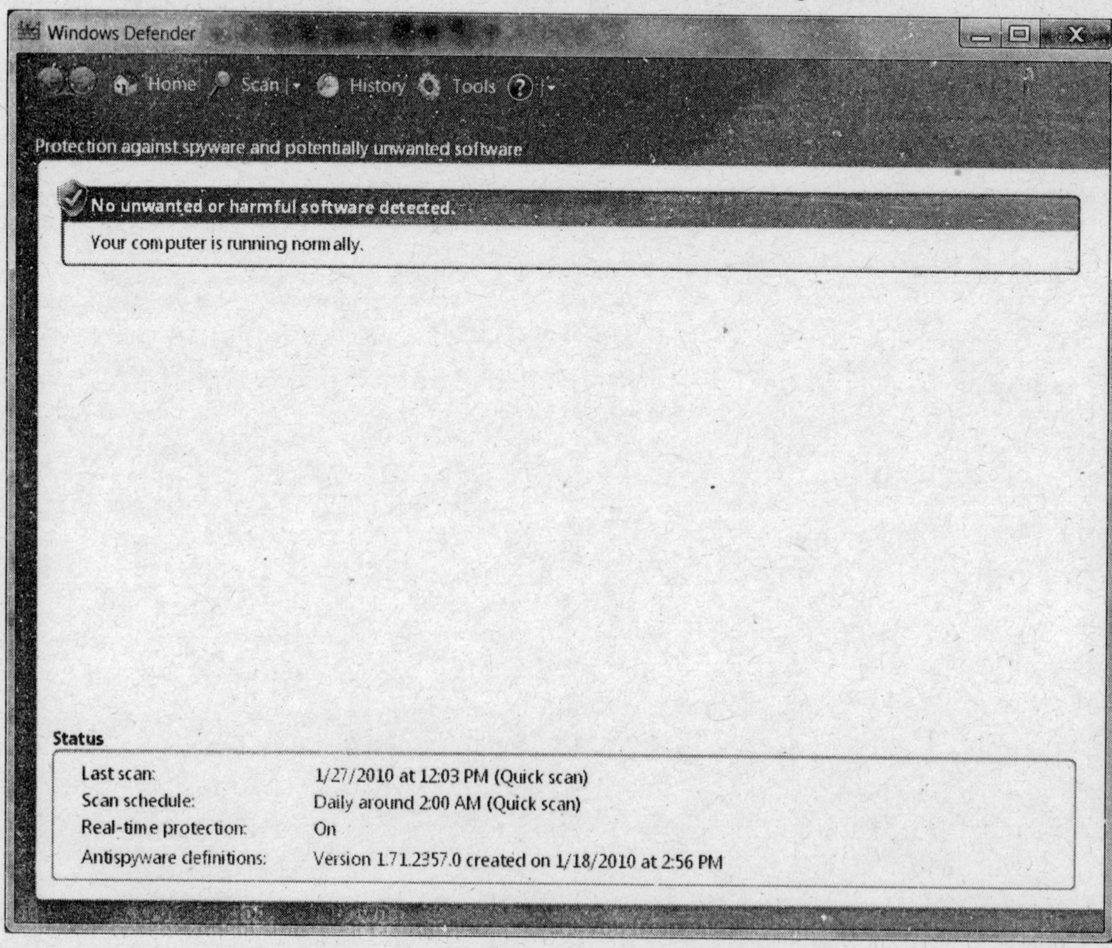

When you use Windows Defender, it's important to have up-to-date definitions. Definitions are files that act like an ever-growing encyclopedia of potential software threats. Windows Defender uses definitions to determine if software that it detects is spyware or other potentially unwanted software, and then to alert you to potential risks. To help keep your definitions up to date, Windows Defender works with Windows Update to automatically install new definitions as they are released. You can also set Windows Defender to check online for updated definitions before scanning.

Windows Firewall

A firewall is software or hardware that checks information coming from the Internet or a network, and then either blocks it or allows it to pass through to your computer, depending on your firewall settings.

A firewall can help prevent hackers or malicious software (such as worms) from gaining access to your computer through a network or the Internet. A firewall can also help stop your computer from sending malicious software to other computers.

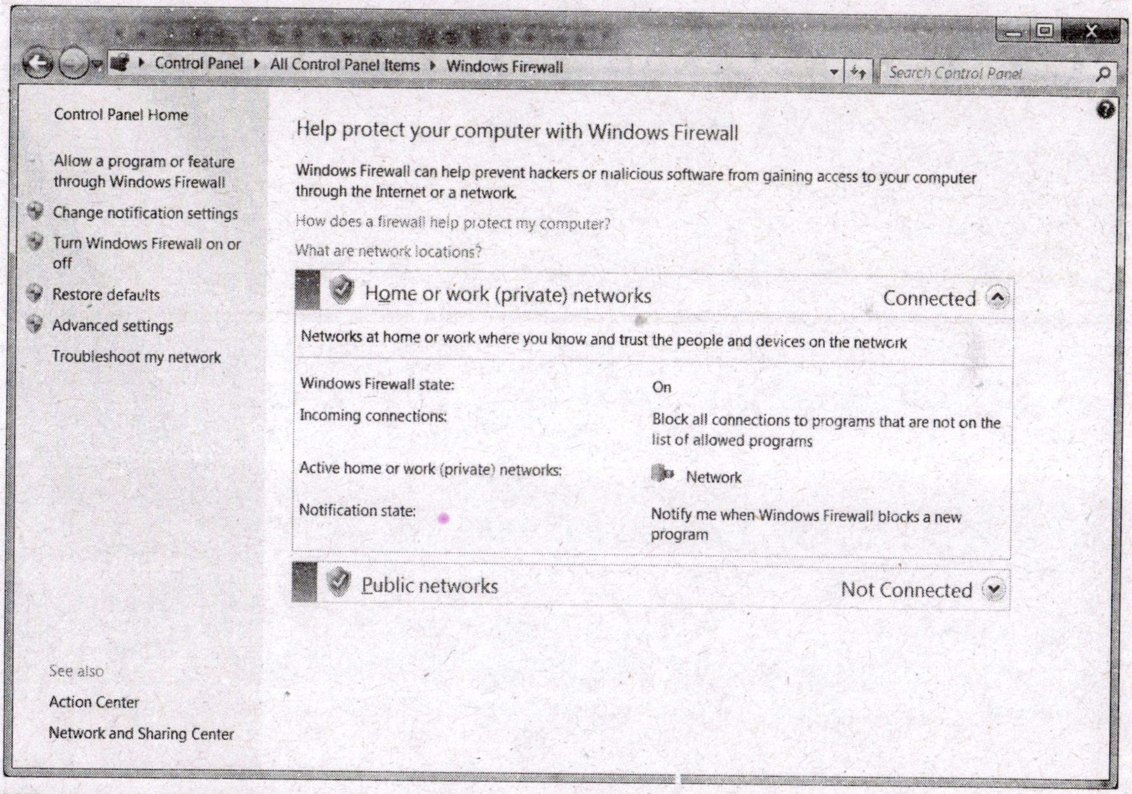

Windows Update

Because Windows is a constant work in progress, Microsoft frequently releases updates, fixes, patches, and drivers, in hope of constantly improving your computer's speed and security all the time.

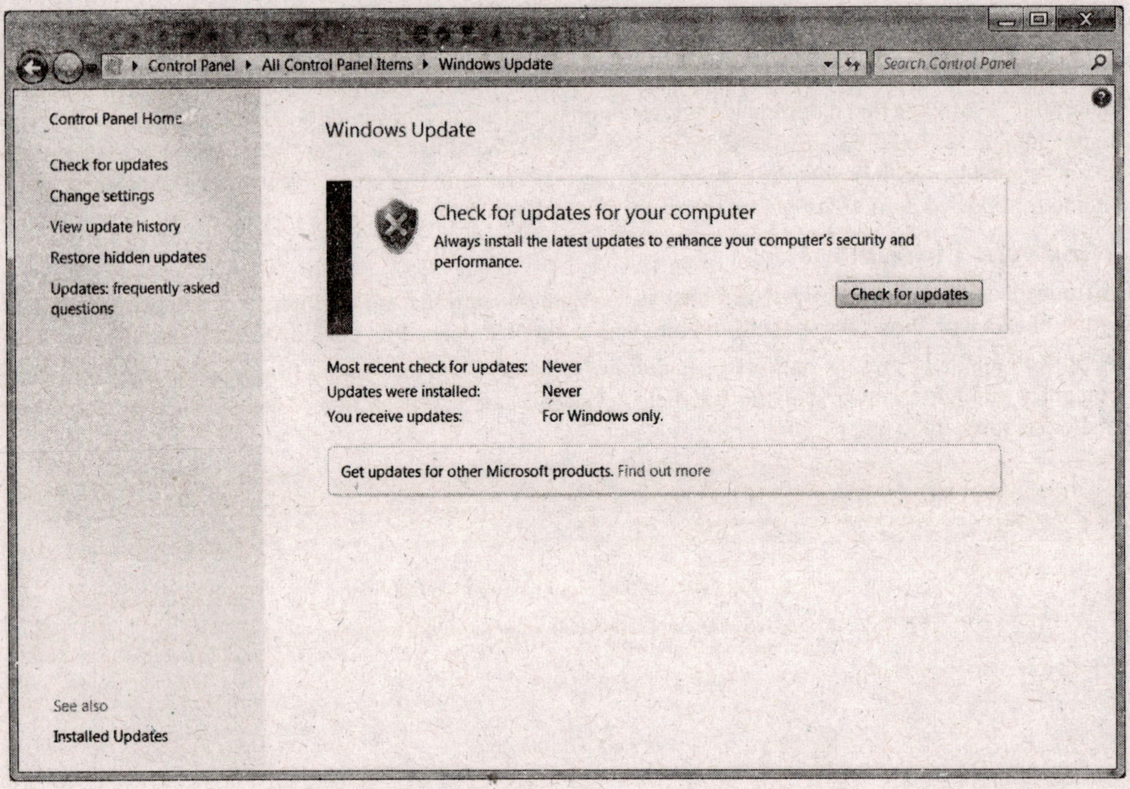

Control Panel
All Control Panel Items
Windows Update
Search Control Panel
Control Panel Home
Check for updates
Change settings
View update history
Restore hidden updates
Updates: frequently asked questions
See also
Installed Updates
Windows Update
Check for updates for your computer
Always install the latest updates to enhance your computer's security and performance.
Check for updates
Most recent check for updates: Never
Updates were installed: Never
You receive updates: For Windows only.
Get updates for other Microsoft products. Find out more

4 Accessories of Windows 7

Introduction

As in earlier versions of Windows, Windows 7 too has its own set of accessories for making the working under Windows Vista easier. Most of the earlier one have been retained but some new ones have also been added.

As was in the eariler versions, few of the accessories are clubbed together in a group. These groups are:

Ease of Access

System Tools

Tablet PC

Windows Power Shell

Then there are few others which are: Calculator, Command Prompt, Connect to a Network Projector, Getting Started, Math Input Panel, Notepad, Paint, Remote Desktop Connection, Run, Snipping Tool, Sound Recorder, Sticky Notes, Sync Center, Windows Explorer, and WordPad.

Let us see the working of each one of them.

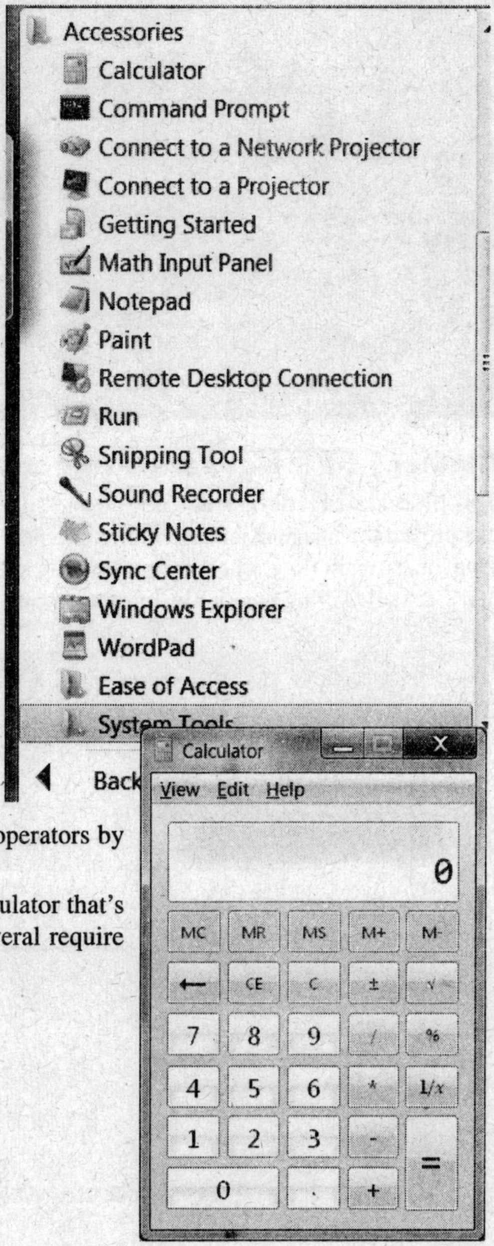

Calculator

You can use Calculator to perform addition, subtraction, multiplication, and division. Calculator also offers the advanced capabilities of scientific and statistical calculators.

You can perform calculations by clicking the calculator buttons, or you can type calculations by using your keyboard. You can also use the numeric keypad to type numbers and operators by pressing NUM LOCK.

Most of the button look just like the ones on the plastic calculator that's probably in your desk drawer at this very moment, but several require special explations:

Slash /	means divided by in computer language.
Asterisk *	is used for multiplication.
Sqrt	click this button to find the square root
%	click this to find the percentage

Command Prompt

This is for running the old DOS based commands

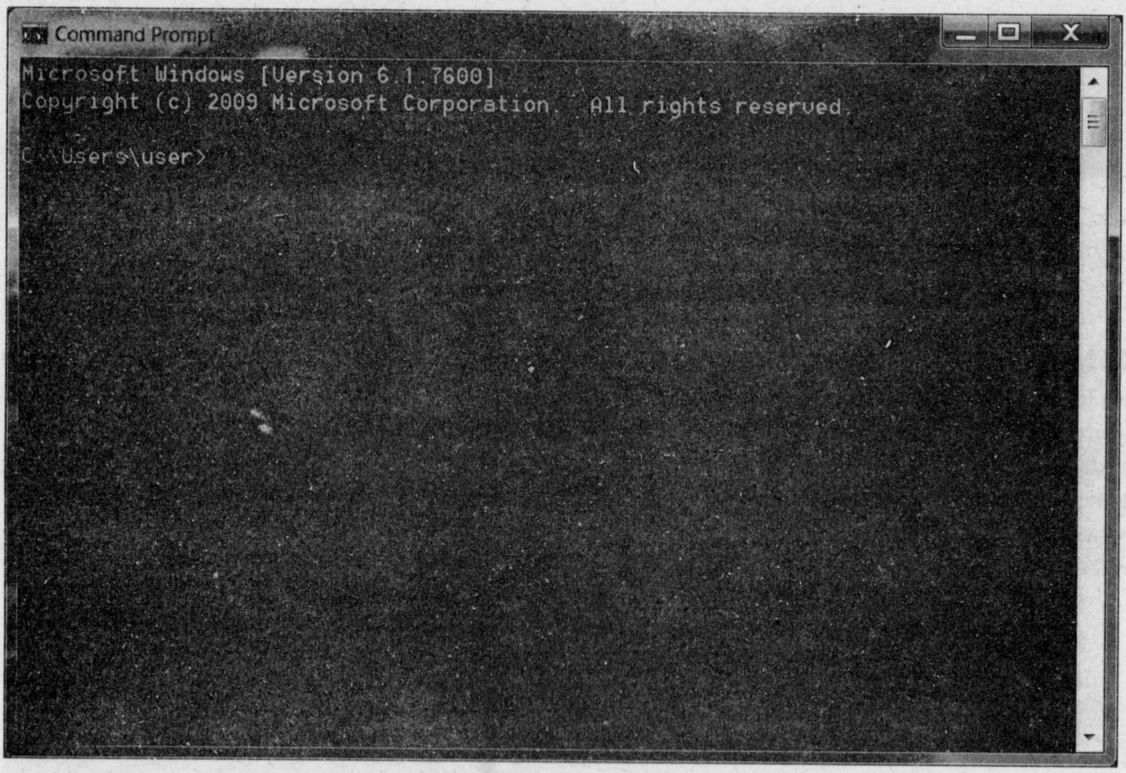

Connect to a Network Projector

This little wizard is designed to detect, and connect your PC to a network projector—a video projector that can project the image from any computer on the network. You, the pitchmaster, can stand in the conference room on the eight floor, where the projector is, showing your awestruck co-workers a PowerPoint presentation that's actually sitting on your PC in Accounting down on the fourth.

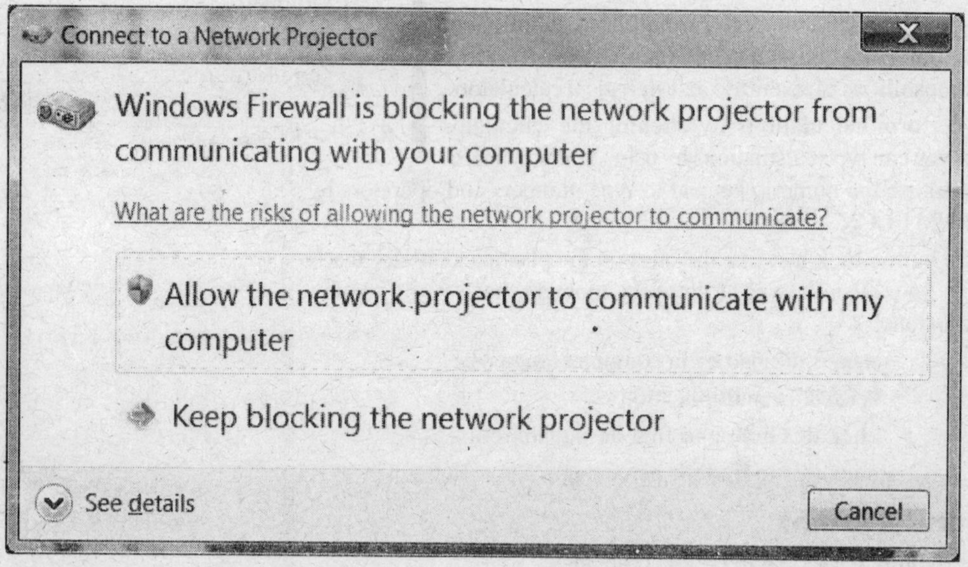

Getting Started

It is a place from where you can find out everything you need to know about setting up your computer. Also, discover the new features of Windows 7, which can help you in production, staying safe and of course, having fun.

Also you can do lots of other things as shown in the figure next.

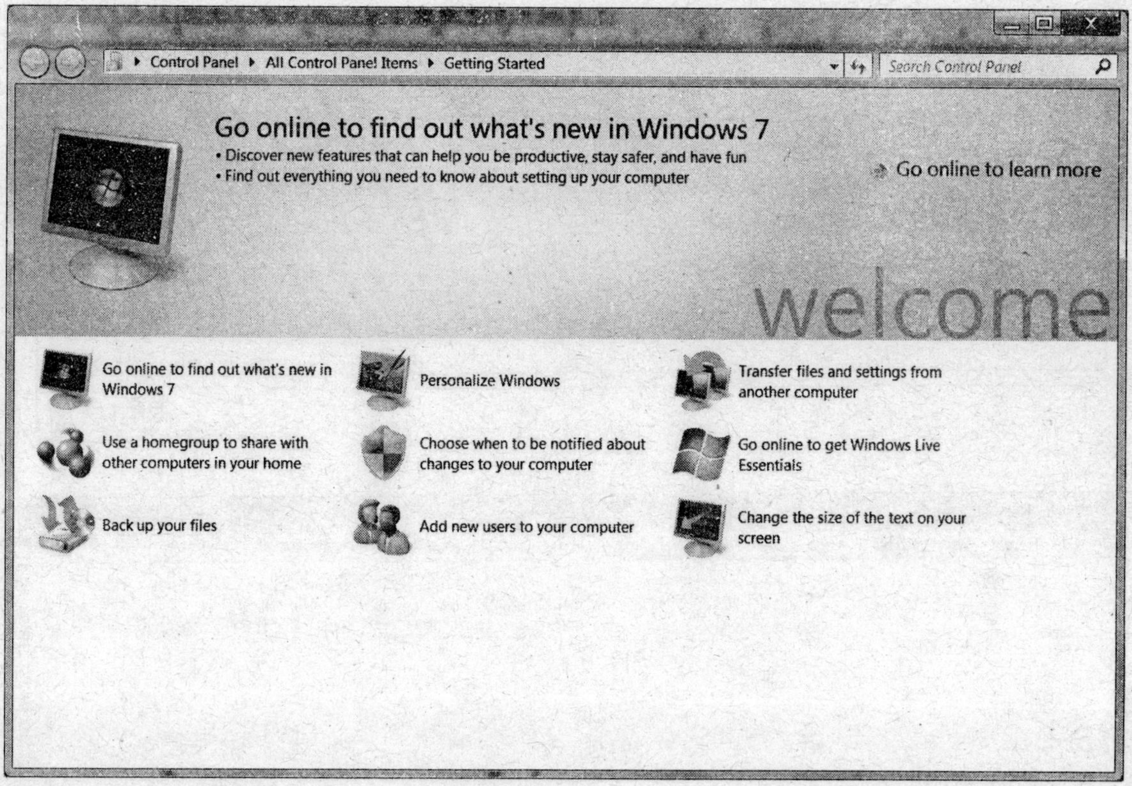

Math Input Panel

There are times when you need to type the text in the form of equations, and other mathematical and chemical symbols. This feature had been there in word processing software, like Microsoft Word, etc. This feature is definitely very useful for creating such type of text.

The screen is shown on the next page.

Notepad

It is a text editor, which means that it lets you open, create, edit files that contain plain, unformatted text, like the Read Me text files that usually accompany new programs. You can also use Netepad to write about short notes or edit text that you intend to paste into your email program after editing it.

Paint

You can use Paint to create simple artwork or edit graphc files from other sources. Common tasks for this program include making quick sketches, fixing dust specks on scanned photos, and entertaining kids for hours.

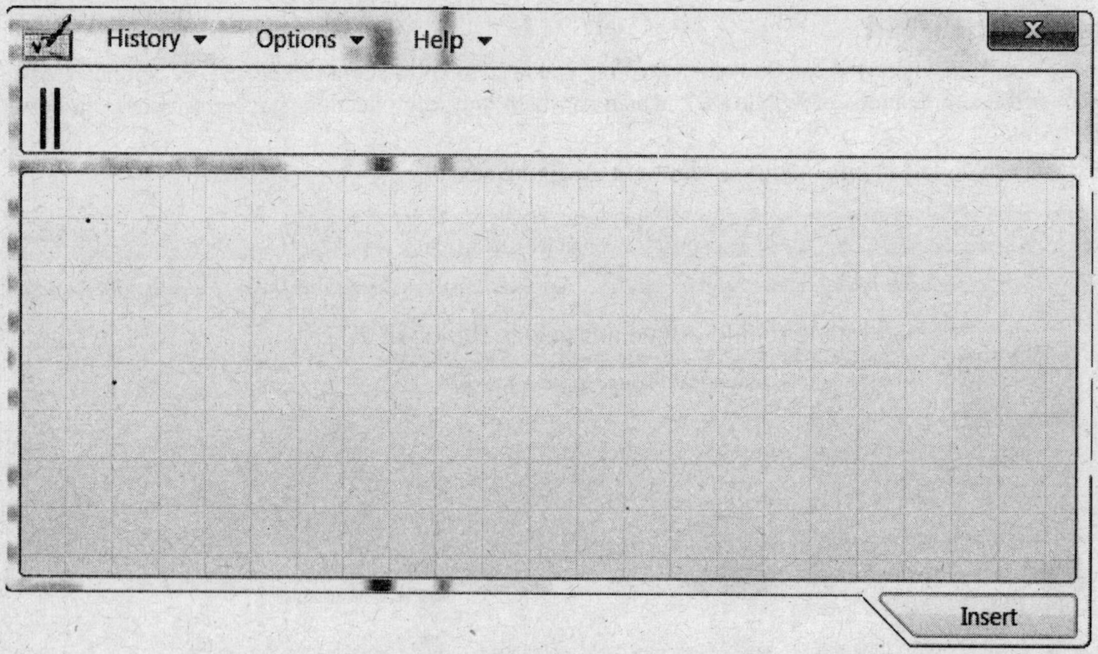

Specifically, for the earlier users of Paint. This time the Paint software is very different from the earlier ones. Now you see most of the commands on the screen, and apply them when neededx

Remote Desktop Connection

This allows you to site at home PC and run your office PC by remote control. The following information will

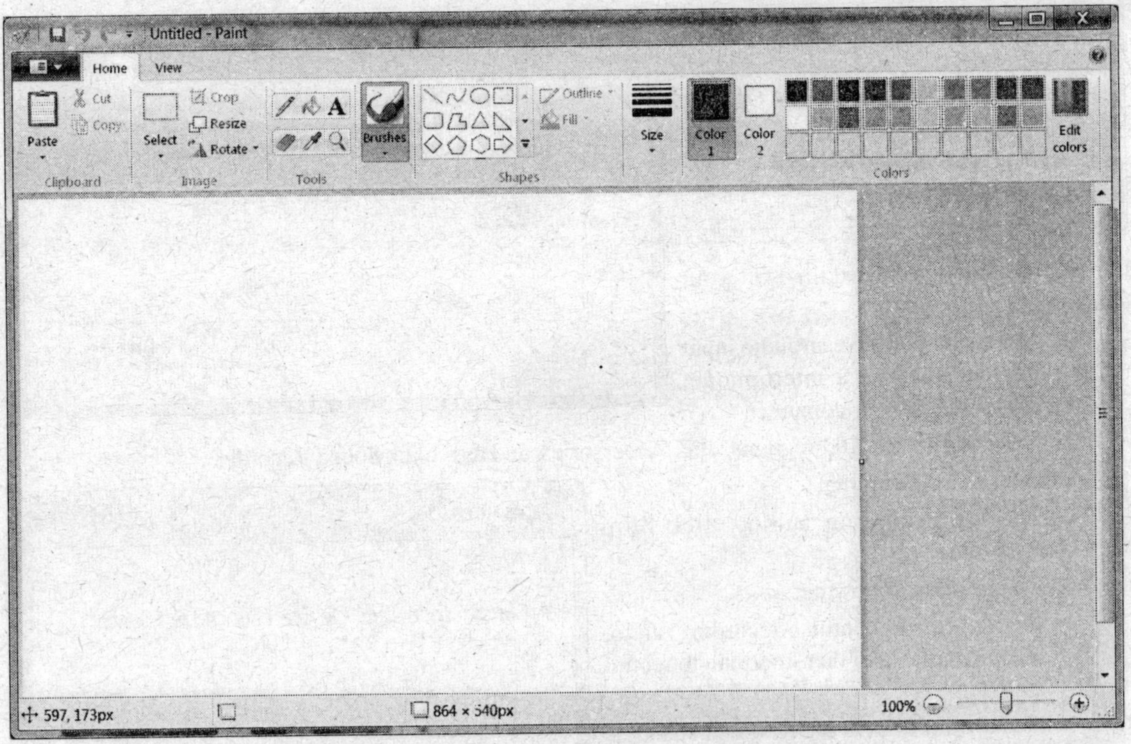

help you decide which setting to choose on the Remote tab in System Properties:

Run

When you want to open somthing with just a few keystrokes, the little Run command-line window is there for you.

Snipping Tool

It takes pictures of your PC's screen, for use when you're writing up instructions, illustrating a computer book, or collecting proof of some secret screen you found buried in a game. You can take pictures of the entire screen or capture only the contents of a rectangular selection. When you are finished, Snipping tools displays your snapshot in a new windows, which you can print, close without saving, edit, or save, ready for emailing or inserting into a manuscript or page-layout program.

Sound Recorder

Using Sound Recorder, you can record sound as a digital media file on your computer from a variety of devices, such as a microphone that is plugged in to your sound card. The types of audio input sources you can record from depend on the audio devices you have, as well as on the input sources that are available on

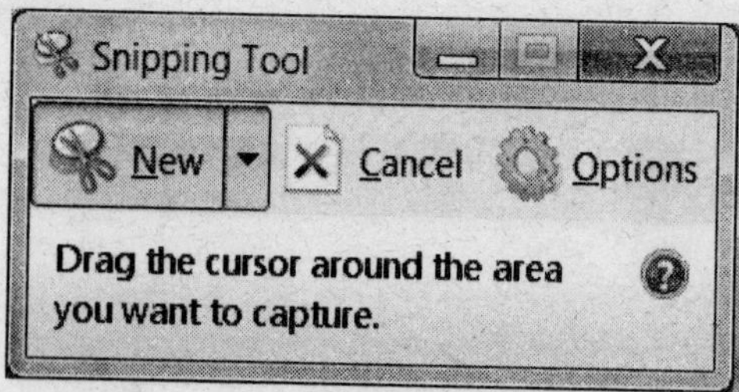

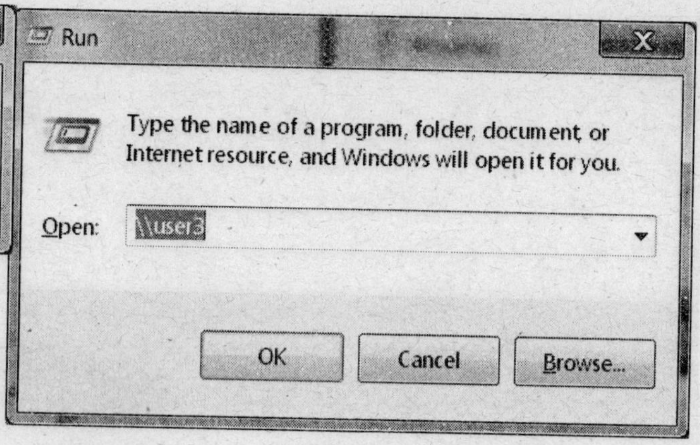

the sound card that is installed on your computer.

1. Make sure you have an audio input device, such as a microphone, connected to your computer.
2. Click Start, click All Programs, click Accessories, and then click Sound Recorder.
3. Click Start Recording.
4. To stop recording audio, click Stop Recording.
5. Do one of the following:

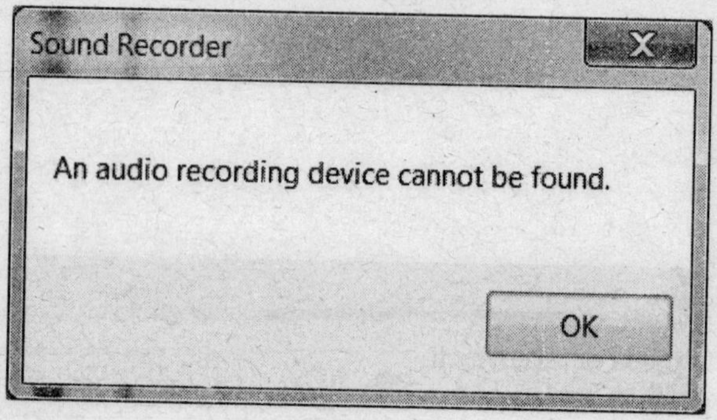

- If you want to continue recording audio, click Resume, and then continue to record sound.
- If you want to save the recorded sound as an audio file, click the File name box, type a file name for the recorded sound, and then click Save.
- To use Sound Recorder, you must have a sound card and speakers installed on your computer. If you want to record sound, you also need a microphone.
- By default, the recorded audio is saved as a Windows Media Audio (WMA) file.

  If you are using Windows Vista Home Basic N or Windows Vista Business N, your Sound Recorder files are saved as .wav files rather than .wma files.
- You can play your recording in a digital media player program that supports playback of WMA files.

Sticky Notes

I am quite sure that you must have seen these sticky notes in real life. This time you have them in the computer. Write something and stick it on any wall that you see in the Windows or any other software which you are using.

Tablet PC accessory that you can use to create short handwritten or voice notes. The small, yellow notes are arranged in a stack on the desktop; similar to paper sticky notes.

Open Sticky Notes

You can open Sticky Notes quickly by using the Start button, or specifying that Sticky Notes opens automatically when you start your computer. You can also keep Sticky Notes always visible on your desktop.

To open Sticky Notes

- On the Windows taskbar, tap the Start button , point to All Programs, and then tap Sticky Notes.

To make Sticky Notes open automatically at startup

- Tap the Tools menu, point to Options, and then tap Open at Startup.

To keep Sticky Notes always visible on the desktop

- Tap the Tools menu, point to Options, and then tap Always on Top.

To close Sticky Notes

- On the title bar, tap the Close button.

Your notes are automatically saved when you close Sticky Notes.

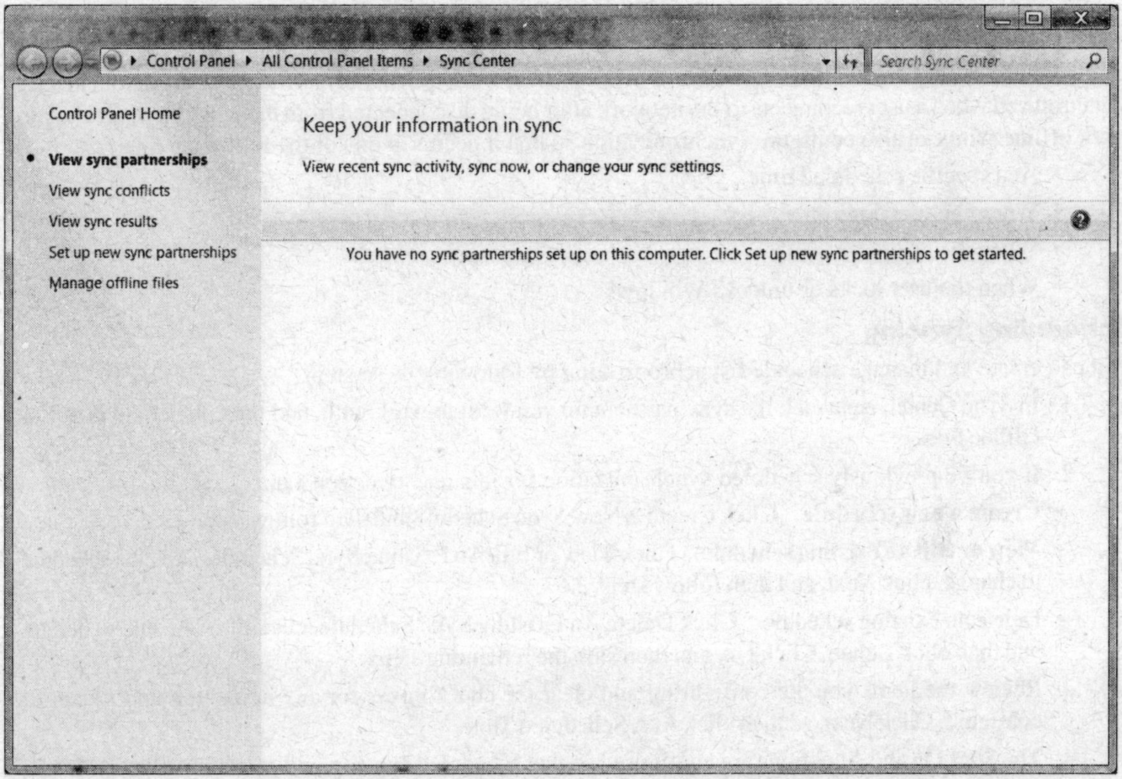

Sync Center

Sync Center, as shown above, simplifies the management of cached offline files and folders. In Sync Center, a sync partnership is established for every shared folder that has locally cached contents. Each sync partnership has a set of properties that enables you to control whether and how syncing occurs.

Biewing Current Sync Parterships

You can view current sync partnerships in Sync Center by following these steps.

1. Access Sync Center by clicking Start, pointing to All Programs, Accessories, and then clicking Sync Center.
2. In Sync Center, sync parternships are listed according to name, status, progress, conflict count, error count, and category

After you display Sync Center, you can easily check for synchronization problems start or stop syncing, and configure syncing.

Syncing Offline Manually

You can manually synchronize offline files by using either of the following techniques.

- **Sync all offline files and folders** When multiple sync partnership have been established, you can sync all offile files and folders by operating Sync Center and then clicking Sync All. Sync All is available only when no individual sync partnerships are selected.
- **Sync a specif network share** When you want to sync the offline files and folders for a particular shared network folder, opne Sync Center, click the sync partnership that you want to work with and then click Sync.

Syncing Offline Files Automatically

Group Policy settings control how offline file synchronization works. Generally, offline files are automatically synchronized when a user reconnects to the network after being disconnected from the network or electing to work offline. You can also configure synchronization so that it occurs at one of the following times.

- At a specific scheduled time
- When the user logs on
- When the computer is idle
- When the user locks or unlocks Windows

Scheduling Syncing

You can create and manage scheduled synchronization by following these steps.

1. In Sync Center, right clck the sync partnership you want to work with, and then click Schedule For Offline Files.
2. If you've previously scheduled synchronization for this resource, you can.
   - **Create a new schedule** Click Create A New Sync Schedule and then follow steps 3 - 7.
   - **View or edit an existing sche**dule Click View or Edit An Existing Sync Schedule, click the schedule to change, click Next, and then follow steps 3 - 7.
   - Delete an existing schedule Click Delete An Existing Sync Schedule, click the schedule to delete, and then click Delete. Click Ok, and then skip the remaining steps.
3. Review the items you are configuring and clear the check boxes for any items you don't want to configure. Click Next, ad then click At A Scheduled Time.
4. The Start On and At options are configured so that scheduled syncing will start immediately. If you want to start scheduled syncing on a different date and time, use the options provided to change the start date and time.
5. The Repeat Every option sts the sync interval. The default interval is once everyday. You can set the repeat interval to a value in minutes, hours, days, weeks, or months. Because only changes are synced, you might want to sync more frequently that you would with Wndows XP. For example, with important files, you might want to sync every 3 to 4 hours.
6. Click Next.
7. Type a descriptive name for the scheduled synchronization, and then click Save Schedule.

Syncing on an Event or Action

You can create and anage synchronzation based on events or actions by following these steps.

1. In Sync Center, click the sync parternship you want to work with, and then click Schedule.
2. If you've previously scheduled synchronization for this resource, you can.
   - **Create a new schedule** Click Create A New Sync Schedule, and then follow steps 3 through 6.

- **View or edit an existing schedule** Click View Or Edit An Existing Sync Schedule, click the schedule to change, click Next, and then follow steps 3 through 6.
- **Delete an existing schedule** Click Delete An Existing Sync Schedule, click the schedule to delete, and then click Delete. Click Ok, and then skip the remaining steps.

3. Review the items you are configuring, clear the check boxes for any items you don't want to configure, and then click Next. Click When An Event Occurs.
4. Use the checked boxes provided to specify the events and actions that start automatic syncing.
5. Click Next.
6. Type a descriptive name for the schedule sync, and then click Save Schedule.

Windows Explorer

When you think about, most of your time working with a computer is spent managing files and folders. You create files and folders to store and organize information. You set file and folder properties, and so on. Because you spend so much time working with files and folders, a few simple techniqes for effective management can go a long way toward saving you time and effort.

You can customize Windows Explorer setting by using any of the following options.

- **Always Show Icons, Never Thumbnails** By default, Windows Explorer shows large thumbnail images of the actual content for pictures and other type of files. For folders that have many pictures, this option can be annoying because Windows Explorer has to render the thumbnail representation of each image. To disable thumbnails except when you select the Thumbnails option on the View menu, slect this option.
- **Always Show Menus** By default, Windows Explorer hides the menu bar, and you must choose to

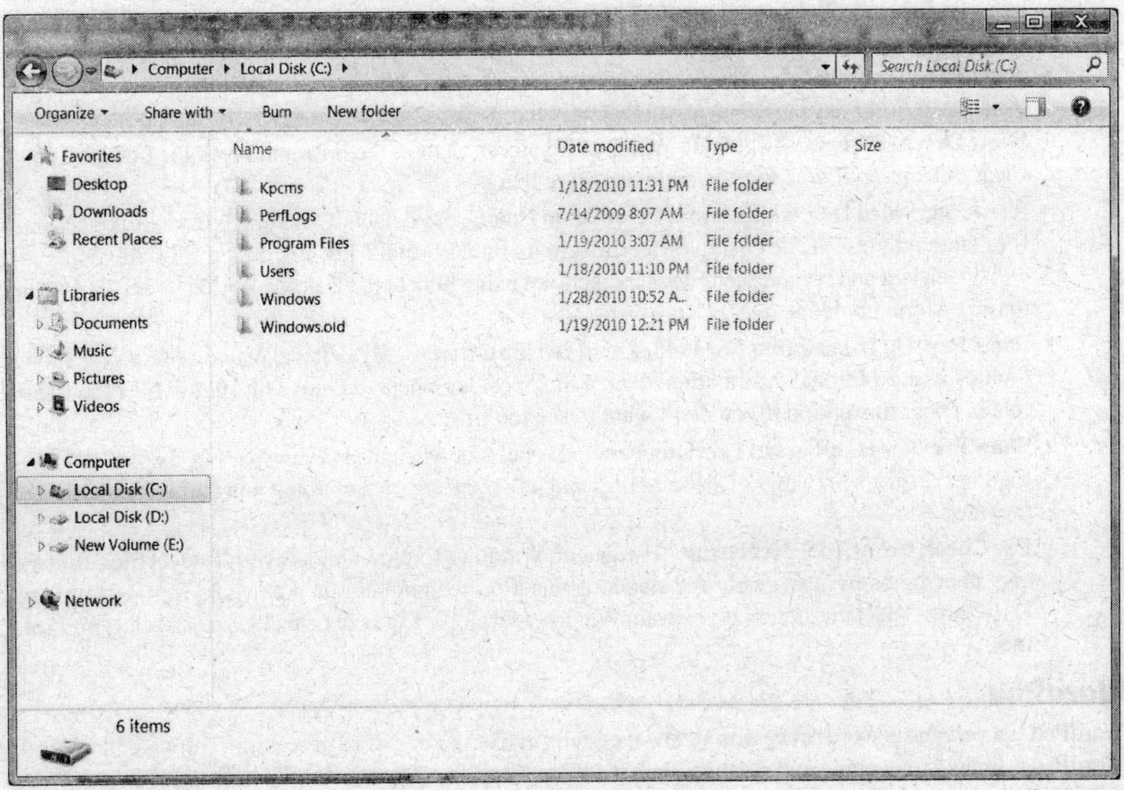

display it by clicking Organize, pointing to Layout, and then clicking Menu Bar. To always display the menu bar, select this option.

- **Display File Icon On Thumbnails** By default, Windows Explorer adds file icons to the thumbnails it displays. To display thumbnails without file icons, clear this option.
- **Display File Size Information in Folder Tips** By default, when you move the mouse pointer over a folder name or folder icon, Windows Explorer displays a tooltip showing the folder's creation date and time, the size of the folder, and a partial list of files. To display less information (only the creation date and time), clear this option.
- **Display The Full Path In The Title Bar** By default, when you press Alt+Tab to access the filp view, Windows displays the folder name when you move the mouse pointer over a Windows Explorer window. To display the actual file path insteaqd, select this option.
- **Hidden Files And Folders** By default, Windows Explorer does not display hidden files, folders, or drives. To display hidden files, folders, and drives, select Show Hidden Files, Folders, And Drives.
- **Hide Empty Drives in The Computer Folder** By default, Windows Explorer does not display information about empty drives in the Computer window. To display information about empty drives, clear this option.
- **Hide Extensions For Known File Types** By default, Windows Explorer does not display file extensions for known file types. To display operating system files, clear this option.
- **Hide Protected Operating System Files** By default, Windows Explorer does not display operating system files. To display operating system files extensions for all file types clear this option.
- **Launch Folder Windows In A Separate Process** By default, Windows runs all instances of Windows Exxplorer in the same process. This saves memory and generally speeds up the process of opening new windows, but it also means that all instances of Windows Explorer are dependent on each other. If one instance crashes, they all crash, and if one instance is in a pending or wait state, all instances could become locked. To modify this behaviour and have Windows start a new process for each instance of Windows Explorer, select this option.
- **Show Drive Letters** By default, Windows Explorer as art of the information on the Locations bar. Clear this option if you don't want to see drive letters.
- **Show Encrypted Or Compressed NTFS Files in Color** By default, Windows Explorer lists encrypted files and compressed files using different colours than normal files. Encrypted files are displayed with green text and compressed files are displayed using blue text. Clear this option if you don't want to use different colours.
- **Show Pop-Up Description For Folder And Desktop Items** By default, Windows Explorer shows tooltips with additional information about a file or folder when you move the mouse over the file or folder. Clear this option if you don't want to see tooltips.
- **Show Preview Handlers in Previous Pane** By default, when the Preview pane is visible, Windows Explorer displays previews of selected files and folders. Clear this option if you don't want to see the previews.
- **Use Check Boxes To Select Items** By default, Windows Explorer allows you to select files, folders, and other items by using only the standard selection techniques, such as click, Shift+Click, and Ctrl+Shift. Select this option if you want Windows Explorer to display check boxes to select multiple files.

WordPad

WordPad is a very basic word processor. It however, fails in front of big word processing software like Word. WordPad is limited to opening and creating plain text files, Rich Text Format documents and Microsoft Write documents.

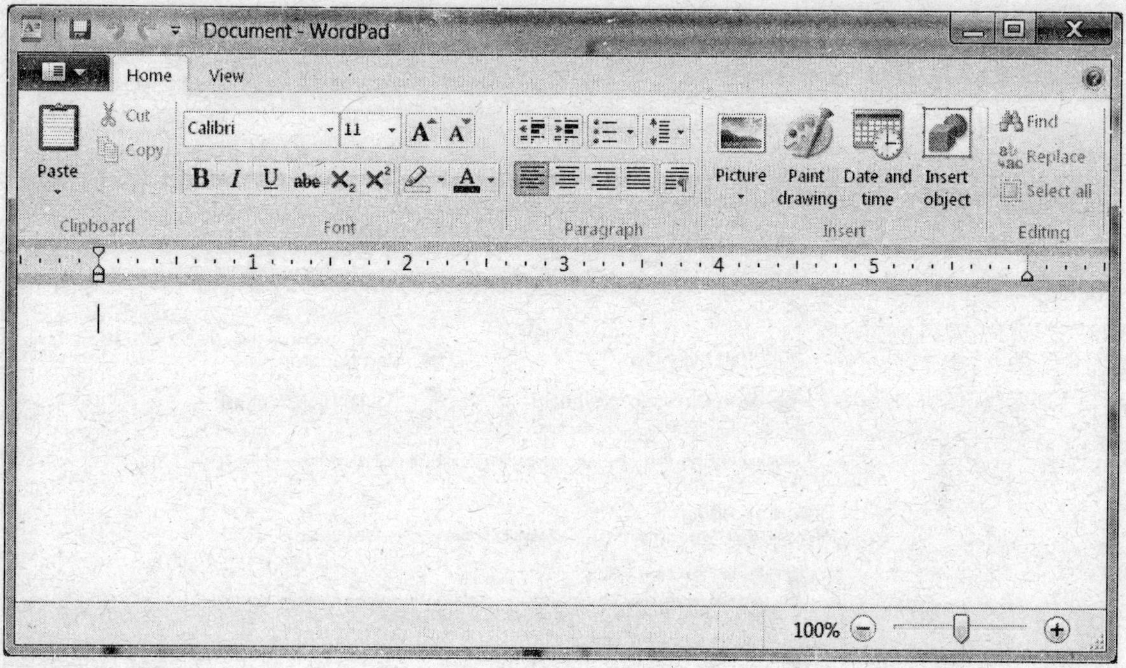

Ease of Access

It has the following programs: Ease of Access Center, Magnifier, Narrator, On-Screen Keyboard and Windows Speech Recognition.

Ease of Access Center

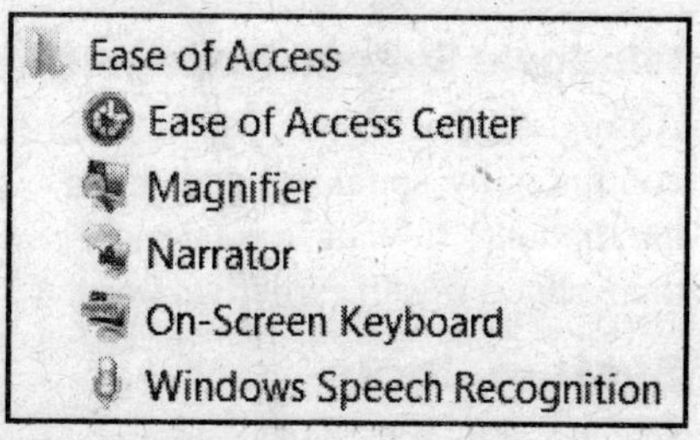

From here you can use the tools under this section to help you started. Windows can read and scan this list automatically. Press the SPACEBAR to select the highlighted tool.

Magnifier

Magnifier is like a software magnifying glass that fills the top portion of your screen. The actual size version appears in the bottom half. The magnified area scrolls as you mover your cursor, tab through a dialog box, or type, enlarging whatever part of the screen contains the action. Using the Magnifier Settings dialog box shown here, you can specify how much magnification you want, which area on the screen gets magnified, and so on.

Narrator

Narrator is a program that can read aloud whatever text appears on the screen—dialog boxes, error messages, menus, text you have typed, and so on. Narrator does not work in all programs, and it sounds a little bit like a Norwegian who has had few drinks. Still, if you have trouble reading text on the screen, or if you just like to hear you email read back to you, it's better than nothing.

On-Screen Keyboard

If you are having trouble typing keep the On-Screen Keyboard program in mind. It lets you type just by cliking the mouse—an option you may find useful.

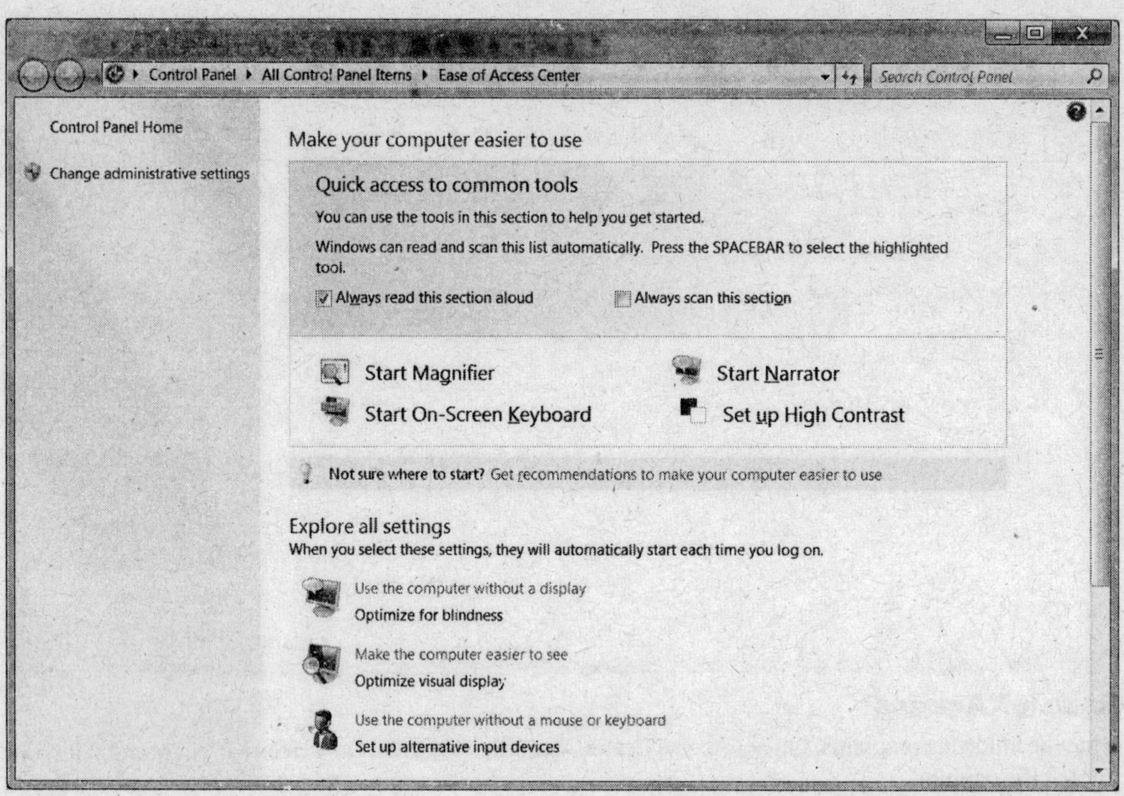

Windows Speech Recognition

A program that allows you to control your computer by speaking commands into a microphone. In Vista, it is far more powerful than what it was in earlier versions.

System Tools

Next set of tools help you in maintaining and troubleshooting the computer. They are: Character Map, Computer, Control Panel, Disk Cleanup, Disk Defragmenter, Internet Explorer (No Add-ons), Private Character Editor, System Information, System Restore, Task Scheduler, Windows Easy Transfer Reports, and Windows Easy Transfer.

Character Map

A special character is a character that cannot be found on your keyboard. You can insert special characters by using Character Map or by pressing a combination of keys on your keyboard.

Character Map enables you to view the characters that are available in a selected font. Using Character Map,

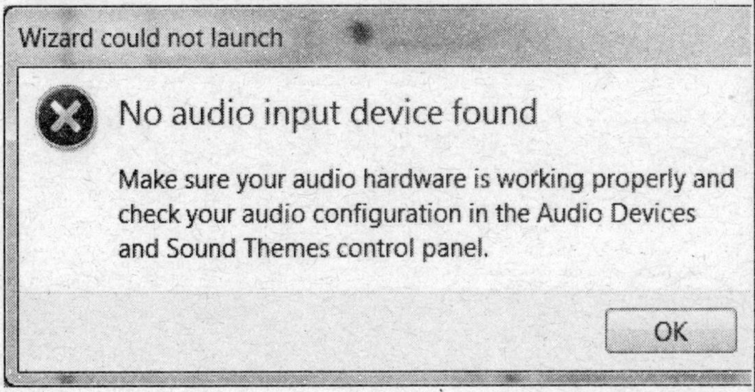

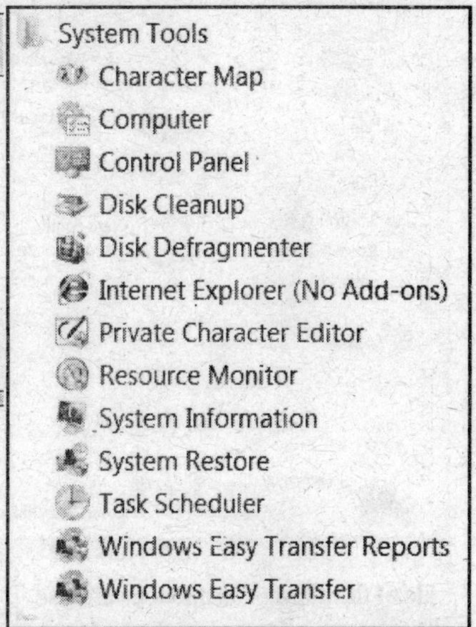

you can copy individual characters or a group of characters to the Clipboard and paste them into any program that can display them.

How to insert a special character into a document?

1. In Character Map, click the Font list, and then click the font you want to use.
2. Click the special character you want to insert into the document.
3. Click Select, and then click Copy.
4. Open your document and click the location in the document where you want the special character to appear.
5. Click the Edit menu, and then click Paste.

Computer

It helps you browse the contents of your computer, open folders, open documents and run your favourite applications. As shown here, it is divided into 2 sections, Favorite Links and Details. You click at any icon on the right hand

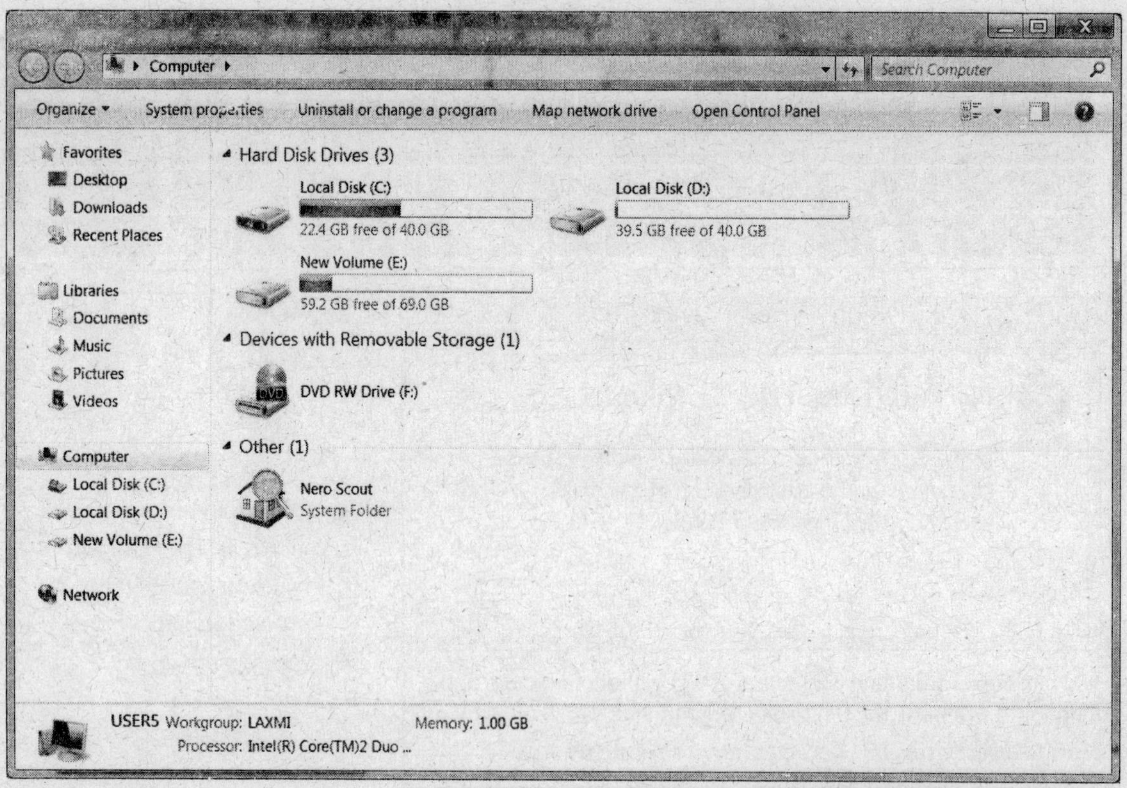

side of the dialog box and then choose the option on the left hand side. Details will give you the detail of the item selected. You can access other places by clicking at any one of them.

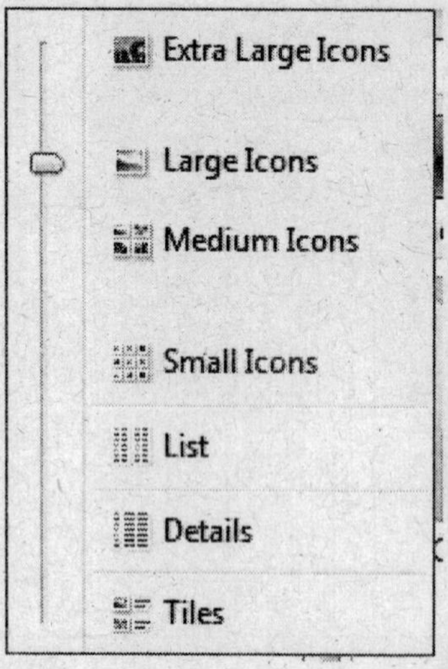

On the right hand side, you have the options of the followings:

Name: It gives you the option of sorting the icons by Name or by from A to H and I to Z.

Type: You can choose the type from CD Drive, Local Disk and System Folder and then Stack by Type.

Total Size: You can set the drives according to their size.

Free Space: You can set the drive to show how much space is available in them and list them according to the size, as shown below.

On the top there are buttons like this:

Organize: This allows you to organize the folders and files according to your liking. Like creating a New Folder, Cutting, copying, pasting of folders/files. Other options are shown here.

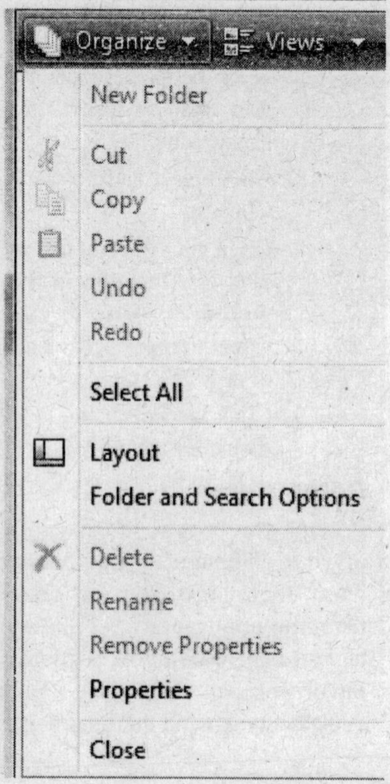

Views: It gives the option of viewing the folders/files in different views.

System properties: Shows information about your computer, such as the processor speed and the amount of installed memory.

Uninstall or change a program: Allows you to uninstall or change any program in the fixed drive.

Map network drive: It allows you to map a network drive.

Now let us see how **Computer** is used for working with files.

Copying of Files

Supposing you have to copy a file from one drive to another. Open the folder of hard disk and the particular file where it exists. Click the file to make it selected. Now click at Copy in the Organize menu.

Now click the other folder/hard disk where you want to copy the file. Let us say disk drive F:. Now again go to the Organize menu and click at Paste, this time. The file will be pasted in the disk drive F:, as shown next. Similary you can copy and paste folders from one place to another.

However, if you want to copy without leaving the copy of the file in the source, press **Control Key** and then click the mouse to drag the file. This will copy the file and not leave the copy behind.

Control Panel

You will read about Control Panel in a separate chapter.

Disk Cleanup

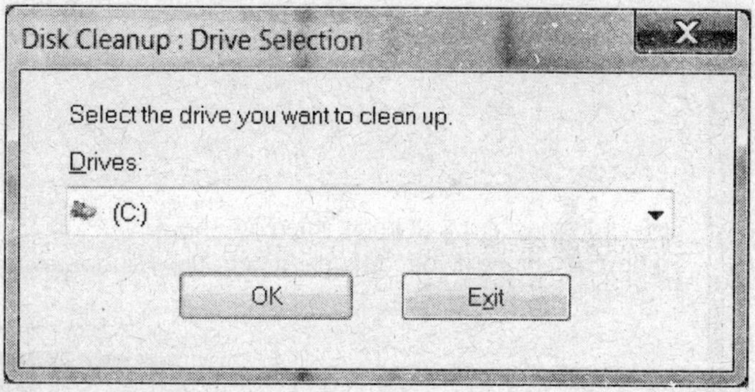

As you use your computer, Windows litters your hard disk with temporary files, programs, utilities, and Web sites scatter disposable files everywhere. If you could see your hard drive surface, it would eventually look like the floor of a minivan whose owners eat a lot of fast food.

Disk Defragmenter

Disk defragmentation describes the process of consolidating fragmented files on your computer's hard disk.

Fragmentation happens to a hard disk over time as you save, change, or delete files. The changes that you save to a file are often stored at a location on the hard disk that's different from the original file. Additional changes are saved to even more locations. Over time, both the file and the hard disk itself become fragmented, and your computer slows down as it has to look in many different places to open a file.

Disk Defragmenter is a tool that rearranges the data on your hard disk and reunites fragmented files so your computer can run more efficiently. In this version of Windows, Disk Defragmenter runs on a schedule so you don't have to remember to run it, although you can still run it manually or change the schedule it uses.

To start the Disk Defragmenter

1. Choose Start > Control Panel. Click System and Maintenance > "Defragment your hard drive".
2. Right-click the icon of a hard drive in Windows Explorer: from the shortcut menu, choose Properties. In the Properties window, click the Tools tab and then click Defragment Now.
3. In the Start menu's search box, or at a command prompt, type dfrgui.exe and press Enter.
4. Adjust the schedule. Click Modify Schedule. A screen appears, showing that Vista ordinarily defrags your disk late every Wednesday night. You can use the pop-up menus here to specify a Weekly, Daily, or Monthly schedule, complete with day-of-week and time-of-day options. Click OK and then OK again.

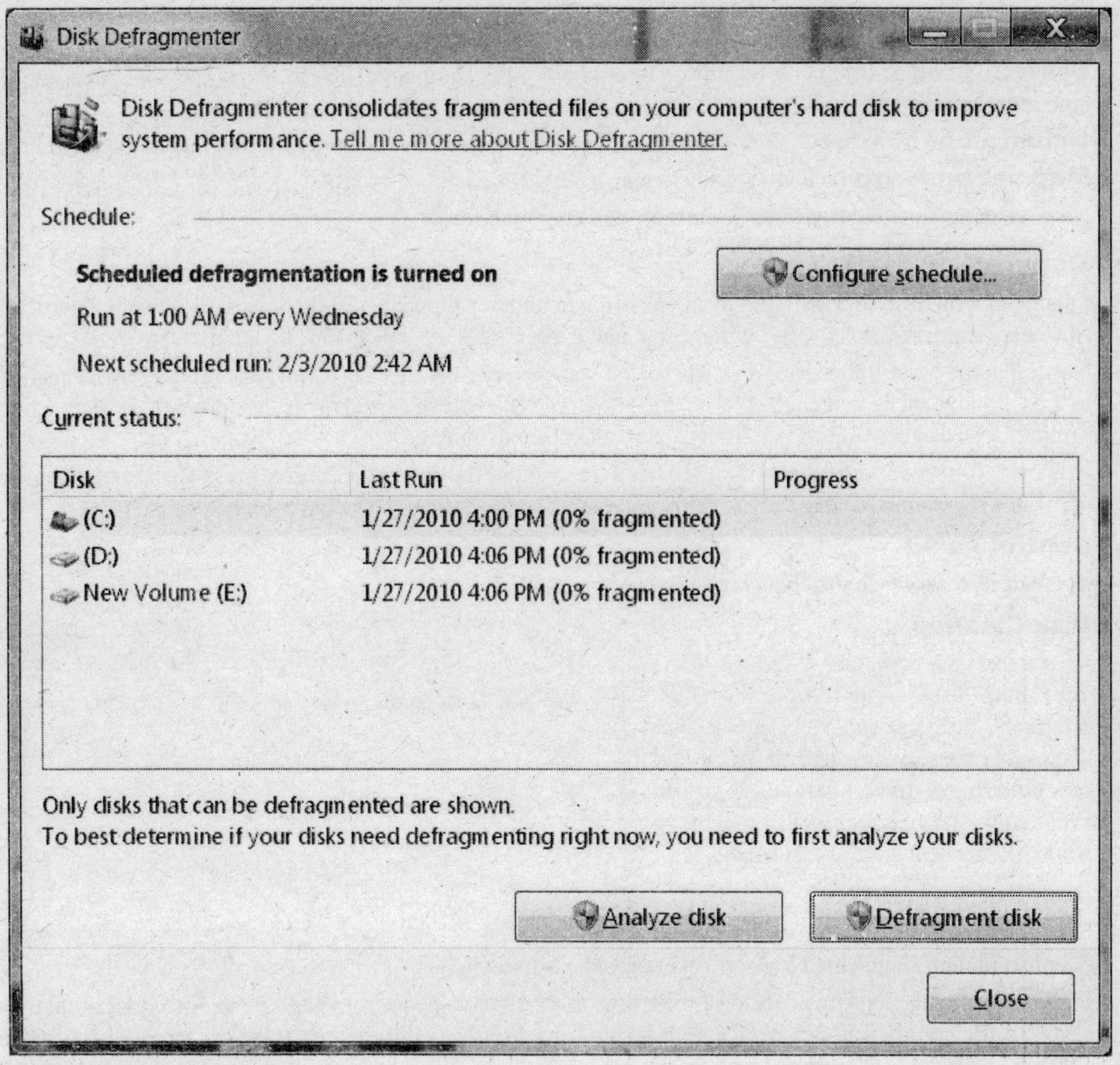

Internet Explorer

Here are some of the ways that Internet Explorer makes browsing the web easier, safer, and more enjoyable.

Increased security and privacy

New security and privacy features allow you to browse the web more safely.

- Phishing Filter can help protect you from phishing attacks, online fraud, and spoofed websites.
- Protected mode can help protect your computer from websites that try to install malicious software or to save files on your computer without your consent.
- Higher security levels can help protect you from hackers and web attacks.
- The Security Status bar displays the identity of secure websites to help you make informed decisions when using online banking or merchants.
- Internet Explorer's lets you start Internet Explorer without toolbars, ActiveX controls, or other add-ons that might slow your computer or prevent you from getting online.

New features

- Tabbed browsing is a new feature in Internet Explorer that allows you to open multiple websites in a single browser window. If you have a lot of tabs open, use Quick Tabs to easily switch between open tabs.
- The new Instant Search box lets you search the web from the Address bar. You can also search using different search providers to get better results.
- Internet Explorer now lets you delete your temporary files, cookies, webpage history, saved passwords, and form information from one place. Delete selected categories, or everything at once.
- Click the Favorites Center button to open the Favorites Center to manage favorites, feeds, and history in one place.
- Printing now scales webpages to fit the paper you're using. Print Preview gives more control when printing, with manual scaling and an accurate view of what you're about to print.
- The Zoom feature lets you enlarge or reduce text, images, and some controls.

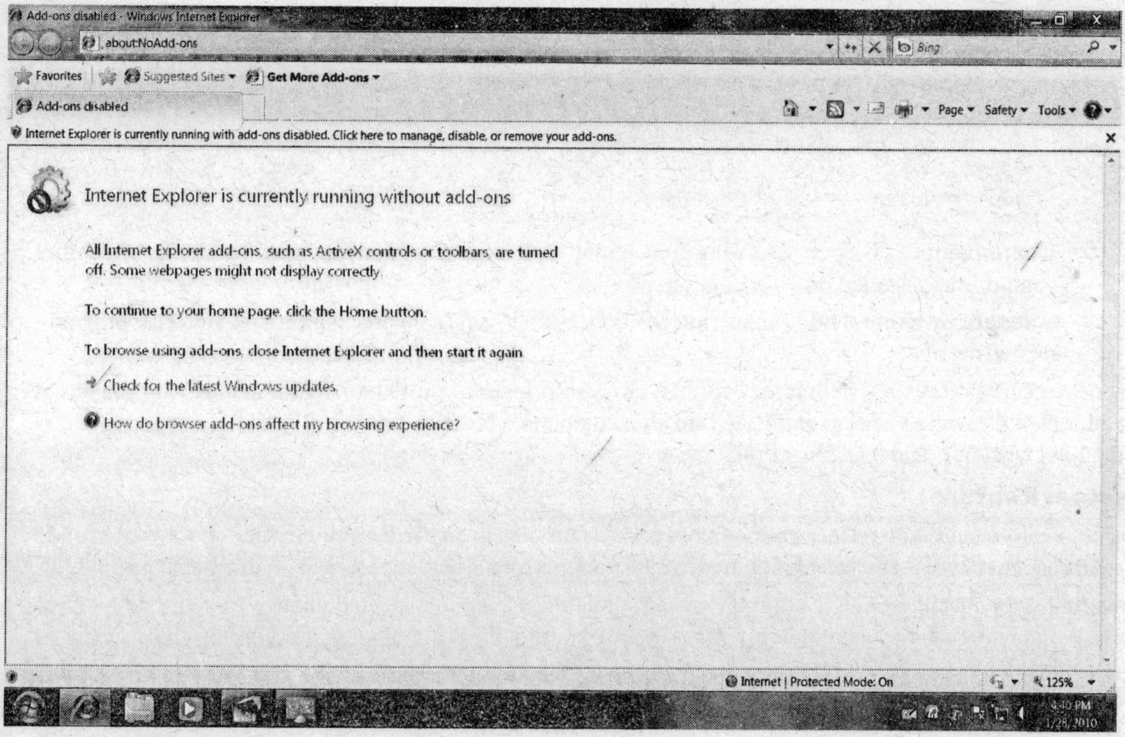

System Information

System Information shows details about your computer's hardware configuration, computer components, and software, including drivers.

System Information lists categories in the left pane and details about each category in the right pane. The categories include:

- **System Summary.** Shows general information about your computer and the operating system, such as the computer name and manufacturer, the type of basic input/output system (BIOS) your computer uses, and the amount of memory that is installed.
- **Hardware Resources.** Displays advanced details about your computer's hardware for IT professionals.

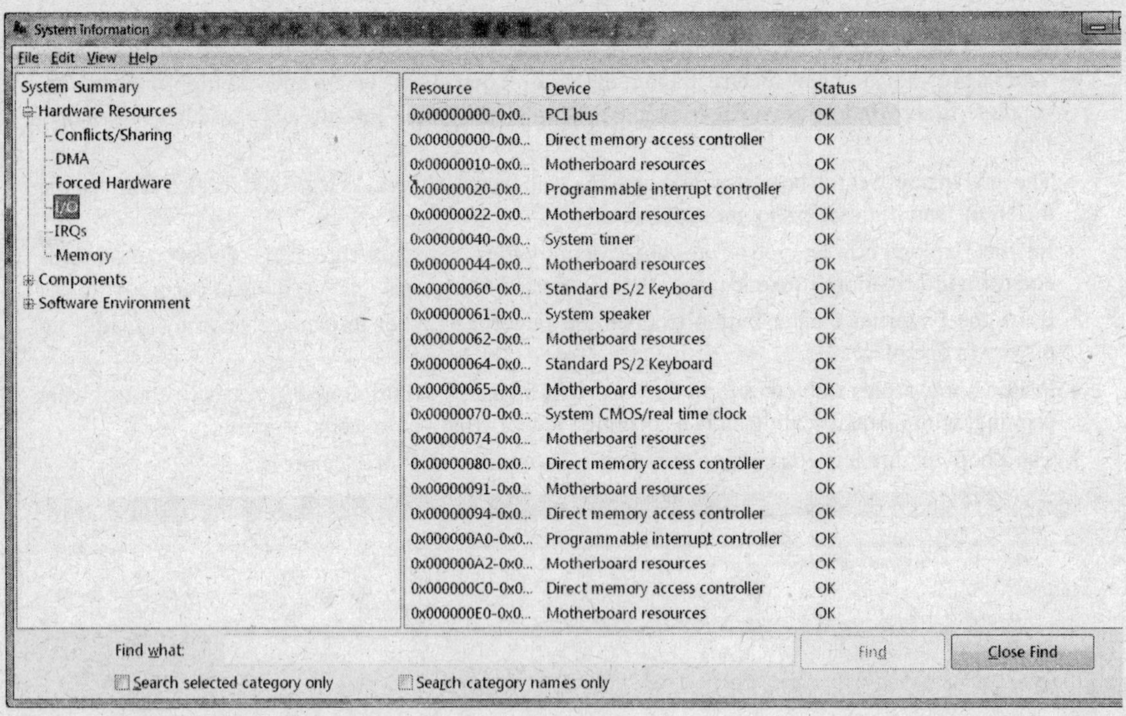

- **Components.** Displays information about disk drives, sound devices, modems, and other components installed on your computer.
- **Software Environment.** Shows information about drivers, network connections, and other program-related details.

To find a specific detail in System Information, type the information you're looking for in the Find what box at the bottom of the window. For example, to find your computer's Internet protocol (IP) address, type ip address in the Find what box, and then click Find.

System Restore

System Restore helps you restore your computer's system files to an earlier point in time. It's a way to undo system changes to your computer without affecting your personal files, such as e mail, documents, or photos.

Sometimes, the installation of a program or a drivercan cause an unexpected change to your computer or cause Windows to behave unpredictably. Usually, uninstalling the program or driver corrects the problem. If uninstalling does not fix the problem, you can try restoring your computer's system to an earlier date when everything worked correctly.

System Restore uses a feature called System Protection to regularly create and save restore points on your computer. These restore points contain information about registry settings and other system information that Windows uses. You can also create restore points manually.

System Restore is not intended for backing up personal files, so it cannot help you recover a personal file that has been deleted or damaged. You should regularly back up your personal files and important data using a backup program.

Task Scheduler

You must be logged on as an administrator to perform these steps. If you are not logged on as an administrator, you can only change settings that apply to your user account.

If you use a specific program on a regular basis, you can use the Task Scheduler Wizard to create a task that

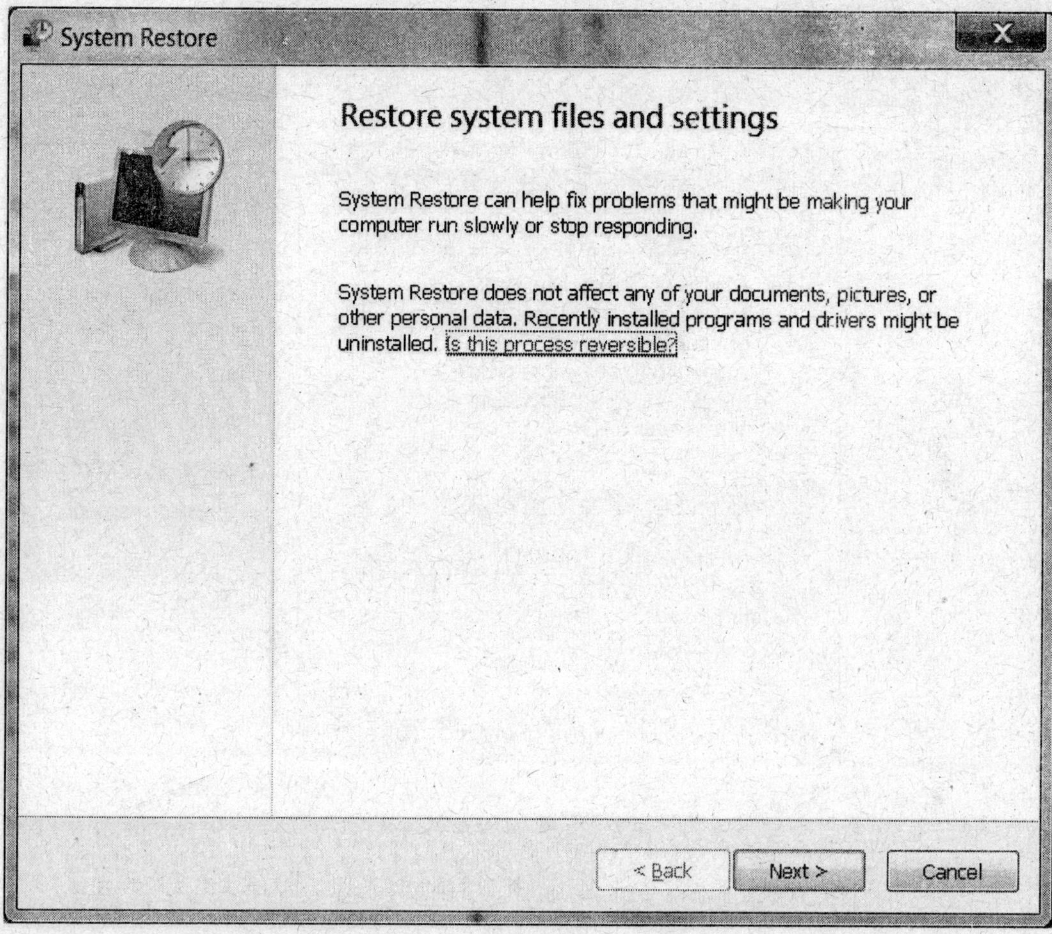

opens the program for you automatically according to the schedule you choose. For example, if you use a financial program on a certain day each month, you can schedule a task that opens the program automatically so you don't risk forgetting to open it yourself.

1. Click to open Task Scheduler.
2. If you are prompted for an administrator password or confirmation, type the password or provide confirmation.
3. Click the Action menu, and then click Create Basic Task.
4. Type a name for the task and an optional description, and then click Next.
5. Do one of the following:
   - To select a schedule based on the calendar, click Daily, Weekly, Monthly, or One time, click Next, specify the schedule you want to use, and then click Next.
   - To select a schedule based on common recurring events, click When the computer starts, or When I log on, and then click Next.
   - To select a schedule based on specific events, click When a specific event is logged, click Next, specify the event log and other information using the drop-down lists, and then click Next.
6. To schedule a program to start automatically, click Start a program, and then click Next.
7. Click Browse to find the program you want to start, and then click Next.

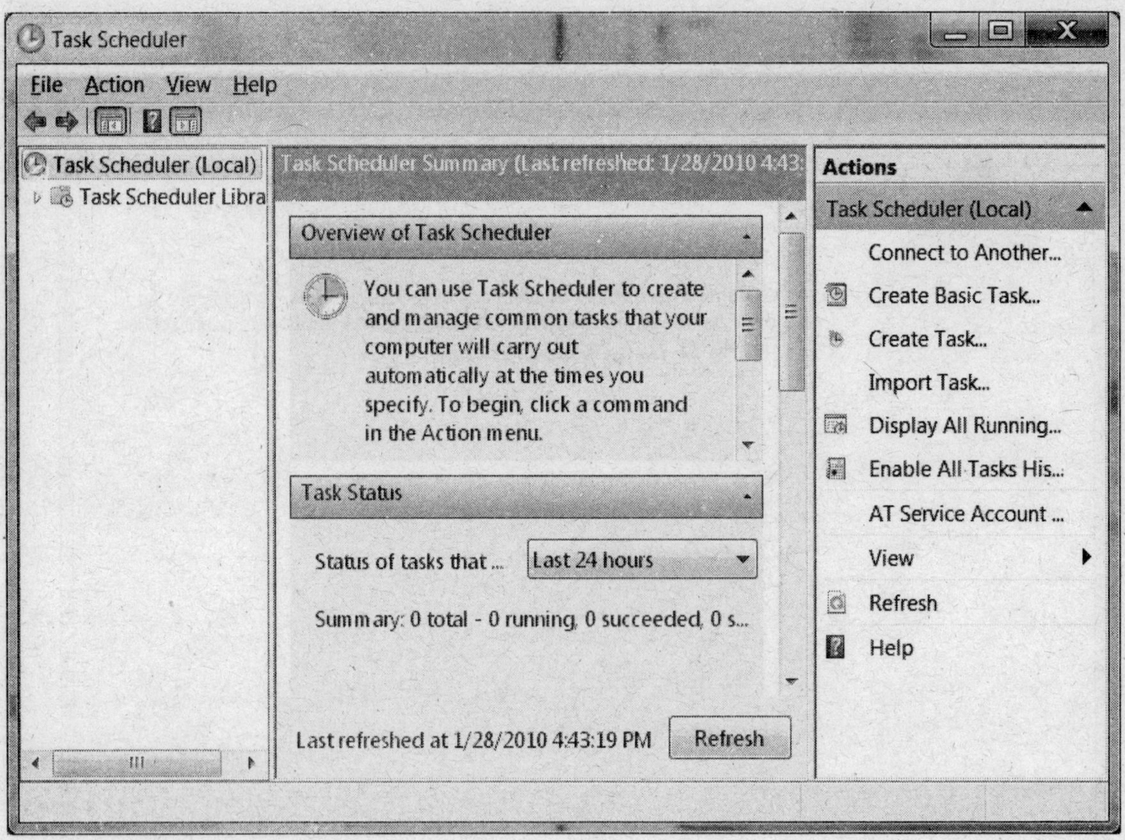

8. Click Finish.

Windows Easy Transfer Reports

Windows Easy Transfer guides you through the process of transferring files and settings from one Windows computer to another. Using Windows Easy Transfer, you can choose what to transfer to your new computer and how to transfer it.

You can transfer most files and program settings. Specifically:

- **Files and folders.** Everything within the Documents, Pictures, and Shared Documents folders. Using advanced options, you can select additional files and folders to transfer.
- **E mail settings, contacts, and messages.** Messages, account settings, and address books from Microsoft Outlook Express, Outlook, Windows Mail, and other e mail programs.
- **Program settings.** Settings that keep your programs configured as you had them on your old computer. You must first install the programs on your new computer, because Windows Easy Transfer does not transfer the programs themselves. Some programs might not work on this version of Windows, including security programs (which are often not compatible with all versions of Windows), antivirus programs, firewall programs (your new computer should already have a firewall running to help ensure safety during the transfer), and programs with software drivers (some are not compatible with all versions of Windows).
- User accounts and **settings.** Color schemes, desktop backgrounds, network connections, screen savers, fonts, Start menu options, taskbar options, folders, specific files, network printers and drives, and accessibility options.

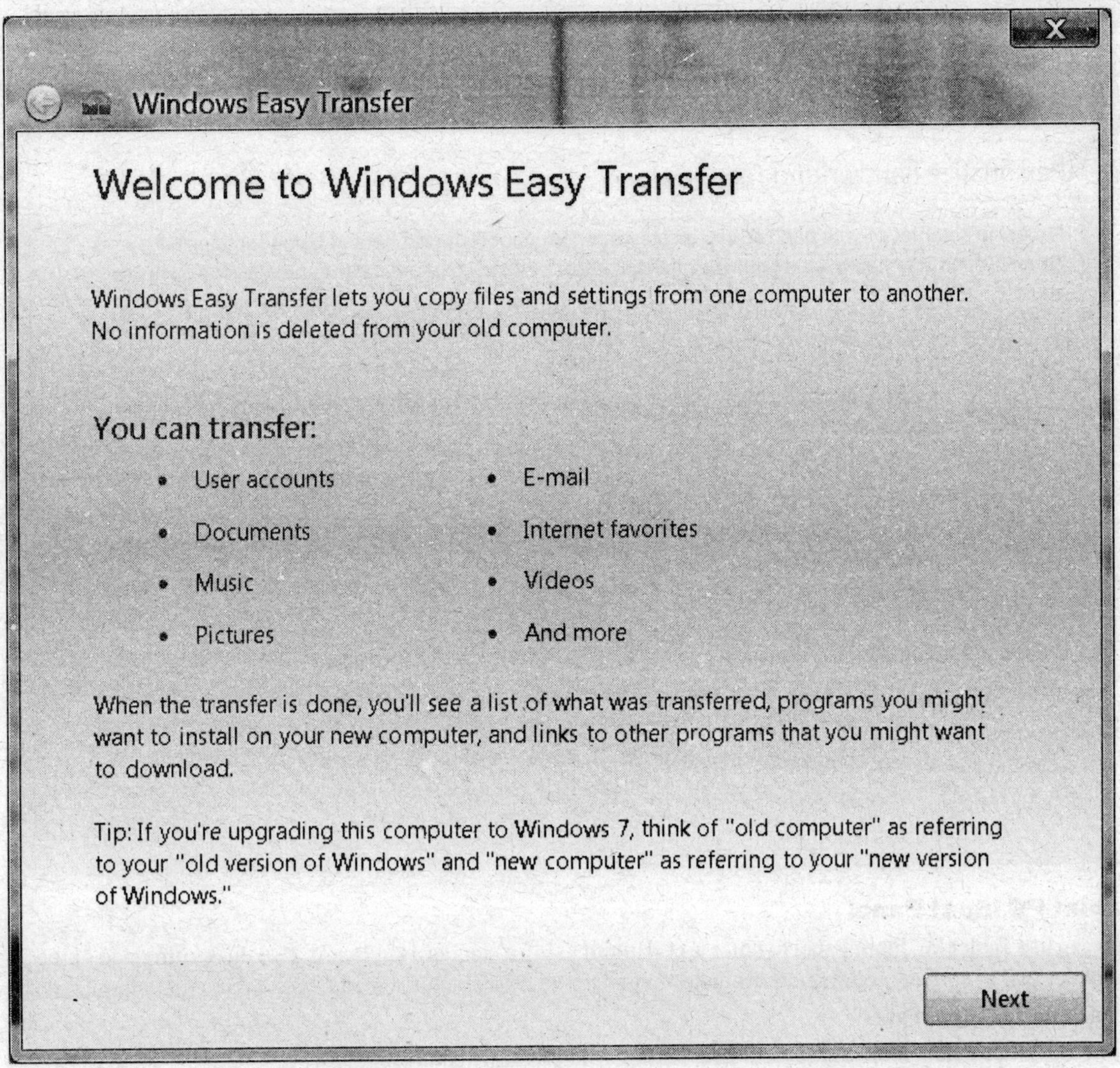

- **Internet settings and favorites.** Internet connection settings, favorites, and cookies.
- **Music.** Electronic music files, playlists, and album art.
- **Pictures and video.** Pictures—which includes any visual file type (for example, .jpg, .bmp, .gif)—and personal videos.

Tablet PC

This is the next set of accessories. It includes: Personalize Handwriting Recognition, Tablet PC Input Panel and Windows Journal.

Personalization Handwriting Recognition

This provides samples of your handwriting increases the likelihood of your writing being recognized correctly. For better results, you must start with specific characters or words that are causing recognition errors for you.

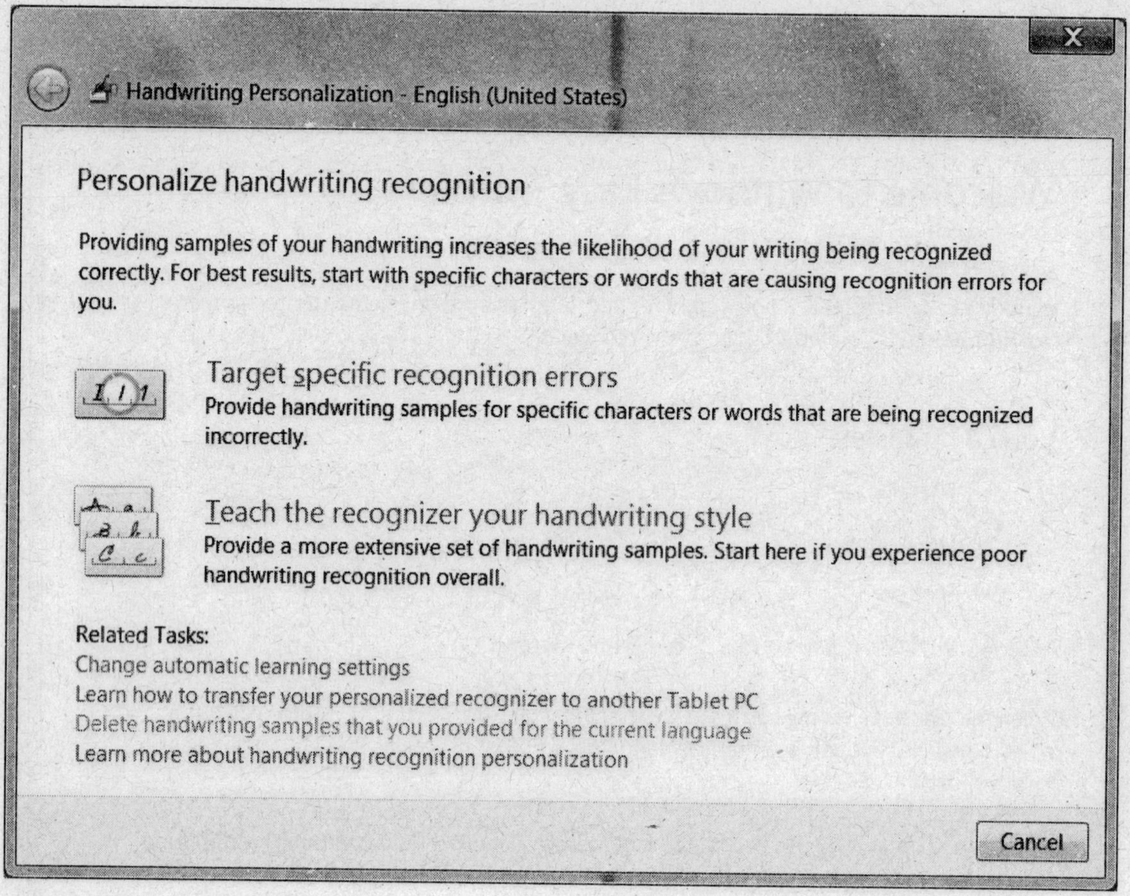

Tablet PC Input Panel

You can use Tablet PC Input Panel to enter text without using a standard keyboard. Use the writing pad or the character pad to convert your handwriting into typed text, or use the on-screen keyboard to enter characters.

What's new in Input Panel?

Input Panel has a new look and several new features. These new features include:

- AutoComplete
- Input Panel tab
- Back-of-pen erase
- New scratch-out gestures

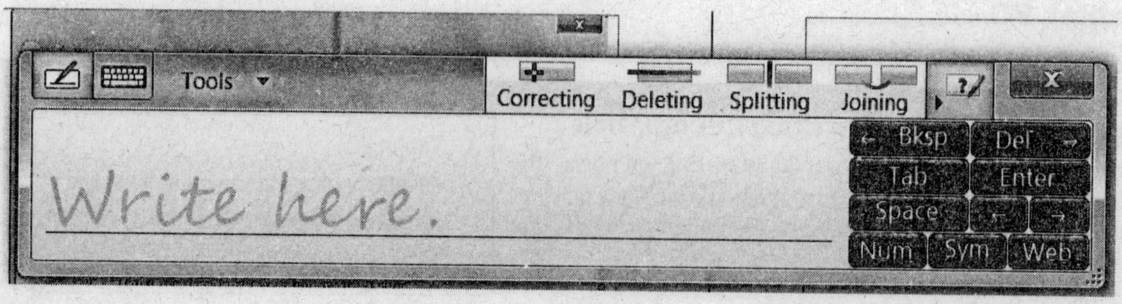

AutoComplete

AutoComplete works just like AutoComplete in common programs, such as Microsoft Internet Explorer. AutoComplete lists possible matches in Input Panel, such as e-mail addresses, URLs, file names, and other items that you've entered before.

When Input Panel recognizes your handwriting, AutoComplete displays possible matches from the program in a list near the writing area. If a suggestion in the list of matches is what you want to enter, tap the suggestion to enter it in the text entry area.

Input Panel tab

The Input Panel tab provides a new way to open and position Input Panel on the screen. When Input Panel is closed, the Input Panel tab appears on the left edge of your screen by default.

To open Input Panel, simply tap the Input Panel tab, and Input Panel will slide out from the edge of your screen. When you close Input Panel, it slides back to the edge of the screen.

You can move the Input Panel tab by dragging it up or down along the edge of the screen. Then, when you tap it, Input Panel opens at the same horizontal location on the screen that the tab appears.

When you open Input Panel by using the Input Panel tab, it floats over any open windows and stays open until you close it.

- Use the Input Panel tab to open Input Panel when you're running a program that uses the entire the screen, such as Remote Desktop.

Back-of-pen erase

If your tablet pen has an eraser, you can use it to delete writing and recognized text from Input Panel. It works in the writing pad, the character pad, and the correction area.

Scratch-out gestures

Windows includes new, more tolerant scratch-out gesture to delete your handwriting or recognized text in Input Panel. These scratch-out gestures are intended to work better with your personal style of crossing out text in Input Panel. The new scratch-out gestures include, but are not limited to:

- Strikethrough, a horizontal line drawn across a word
- Vertical scratch-out, in the pattern of an M or W
- Circular scratch-out
- Angled scratch-out

You can still use the Z-shaped scratch-out gesture that was available in Microsoft Windows XP Tablet PC Edition. If your handwriting is sometimes accidentally deleted by one of the new scratch-out gestures, you can adjust your settings to use only the Z-shaped scratch-out gesture.

Text entry

You can use the writing pad, the character pad, or the on-screen keyboard to enter text. The writing pad and the character pad convert your handwriting into typed text. The on-screen keyboard works just like a standard keyboard except that you enter text by tapping keys with your tablet pen.

The following table describes the different choices for using Input Panel.

- With the writing pad, you can write continuously, as if you were writing on a lined piece of paper.
- The character pad converts your handwriting to typed text, one letter, number, or symbol at a time.
- The on-screen keyboard is similar to a standard keyboard.

The writing pad and character pad have a number pad, a symbol pad, and web quick keys to help you quickly and accurately enter these types of text. These quick keys are hidden when you start to write, but appear after you insert or delete your writing.

- If the password security settings are turned on, Input Panel automatically switches to the on-screen keyboard when you place the insertion point in a text input area where you enter a password.

Text correction

Input Panel provides you with several ways to easily correct the text that you enter.

You can correct your handwriting recognition results directly in the writing pad or the character pad before you insert the text.

To erase a word or a character, use a scratch-out gesture or the back-of-pen erase to remove the word or character, and then start over. In the writing pad for Western languages, you can use the correction area to fix incorrectly recognized text.

You can select an alternate word that Input Panel suggests, or rewrite letters to correct the word in the correction area. To access the correction area, tap the recognized text for the word that you want to correct.

In the character pad, you can write over an incorrectly recognized character or use the drop-down menu to select from a list of characters that the handwriting recognizer has identified as alternates. If you've already inserted the text in a program, you can select the text that you want to correct, and then either select an alternate word that Input Panel suggests or use the correction area to correct the word.

Tips for using Input Panel

Use the following tips to become more efficient with using Input Panel.

- Use the number pad to insert numbers. To open the number pad, tap the Num button on the writing pad or the character pad.
- Use the symbol pad to insert symbols. To open the symbol pad, tap the Sym button

Windows Journal

It is an accessory that enables users who do not have a computer running Windows Journal to view files that were created with Windows Journal.

Tips for working efficiently in Journal

In Windows Journal, you can handwrite by using your tablet pen. You can save your handwriting in a note, convert the writing to typed text, and then enter typed text into your notes. Or, you can just leave your handwriting as ink in a note. You can also create drawings and insert pictures in your notes.

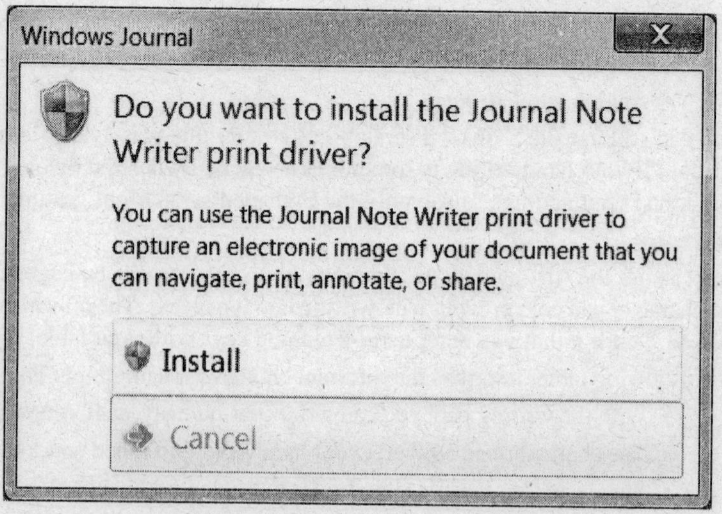

Use the following information to help you work with Journal quickly and efficiently.

Using shortcut menus

The fastest way to do many tasks is to use a right-click equivalent with your tablet pen. The following is a list of places where you can use right-click equivalents:

- Ink on a page
- An empty space on a page
- A picture or a flag
- The area inside a text box

- A text box border
- A column header in the find pane or the note list pane
- A note title in the find pane or note list pane
- A toolbar
- The vertical and horizontal scroll bars on a page

Using keyboard shortcuts

Many of the toolbar buttons and menu commands in Journal have corresponding keyboard shortcuts. You can use these keyboard shortcuts instead of your tablet pen to do things such as create or save notes, open or close recently used notes, and print notes.

The following table shows the various keyboard shortcuts available in Journal.

Action	***Keyboard shortcut***
Start a new note	CTRL+N
Open a recently used note	CTRL+O
Save changes to a note	CTRL+S
Move a note to a specific folder	CTRL+SHIFT+V
Print a note	CTRL+P
Close a note and its Journal window	ALT+F4
Undo a change	CTRL+Z
Redo a change	CTRL+Y
Select all items on a page	CTRL+A
Cut a selection	CTRL+X
Copy a selection to the Clipboard	CTRL+C
Paste a selection from the Clipboard	CTRL+V
Cancel a selection	ESC
Delete a selection	DEL
Start a basic find	CTRL+F
Go to a page	CTRL+G
Refresh find results	F5
Refresh the note list	F5
Toggle between a note list and a note	F6
Display a shortcut menu for column headings in a note list	CTRL+SHIFT+C
View a note in full-screen mode	F11
Open Journal Help	F1

Create and save a Journal note

You can create, save, open, and close notes in Windows Journal. You can export a note to a different file format for a colleague who doesn't have Journal. Journal can also help you to recover note content if a note closes unexpectedly.

To create a note

You should give each new note a note title. When you save a new note, Journal suggests a file name based on the note title that you write. Also, when you view a list of notes in the find pane or the note list pane, you can see the note titles written in your own handwriting.

Journal can suggest a file name based on your note title only when you have enabled handwriting recognition. You can do this on the Other tab in the Options dialog box. (Tap Tools, tap Options, and then tap the Other tab.)

1. On the Standard toolbar, tap New Note.
2. To create a note title, write a note title in the title area at the top of the first page of your note.
3. You can control the appearance of the title area on the Background and Title Area tab in the Page Setup dialog box. (Tap File, tap Page Setup, and then tap the Background and Title Area tab.)

To save a note

Journal notes are saved by default in Journal note format (.jnt). If you want to save a note as a template, you can also save it in Journal template format (.jtp).

1. On the Standard toolbar, tap Save.
2. In the Save in box, browse to the folder in which you want to save your note.
3. In the Save as type list, tap the format that you want.
4. In the File name box, enter a name for your note.
   - How do I enter text without a standard keyboard?
   - To open Input Panel, tap the Input Panel tab, which appears by default on the left edge of the screen.
   - Tap the On-Screen Keyboard button.
   - Make sure that the insertion point is in the File name box, and then use the on-screen keyboard to enter the text.
5. Tap Save.

To save changes to a note

- On the Standard toolbar, tap Save.

To export a note

1. Tap the File menu, and then tap Export As.
2. In the Export dialog box, in the Save in box, browse to the folder to which you want to export your note.
3. In the Save as type list, tap the format that you want.
4. In the File name box, enter a name.
   - How do I enter text without a standard keyboard?
   - To open Input Panel, tap the Input Panel tab, which appears by default on the left edge of the screen.
   - Tap the On-Screen Keyboard button.
   - Make sure that the insertion point is in the File name box, and then use the on-screen keyboard to enter the text.
5. Tap Export.on the writing pad or the character pad.
   - Use web quick keys to enter URLs more quickly. To open the web quick keys, tap the Web button on the writing pad or the character pad.
   - Use gestures to perform common keystroke actions.
   - Do not hyphenate a word if it doesn't fit on one line in the writing pad. Write the entire word on a new line instead.

Windows PowerShell

Automated troubleshooting is a feature made possible by Windows PowerShell and related system services. As long as PowerShell is installed (it is installed by default) and the required services are available, automated troubleshooting will work. Standard troubleshooters include the following:

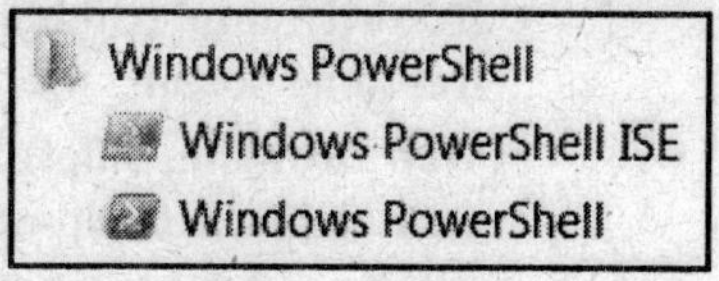

- **Aero troubleshooter** Diagnoses and resolves problems that prevent the computer from properly using Windows Aero.
- **Hardware And Device troubleshooter** Diagnoses and resolves problems that prevent the computer from property using a device.
- **Homogroup Networking troubleshooter** Diagnoses and resolves problems that prevent the computer from sharing files in a homegroup.
- **Internet Connectivity troubleshooter** Diagnoses and resolves problems that prevent the computer from connecting to the internet and accessing the Web.
- **Maintenance troubleshooter** Performs routine maintenance if the user does not.
- **Network Adapter troubleshooter** Diagnoses and resolves problems.
- **Performance troubleshooter** Diagnoses and resolves problems that are impacting the overall performance of the computer.
- **Play Sound troubleshooter** Diagnoses and resolves problems that prevent the computer from plaing sound.
- **Power troubleshooting** Diagnoses and resolves problems that affect power management, sleep, hibernation, and resume.
- **Printer troubleshooting** Diagnoses and resolves problems that prevent the computer from using a printer.
- **Program Compatibility troubleshooter** Diagnoses and resolves problems that prevent a program from running on the computer.

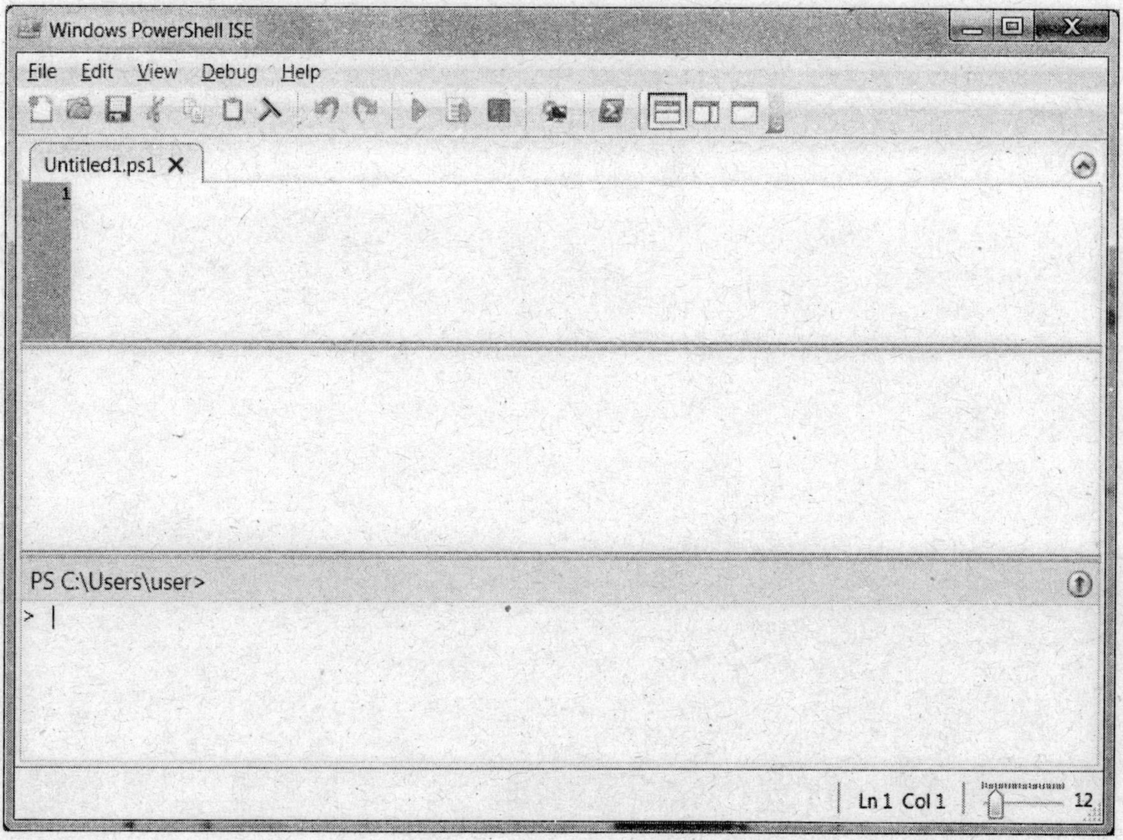

- **Record Sound troubleshooter** Diagnoses and resolves problems that prevent the computer from recording sound.
- **Web Browsing Safety troubleshooter** Identifies issues with settings that could compromise the security of the computer and the safety of the user when browsing the Web.
- **Windows Media troubleshooting** Diagnoses and resolves problems that prevent the computer from playing music or DVDs. Can also be used to reset Windows Media Player to its default settings.

5 Configure and Maintain Your System

Introduction

So far you have studied what all is available in Windows 7, but what all is for you, you have to find out. Not all changes will be appropriate to your system. Some areas may never apply to how you use Windows 7, but you may have need of them in future.

Date and Time Settings

Windows 7 keeps track of the date and time based on the information provided at the time of installation. It even makes the correct adjustment for daylight-saving time. If you elect to show the clock on the Taskbar, positioning the pointer over the time will produce a flyover box with the date inside.

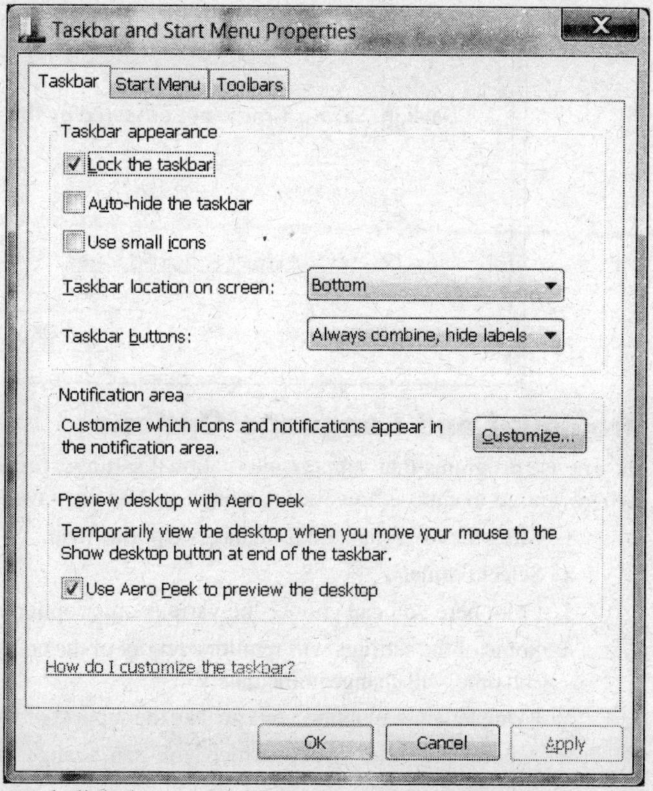

Display clock on the Taskbar

1. Right-click on the Taskbar in a blank spot.
2. Select Properties from the pop-menu.
3. Select the Notification Area panel.
4. Make sure that the Clock is clicked in "Select which system icons to always show".

Change the Date or Time Settings

1. Click the Start button and select Control Panel.
2. Click the Date and Time.
3. Date and Time dialog box appear.
4. To adjust the clock, highlight the portion to be changed in the text box and click the up and down arrows until the time you want is displayed.
6. Click the Time Zone tab to change the time zone, selecting the one you want from the drop-down list.
7. Internet Time can also be changed by clicking at the Internet Time panel.

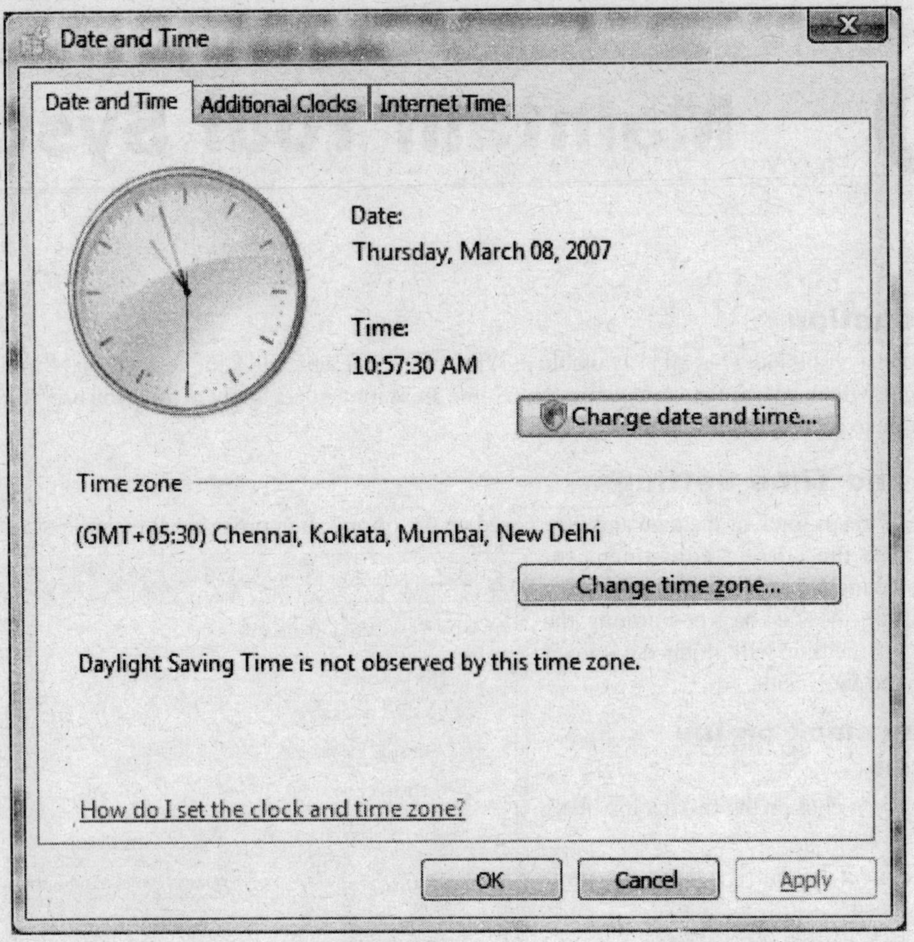

Regional and Language Options

If you use programs that support international settings, the Regional Settings icon in the Control Panel is where you go to choose how these settings will be displayed.

1. Click the Regional and Languages Options icon.
2. Select Formats.
3. From here you can choose the various other options of display.
4. Some of the settings will require a reboot of the computer to take effect, but others, such as the date and time, will change immediately.
5. Using languages option you can take the support of various other languages which Window supports.
6. Among the other panels which you can change are Location, Keyboards and Languages, and Admistrative.

Keyboard Settings

The installation routine of Windows 7 finds the keyboard plugged into your computer and recognizes it. If you need to change keyboards, adjust the keyboard's speed, or install a keyboard designed for another language, do the following:

1. Click the Start button.

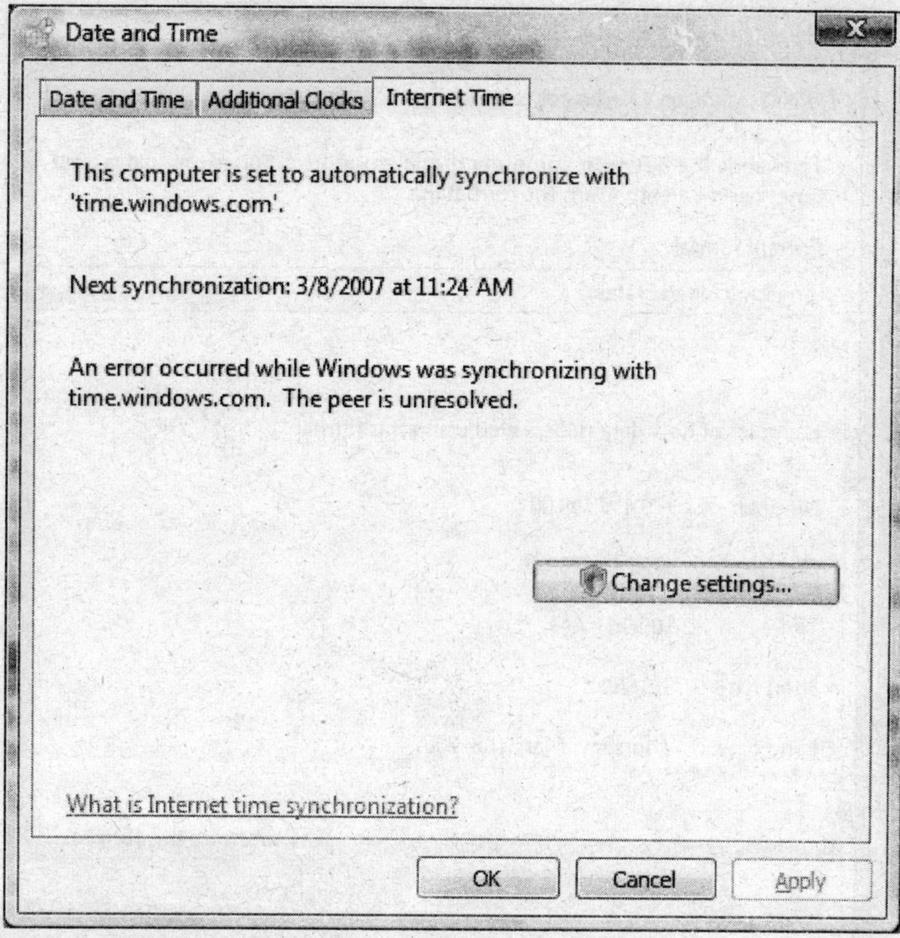

2. Select Control Panel.
3. Click at Keyboard icon to get the keyboard dialog box.
3. One of the feature is Keyboard Speed

Keyboard Speed

In the Keyboard Properties dialog box, click the Speed tab to adjust keyboard rates. Here are the available settings:

Repeat delay Determines how long a key has to be held down before it starts repeating. The difference between the Long and Short setting is only about a second.

Repeat rate Determines how fast a key repeats. Fast means you can hold down a key and almost instantly get a stream of letters. Click in the practice area to test this setting.

Cursor blink rate Makes the cursor blink faster or slower. The blinking cursor on the left demonstrates the setting.

The other one is Hardware, which shows the hardware features of the keyboard.

Managing Fonts

TrueType fonts can be easily managed in Windows. Fonts are located in See Also part of the Appearance and Themes.

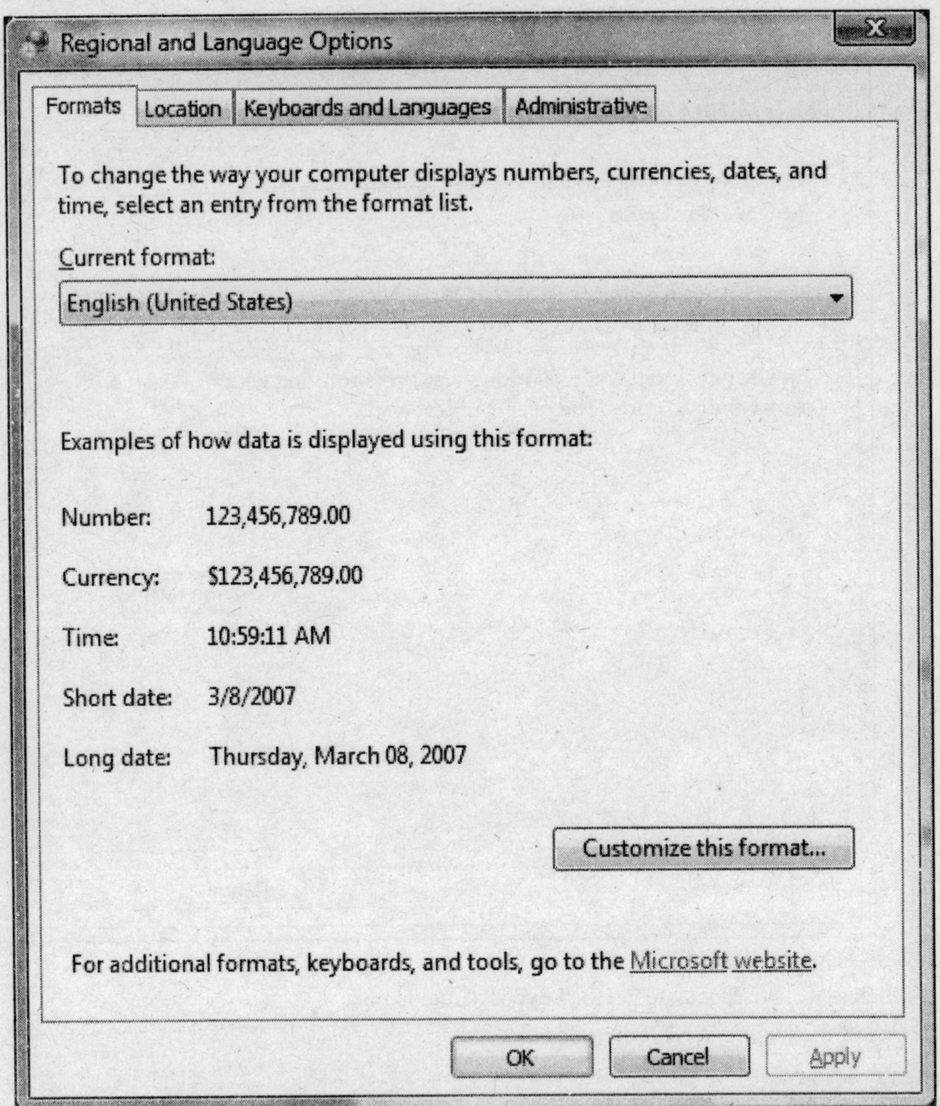
Regional and Language Options
Formats
Location
Keyboards and Languages
Administrative
To change the way your computer displays numbers, currencies, dates, and time, select an entry from the format list.
Current format:
English (United States)
Examples of how data is displayed using this format:
Number: 123,456,789.00
Currency: $123,456,789.00
Time: 10:59:11 AM
Short date: 3/8/2007
Long date: Thursday, March 08, 2007
Customize this format...
For additional formats, keyboards, and tools, go to the Microsoft website.
OK
Cancel
Apply

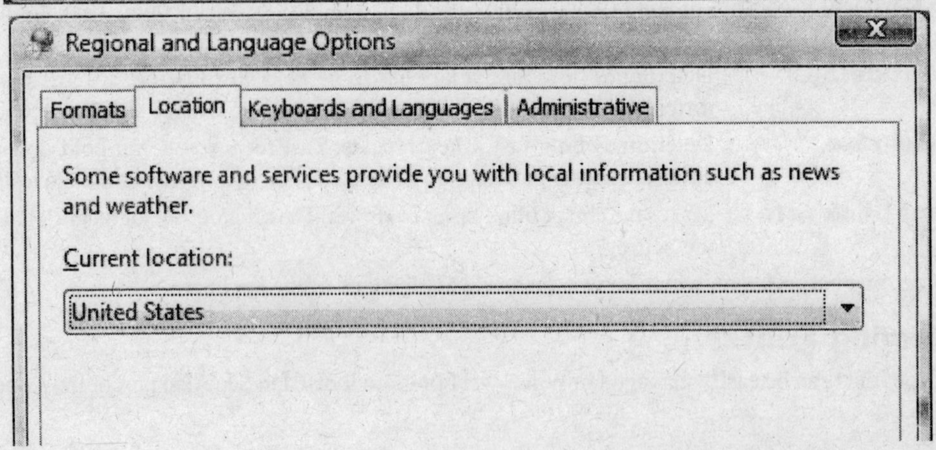
Regional and Language Options
Formats
Location
Keyboards and Languages
Administrative
Some software and services provide you with local information such as news and weather.
Current location:
United States

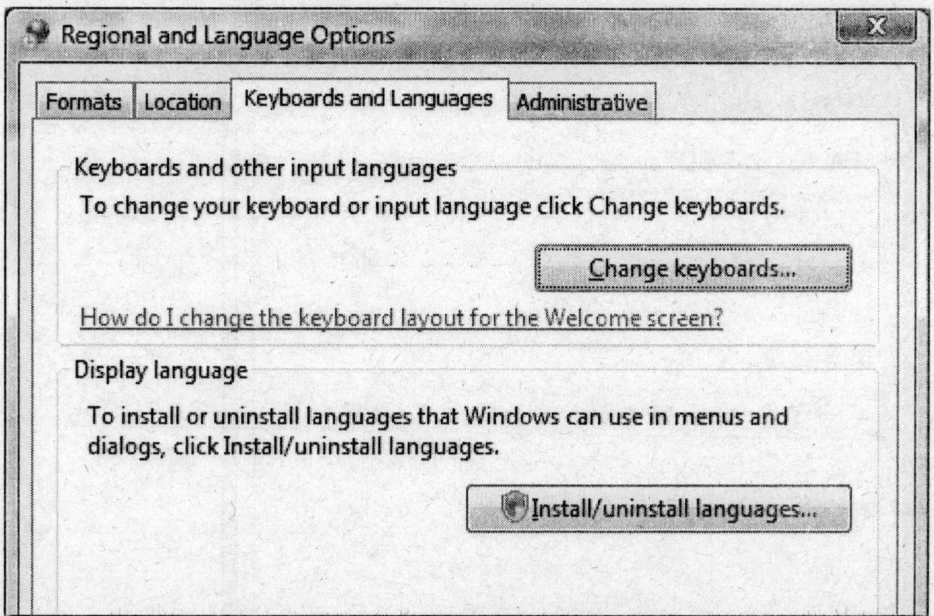
Regional and Language Options
Formats
Location
Keyboards and Languages
Administrative
Keyboards and other input languages
To change your keyboard or input language click Change keyboards.
Change keyboards...
How do I change the keyboard layout for the Welcome screen?
Display language
To install or uninstall languages that Windows can use in menus and dialogs, click Install/uninstall languages.
Install/uninstall languages...

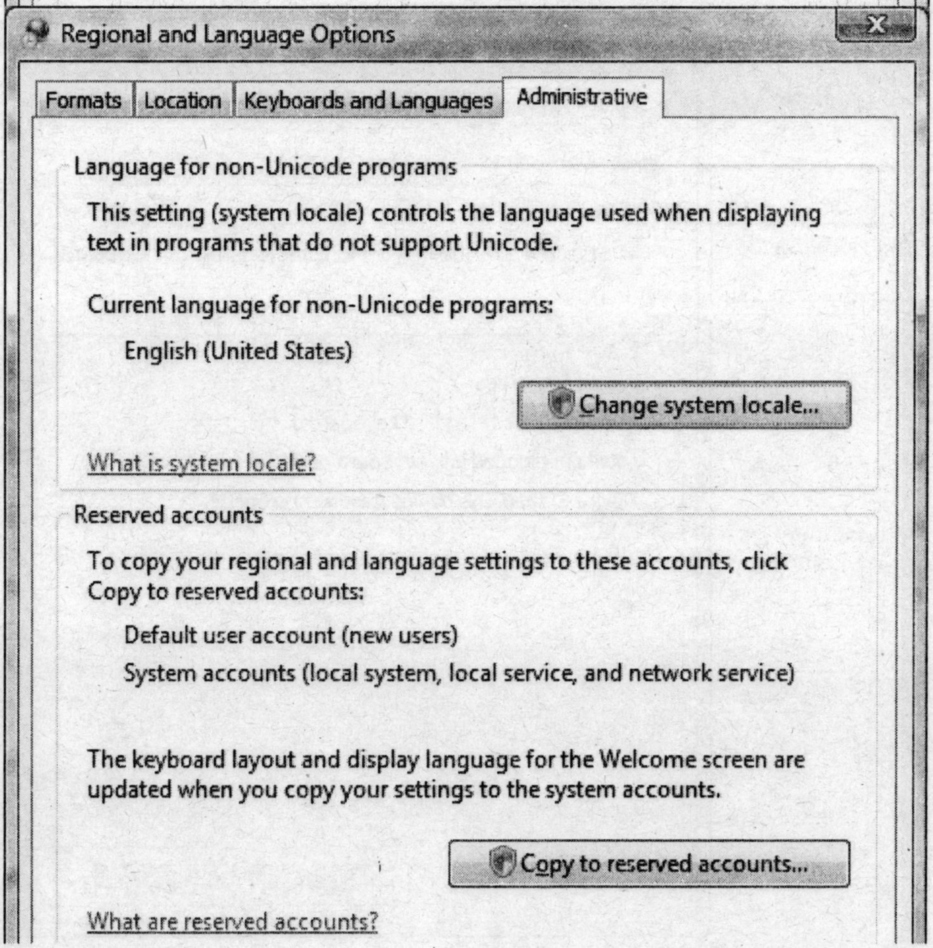
Regional and Language Options
Formats
Location
Keyboards and Languages
Administrative
Language for non-Unicode programs
This setting (system locale) controls the language used when displaying text in programs that do not support Unicode.
Current language for non-Unicode programs:
English (United States)
Change system locale...
What is system locale?
Reserved accounts
To copy your regional and language settings to these accounts, click Copy to reserved accounts:
Default user account (new users)
System accounts (local system, local service, and network service)
The keyboard layout and display language for the Welcome screen are updated when you copy your settings to the system accounts.
Copy to reserved accounts...
What are reserved accounts?

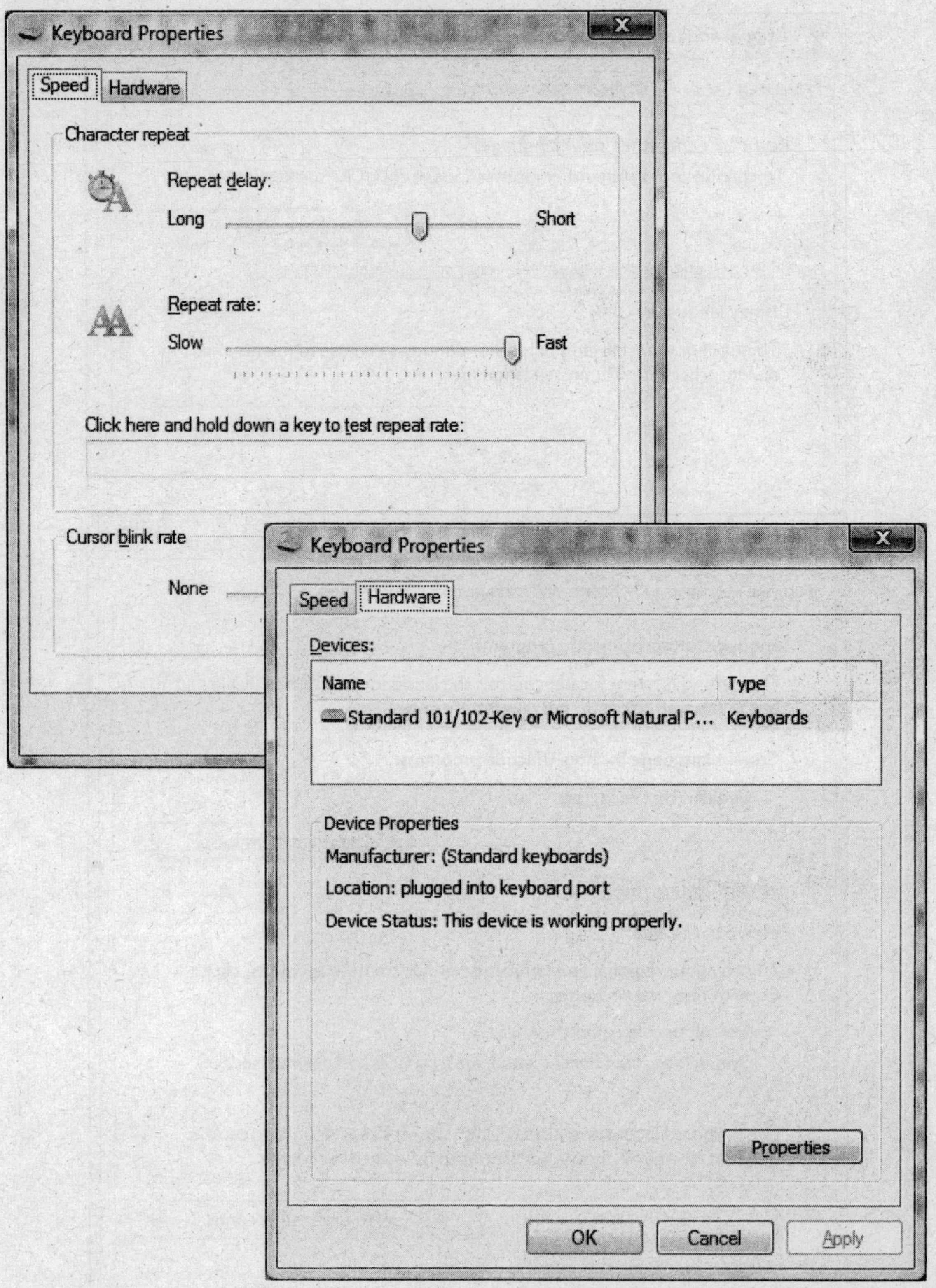
Keyboard Properties
Speed
Hardware
Character repeat
Repeat delay:
Long
Short
Repeat rate:
Slow
Fast
Click here and hold down a key to test repeat rate:
Cursor blink rate
None
Keyboard Properties
Speed
Hardware
Devices:
Name
Type
Standard 101/102-Key or Microsoft Natural P...
Keyboards
Device Properties
Manufacturer: (Standard keyboards)
Location: plugged into keyboard port
Device Status: This device is working properly.
Properties
OK
Cancel
Apply

Selecting and Viewing Fonts

The menus in the Fonts folder are slightly different from the usual folder menus. In the view menu, you will find, in addition to the choices of viewing icons and lists, an option called List Fonts by Similarity. Choose that option to see a view like that is shown below.

Select a font in the drop-down box at the top, and the other fonts will line up in terms of their degree of similarity. To see how similar, you can right-click any of the font names and select Open from the pop-menu menu. Windows will open with a complete view of the font in question. TrueType fonts located elsewhere can be moved into this folder.

Fonts don't have to be physically located in the Windows/Fonts folder to be recognized by Windows 7. You can make a shortcut to a font in another folder and put the shortcut in the Fonts folder. The shortcut is all you need for the font to be installed.

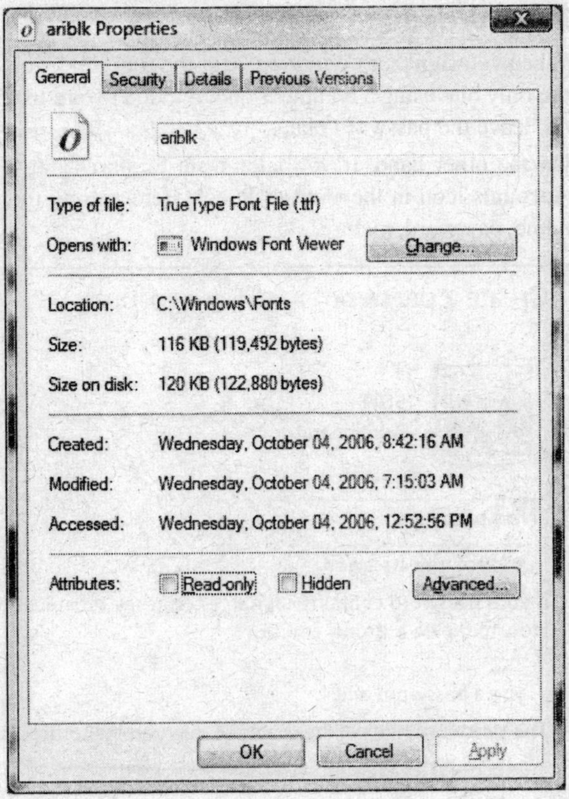

Installing New Fonts

It is quite easy. Select Install New Font from the File Menu in the font dialog box. Once selected you can tell the system where the fonts which you want to add are lying. Highlight the font or fonts which you want to install and click Ok button to install the fonts.

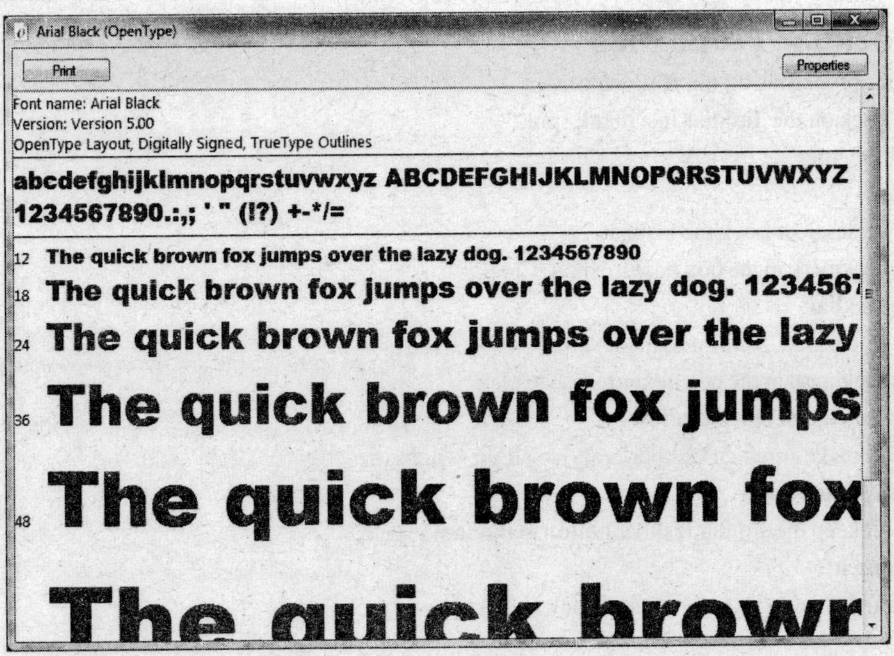

Passwords

When you sign on to Windows 7 for the first time, you are asked to provide a name and password. If you are the only one using a computer and you don't want to deal with a password everytime your turn the machine on, leave the password blank.

On the other hand, if you later want to start using a password or change the one you have, click User Accounts icon in the Control Panel. Here among the other options you have the option of changing user name, password, picture, etc.

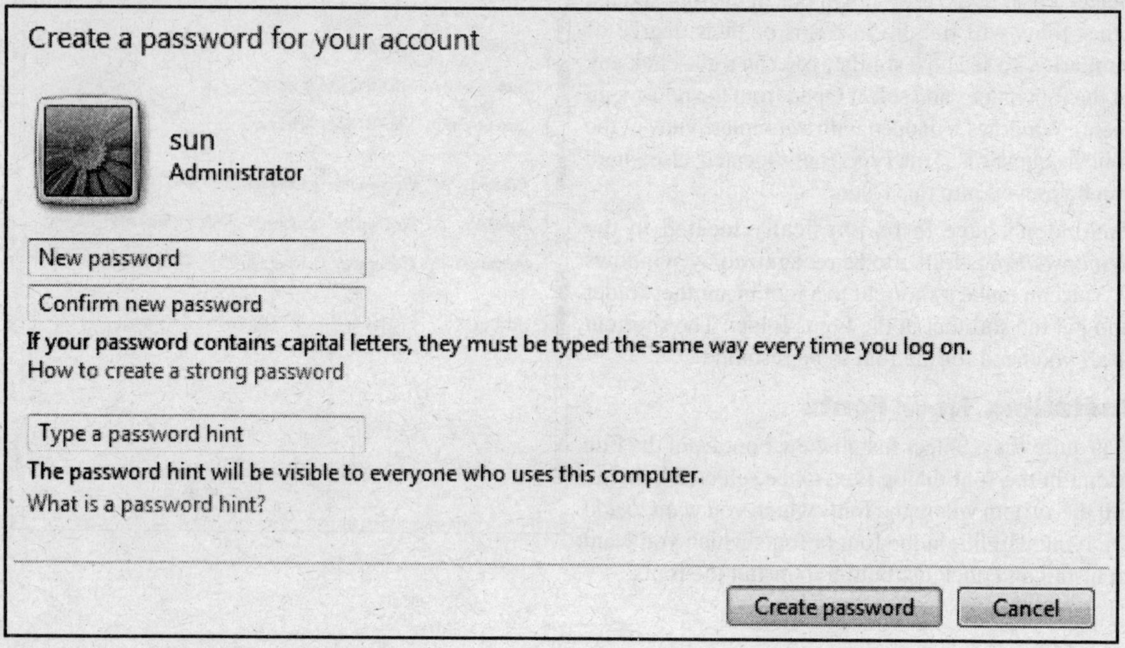

Setting Taskbar Properties

To set the taskbar properties do the following:

1. Right-click on the Taskbar in a blank spot.
2. Click Properties.

Locking taskbar

1. Select or deselect Lock the taskbar.
2. Put a checkmark in the box next to Show Clock.

Autohiding the taskbar

1. Select or deselect Auto-hide the taskbar.
2. Put a checkmark in the box next to Show Clock.

Keep the taskbar on top of other windows

1. This will make sure that taskbar is above all the windows.

Group similar taskbar button

1. This will keep the similar taskbar button at the same place.

Show Quick Launch

1. You can choose to show/hide the Quick Launch.

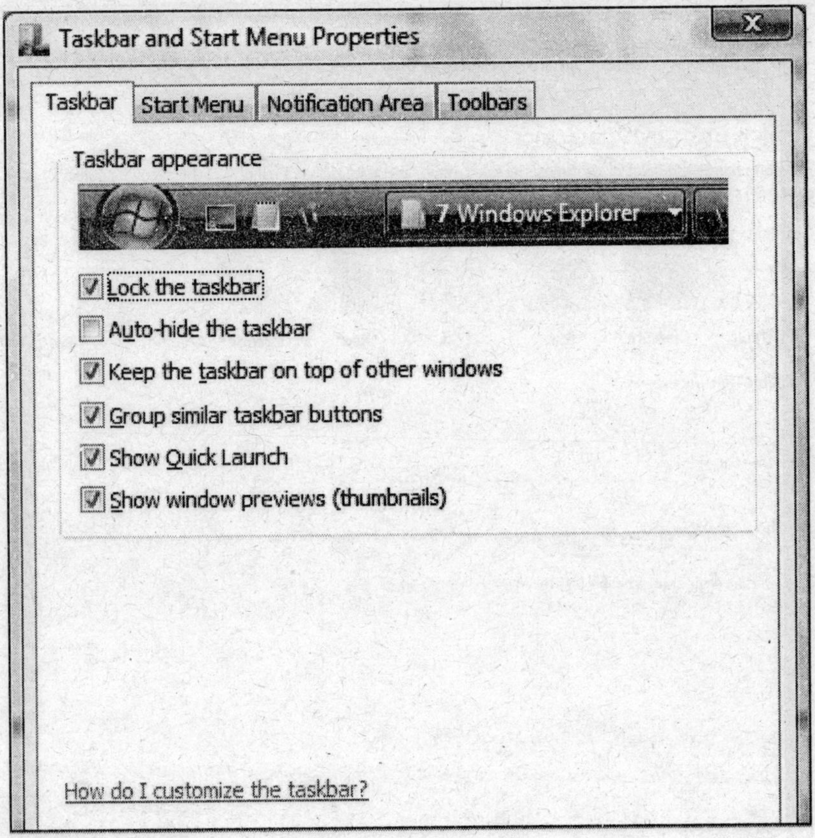

Show window previews (thumbnails)

1. You can show or hide window previews.

Setting Monitor Display Properties

Options here will depend on monitor and adapter type being used.

1. Right-click empty area on desktop.
2. Click Personalize.

Select a colour quality

1. Select the desired palette in Colour palette list.

Set desktop

1. Drag a picture to make it the desktop background.

Setting Screen Saver

1. Select desired screen saver in Screen Saver list, by clicking at Photos.
2. You can also set the time for the screen saver.
3. See the preview of the screen saver.

Setting Sounds

1. Select Sounds.
2. From the Sound dialog box, set the sound for various Windows options.

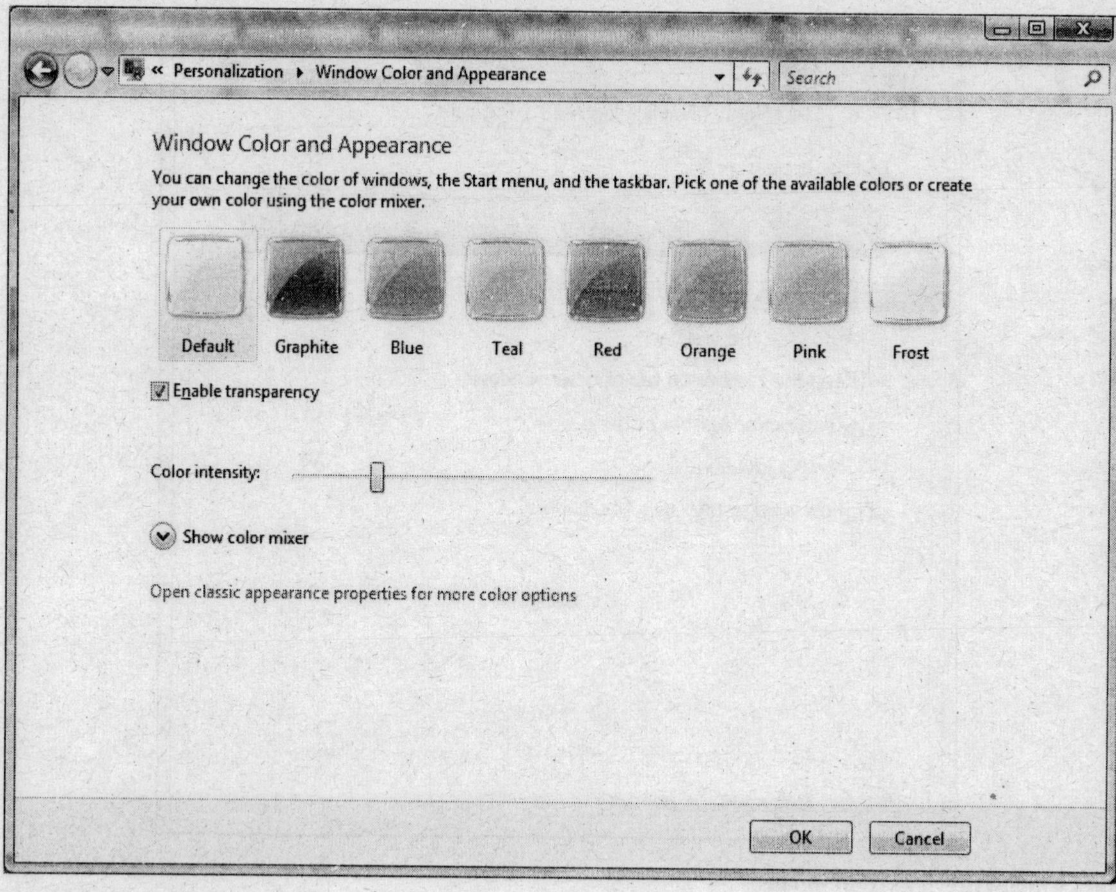

Setting Mouse Pointers

1. Select Mouse Pointers.
2. From the various options select the one which you are comfortable with.

Selecting a Theme

1. Select Sounds.
2. Windows comes with various themes, you can choose the one wanted by you.

Selecting Display Settings

1. Select Display Settings.
2. Choose the resolution to match your monitor.
3. Choose the colors.

Maintain Your System

Computers are capable of producing definite results only when they are properly maintained. It is likely to give some errors if not maintained at regular intervals. For this there are different commands available under Windows 7. I will discuss here few of them.

Disk Fragmentation

As you might know that when you write to a hard disk, it writes at a place where it finds free space and stores

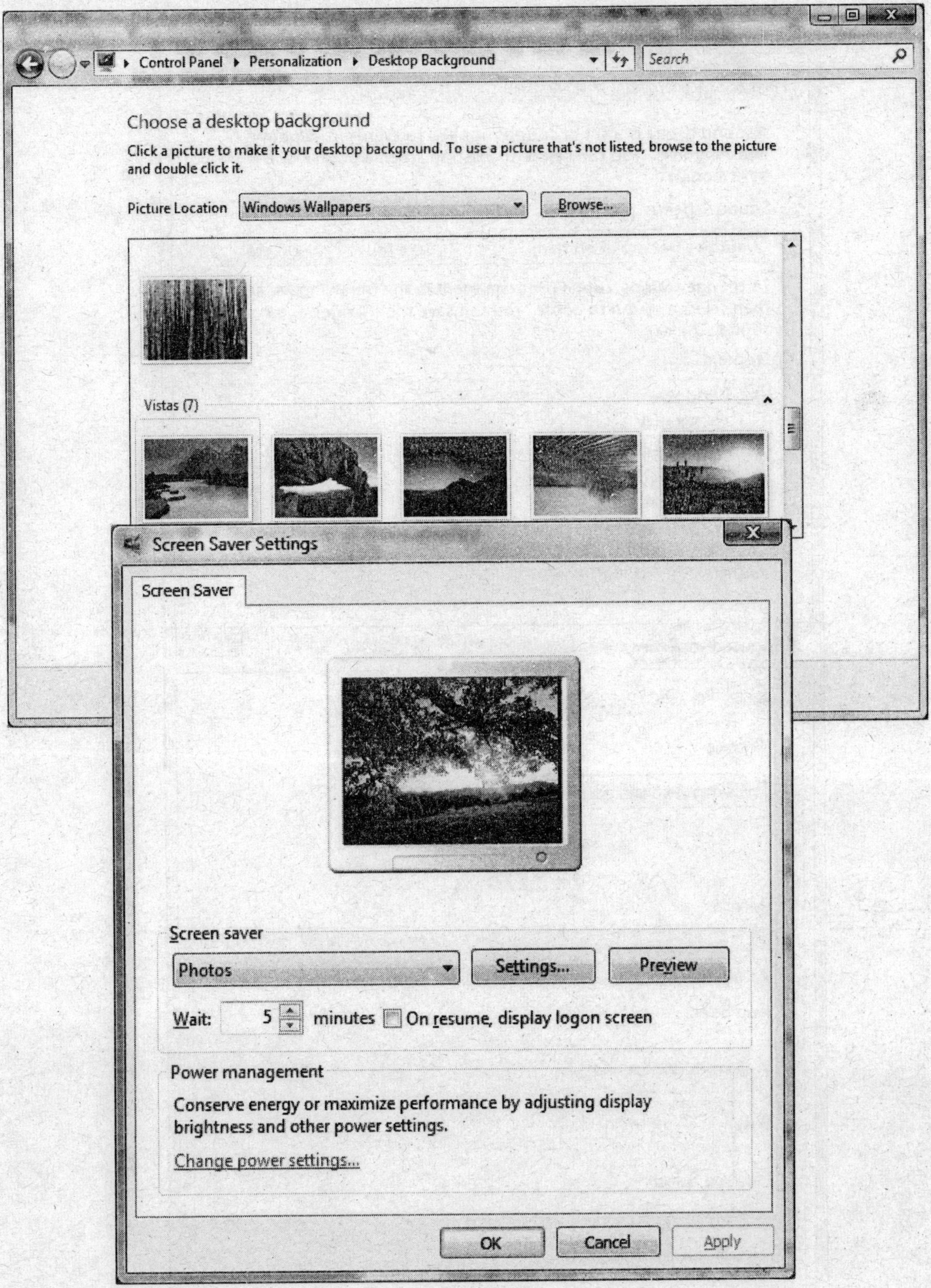
Control Panel ▸ Personalization ▸ Desktop Background
Search
Choose a desktop background
Click a picture to make it your desktop background. To use a picture that's not listed, browse to the picture and double click it.
Picture Location
Windows Wallpapers
Browse...
Vistas (7)
Screen Saver Settings
Screen Saver
Screen saver
Photos
Settings...
Preview
Wait:
5
minutes
On resume, display logon screen
Power management
Conserve energy or maximize performance by adjusting display brightness and other power settings.
Change power settings...
OK
Cancel
Apply

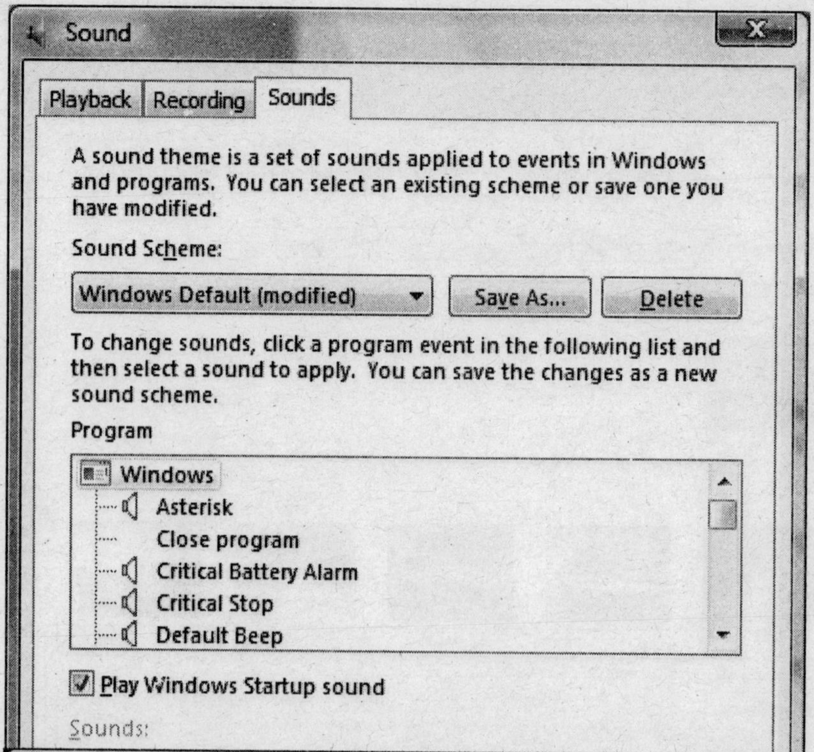
Sound
Playback
Recording
Sounds
A sound theme is a set of sounds applied to events in Windows and programs. You can select an existing scheme or save one you have modified.
Sound Scheme:
Windows Default (modified)
Save As...
Delete
To change sounds, click a program event in the following list and then select a sound to apply. You can save the changes as a new sound scheme.
Program
Windows
Asterisk
Close program
Critical Battery Alarm
Critical Stop
Default Beep
Play Windows Startup sound
Sounds:

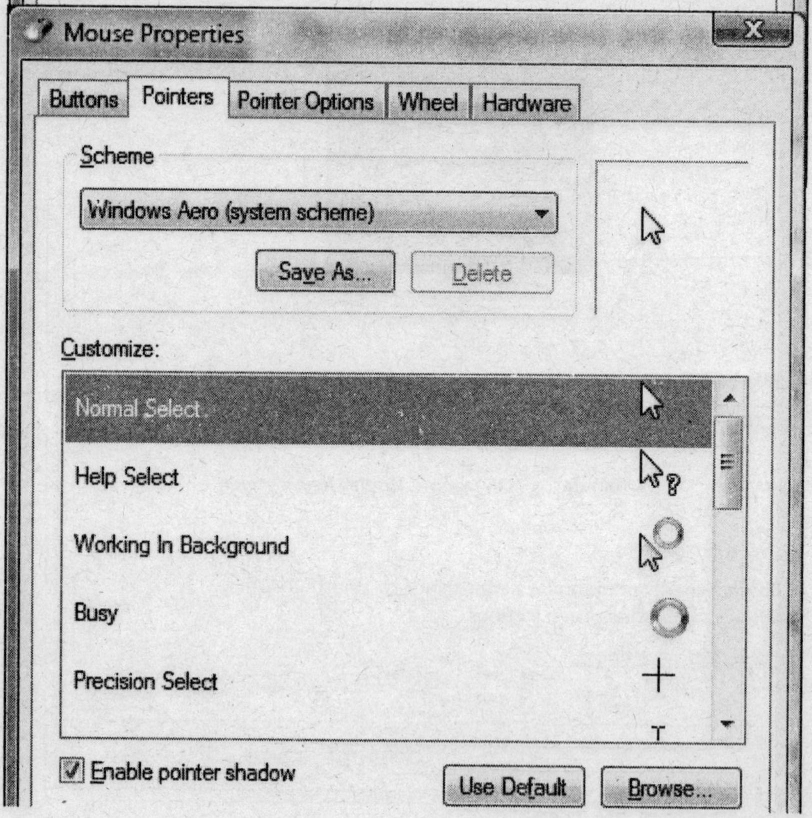
Mouse Properties
Buttons
Pointers
Pointer Options
Wheel
Hardware
Scheme
Windows Aero (system scheme)
Save As...
Delete
Customize:
Normal Select
Help Select
Working In Background
Busy
Precision Select
Enable pointer shadow
Use Default
Browse...

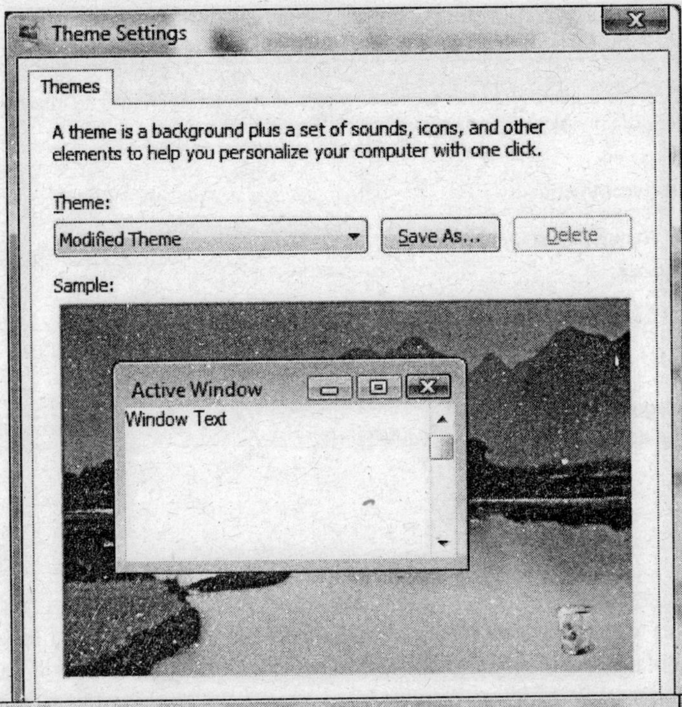
Theme Settings
Themes
A theme is a background plus a set of sounds, icons, and other elements to help you personalize your computer with one click.
Theme:
Modified Theme
Save As...
Delete
Sample:
Active Window
Window Text

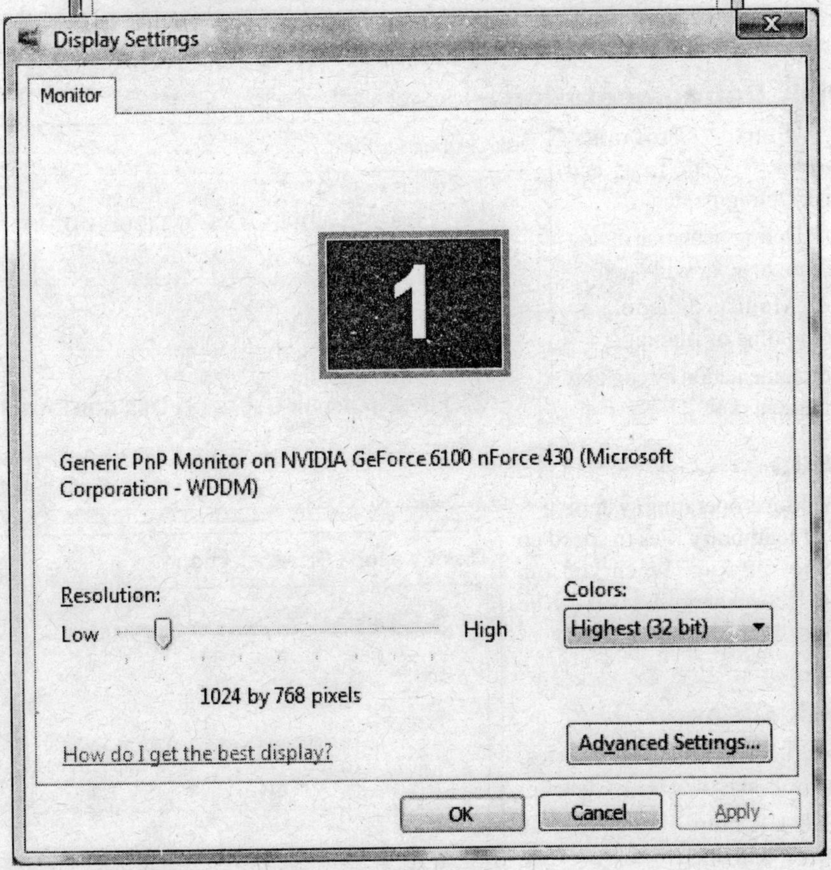
Display Settings
Monitor
1
Generic PnP Monitor on NVIDIA GeForce 6100 nForce 430 (Microsoft Corporation - WDDM)
Resolution:
Low
High
1024 by 768 pixels
Colors:
Highest (32 bit)
How do I get the best display?
Advanced Settings...
OK
Cancel
Apply

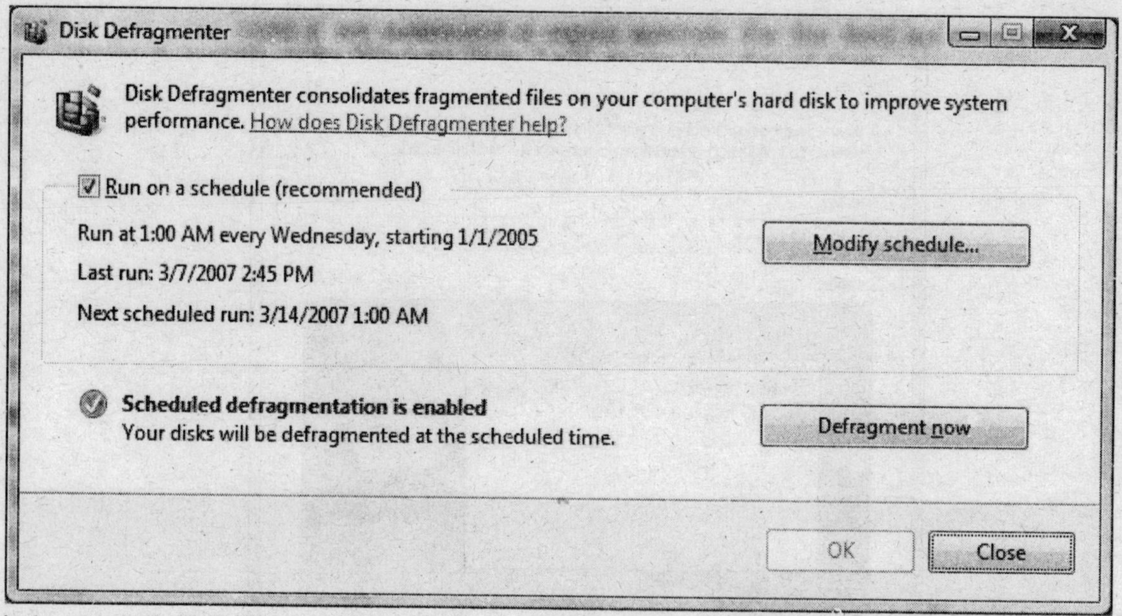

its location in the FAT. This way when you keep on working with deleting and adding files at random, there is bound to be filled up and blank space in hard disk at random. What disk fragmentation does is to put all the blank space at one side and the filled files on the other. This makes the working much faster than before. So to run your hard disk more efficiently, you must run Disk Defragmentation at least once a month.

Running Disk Defragmentation

1. Click Start, Programs, Accessories, System Tools and then Disk Defragmenter.
2. The Disk Defragmentation dialog box, as shown next, will open.
3. Click at Modify Schedule to change the time of running.
4. Start Defragmentation by clicking at Defragment now.

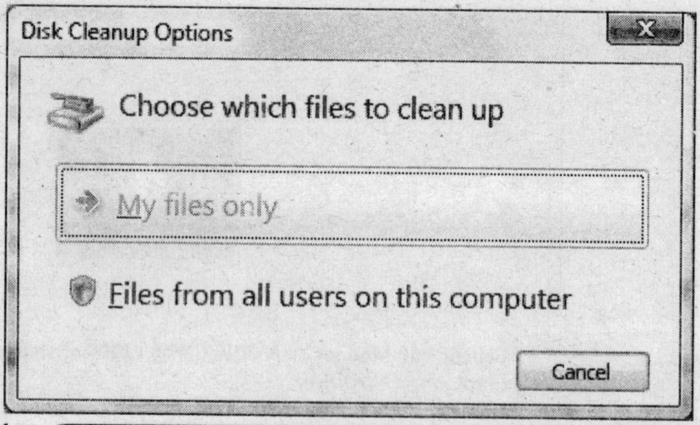

Disk Cleanup

While running Windows operating system does create a lot of temporary files to speed up the working of the software. When you run **Disk Cleanup** it checks for files that can be safely deleted and then presents a listing of such files.

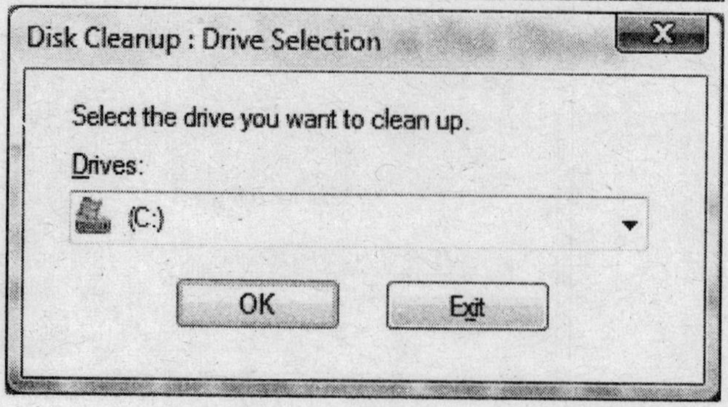

Running Disk Cleanup

1. Click Start, Programs, Accessories, System Tools and then Disk Cleanup.
2. The Disk Cleanup dialog box, as shown here, will open.

3. You have the choice to select "My files only" or "Files from all users on this computer".
4. Click at the drive which you want to clean up, in the next dialog box.
5. Once clicked Ok, it will show you the files which can be deleted, as shown in the dialog box.
6. Put a checkmark next to the categories you want to delete. Various type of files listed here are:

Downloaded program files Downloaded Program Files are ActiveX controls and Java applets downloaded automatically from the Internet when you view certain pages. They are temporarily stored in the Downloaded Program Files folder on your hard disk.

Temporary Internet files These are from various Web sites that you have visited, and they can make reconnecting to a Web site much faster. But there is no point in keeping them around forever.

Offline Webpages Offline pages are webpages that are stored on your computer so you can view them without being connected to the Internet. If you delete these pages now, you can still view your favorites offline later by synchronizing them. Your personalized for webpages will be left intact.

Hibernation File Cleaner The hibernation file contains information about the state of your computer as it enters hibernation. If you do not use the hibernation power setting, you can remove this file to free up disk space. Removing this file disable hibernation. If you use hibernation on this computer, do not remove this file. To adjust power settings or to enable hibernation, click Power Options.

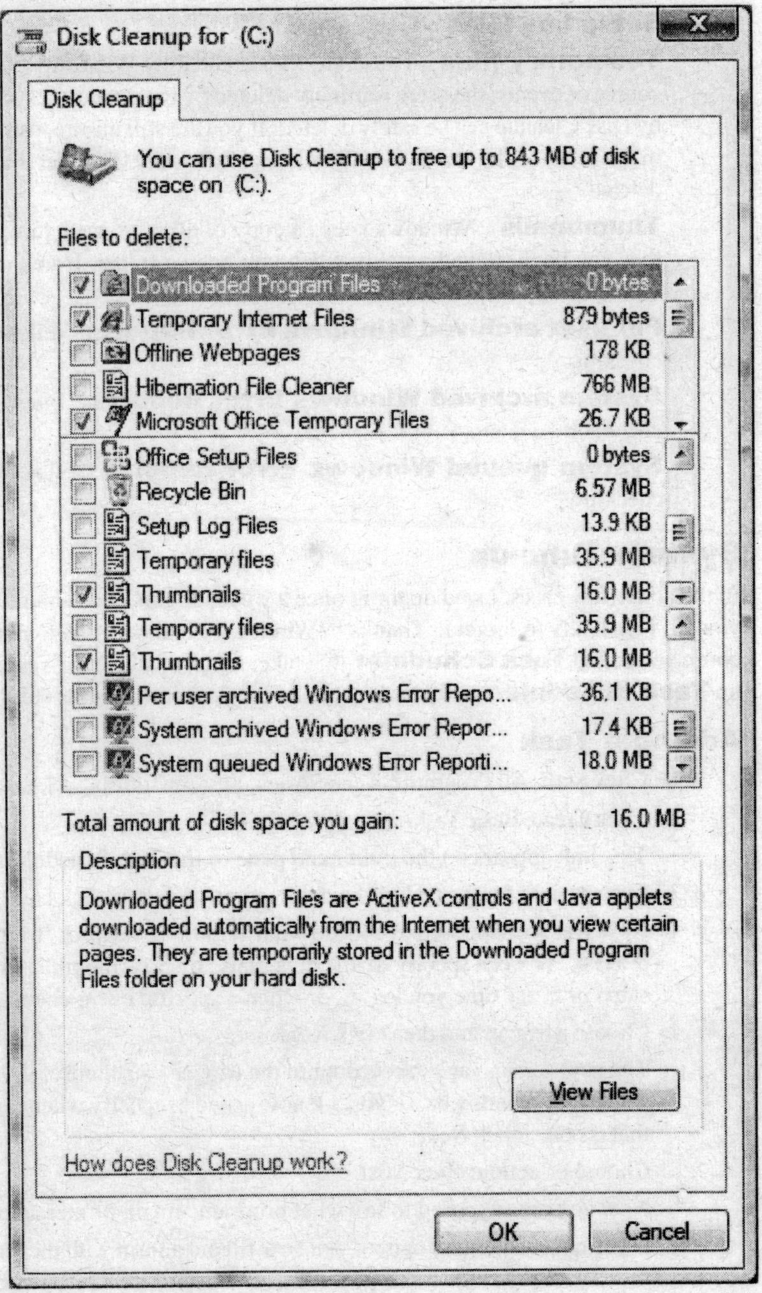

Microsoft Office Temporary Files Microsoft Office maintains log files for diagnostic purposes as well as other temporary data files. These files are left over from a previous Office session and can be deleted.

Office Setup Files Installation files used by Office. If these files are removed from your computer, you may be prompted for your original installation media or source during any Reinstall, Repair, or Patch operation.

Recycle Bin If the Recycle Bin settings are correctly configured, you should not need to empty the bin to clear space on your hard drive. If the Recycle Bin is too large, reset it to some smaller size.

Setup Log Files Files created by Windows.

Temporary files These are files created by Windows and Windows programs. In the normal course of events, these are routinely deleted by the operating system. Any file that remain to be found by Disk Cleanup can be safely deleted. If you are still unsure, use Windows Explorer to look at the files in the Temp folder inside your Windows folder. Any file older than a few days are strays and should be deleted.

Thumbnails Windows keeps a copy of all of your picture, video, and document thumbnails so they can be displayed quickly when you open a folder. If you delete these thumbnails, they will be automatically recreated as needed.

Per user archived Windows Error Reports Files used for error reporting and solution checking.

System archived Windows Error Reports Files used for error reporting and solution checking.

System queued Windows Error Reports Files used for error reporting and solution checking.

System Tune-up

In the above few cases, I said do thing once a week, do this once a month but when it comes to actual doing, you are very likely to forget it. Thanks to Windows 7 it allows you to remember all this. For this we have the command called **Task Scheduler** that takes cares of all the above commands. All you need to do is to set up **Task Scheduler** to run automatically on a schedule you specify.

Adding a Task

1. Click Start, All Programs, Accessories, System Tools and Task Scheduler.
2. Click Create Basic Task.

   This link appears on the right hand pane of the Task Scheduler. A wizard appears.
3. Type a name for the task and a description, and then click Next.

   Now you are supposed to choose what Windows 7 calls a "trigger" —in plain English, when to run the task. You can specify that it runs dialy, weekly, monthly, or just once; every time the computer starts or every time you log in; or when a specific event occurs — like when a program starts.
4. Choose a trigger and then click Next.

   The next screen varies according to the trigger you choose. If you choose to run the task on a daily, weekly, or monthly basis, you are now asked to specify when during that day, week, or month. Once that is done, click Next.
5. Choose an action; click Next.

   Now you are supposed to say what program, email, or message you want the PC to fire up.

   If you chose the email option, you now fill out a form with the recipient's name, address, subject line, message body, and so on; you can even specify an attachment.

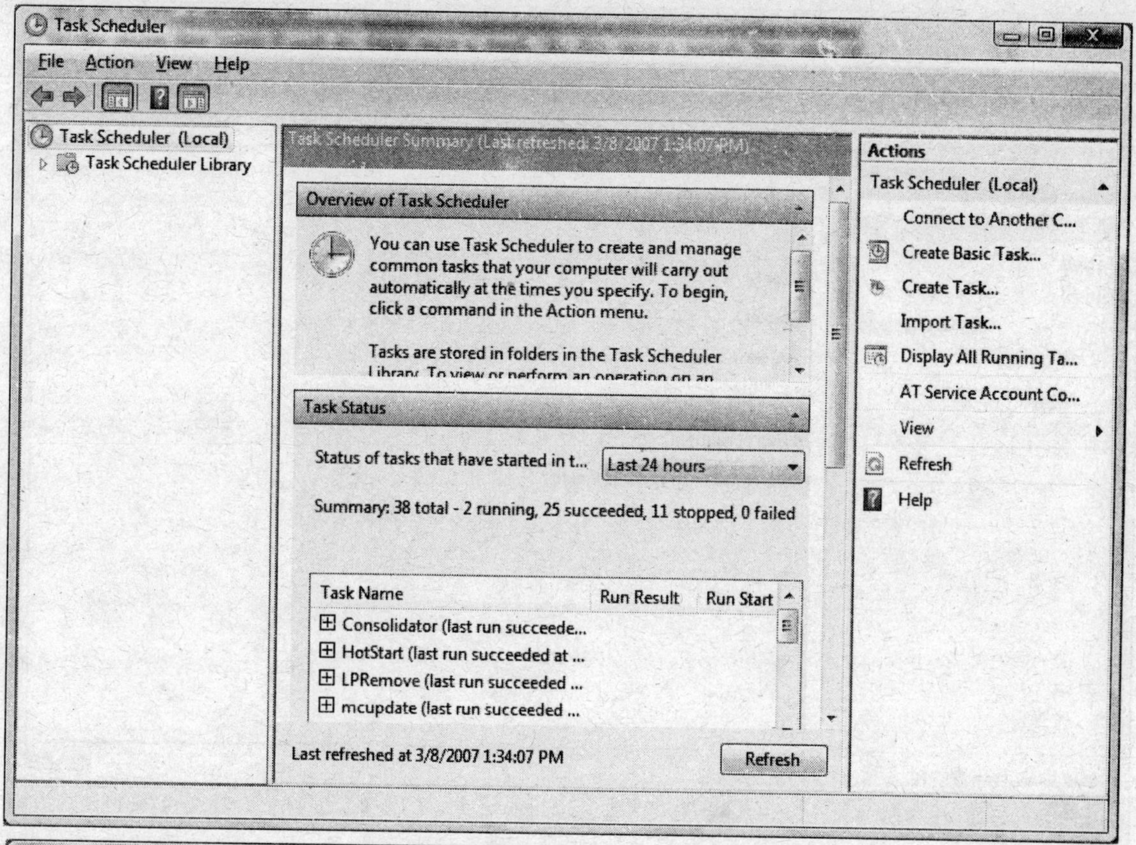
Task Scheduler
File Action View Help
Task Scheduler (Local)
Task Scheduler Library
Task Scheduler Summary (Last refreshed: 3/8/2007 1:34:07 PM)
Overview of Task Scheduler
You can use Task Scheduler to create and manage common tasks that your computer will carry out automatically at the times you specify. To begin, click a command in the Action menu.
Tasks are stored in folders in the Task Scheduler Library. To view or perform an operation on an
Task Status
Status of tasks that have started in t...
Last 24 hours
Summary: 38 total - 2 running, 25 succeeded, 11 stopped, 0 failed
Task Name
Run Result
Run Start
Consolidator (last run succeede...
HotStart (last run succeeded at ...
LPRemove (last run succeeded ...
mcupdate (last run succeeded ...
Last refreshed at 3/8/2007 1:34:07 PM
Refresh
Actions
Task Scheduler (Local)
Connect to Another C...
Create Basic Task...
Create Task...
Import Task...
Display All Running Ta...
AT Service Account Co...
View
Refresh
Help

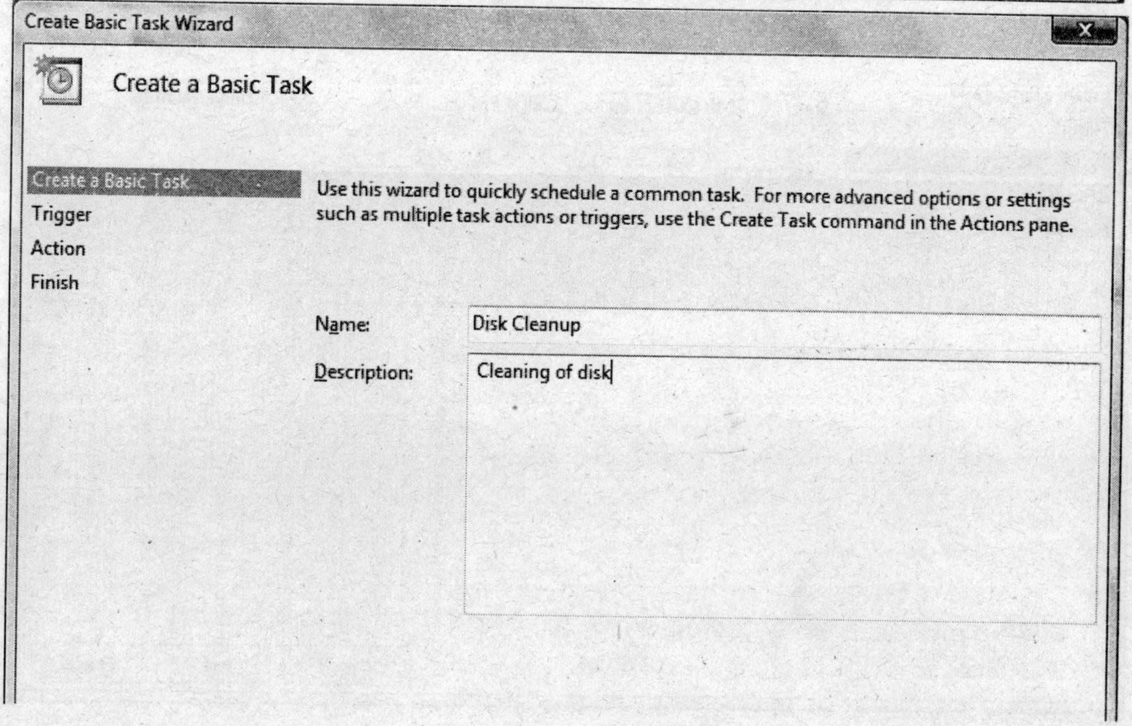
Create Basic Task Wizard
Create a Basic Task
Create a Basic Task
Trigger
Action
Finish
Use this wizard to quickly schedule a common task. For more advanced options or settings such as multiple task actions or triggers, use the Create Task command in the Actions pane.
Name:
Disk Cleanup
Description:
Cleaning of disk

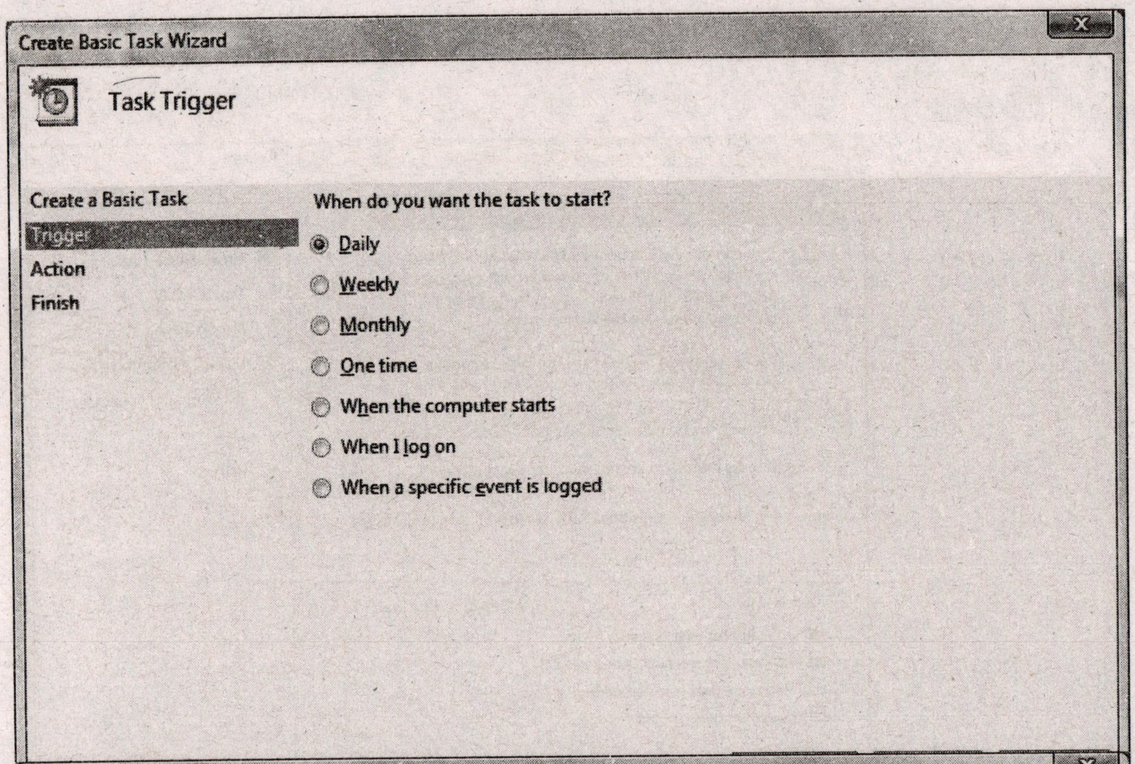

Create Basic Task Wizard
Task Trigger
Create a Basic Task
Trigger
Action
Finish
When do you want the task to start?
Daily
Weekly
Monthly
One time
When the computer starts
When I log on
When a specific event is logged

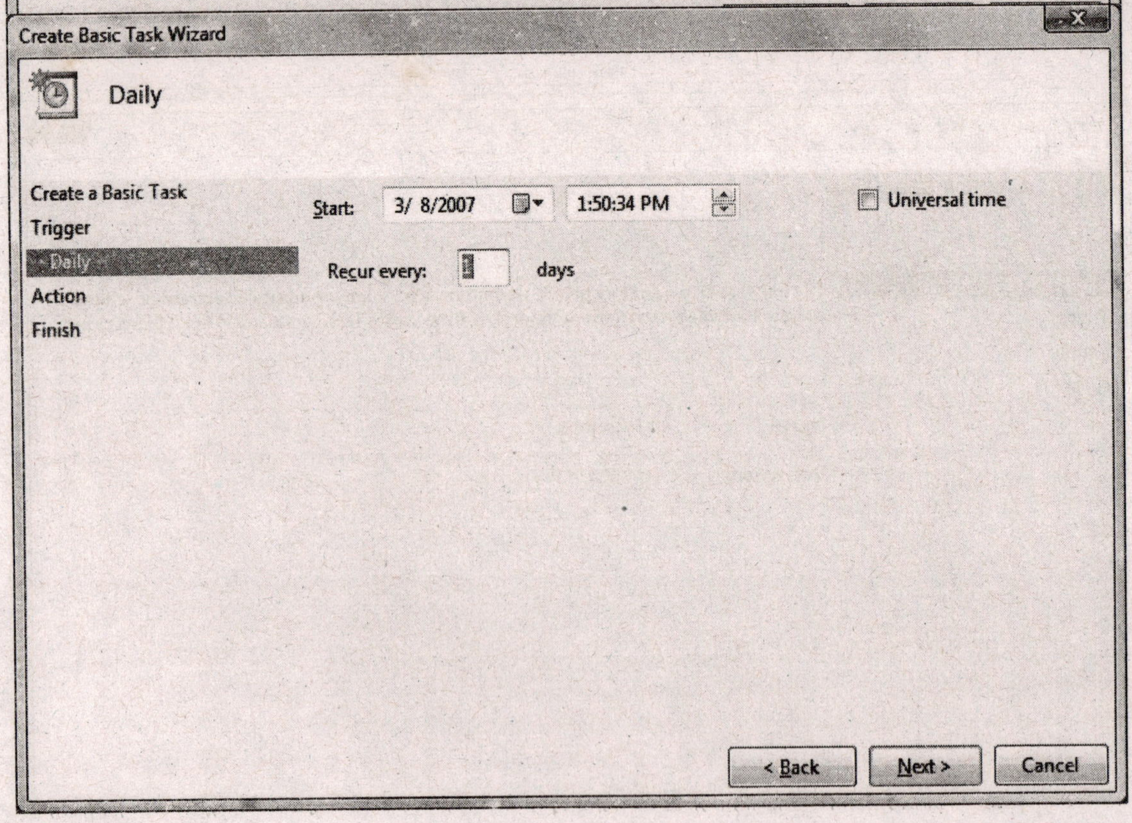

Create Basic Task Wizard
Daily
Create a Basic Task
Trigger
Daily
Action
Finish
Start: 3/ 8/2007
1:50:34 PM
Universal time
Recur every: 1 days
< Back
Next >
Cancel

If you chose to run a program, you now browse to select the program. At this point, programmers can also add arguments, which are codes that customize how the program starts.

And if you opted to display a message, you get to type a name and text for the message. At the appointed time, an actual Window dialog box will appear on the screen—except that it will contain text that you wrote.

6. Complete the details about the email, program, or phony dialog box, and then click Next.

   Finally, a screen appears, summarizing the task, when it will run, and so on. To edit it, click the Back button.

7. To confirm the automated task, click Finish.

   You return to the Task Scheduler window. Although you may have to scroll down to see it, your new task appears in the Active Tasks list at the bottom of the window. If all goes well, 7 will fire it up at the moment you specified.

Checking Disk

In the earlier versions of Windows, you had ScanDisk, which is missing here in 7. Now you can perform the

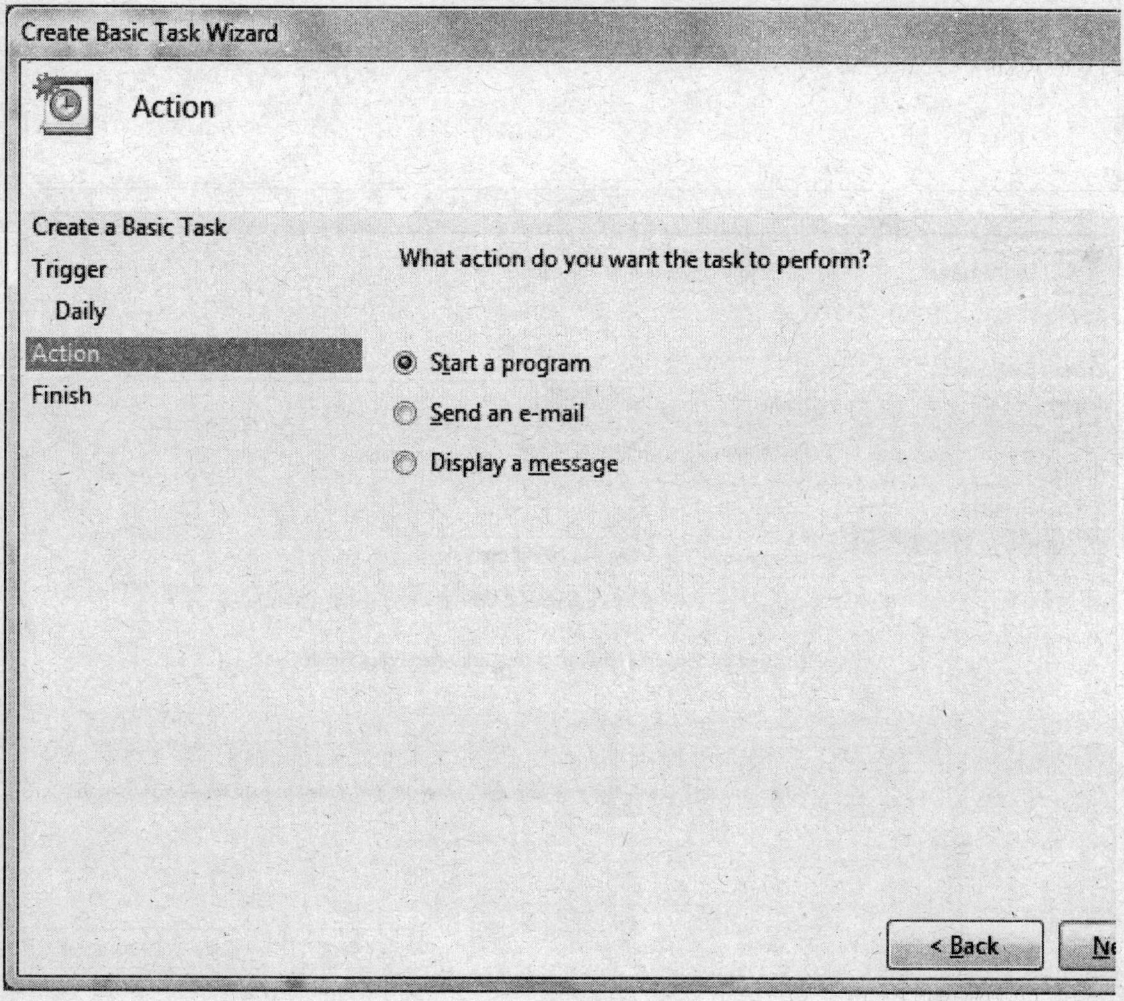

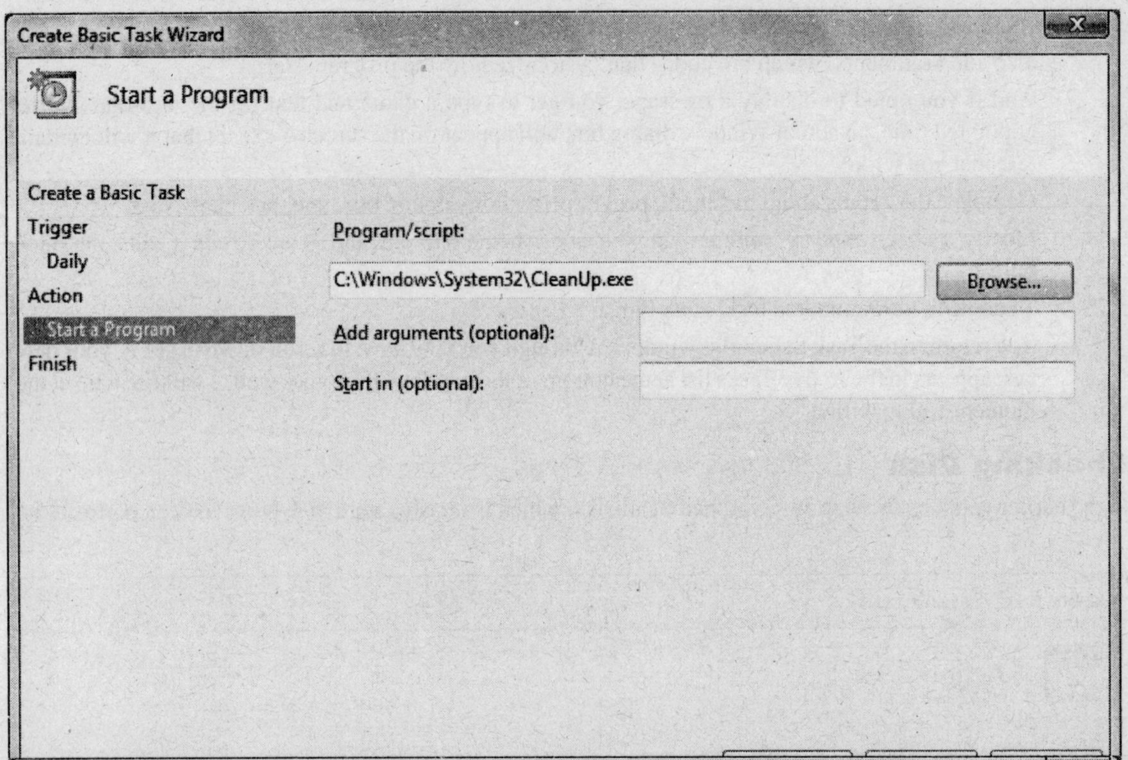
Create Basic Task Wizard
Start a Program
Create a Basic Task
Trigger
Daily
Action
Start a Program
Finish
Program/script:
C:\Windows\System32\CleanUp.exe
Browse...
Add arguments (optional):
Start in (optional):

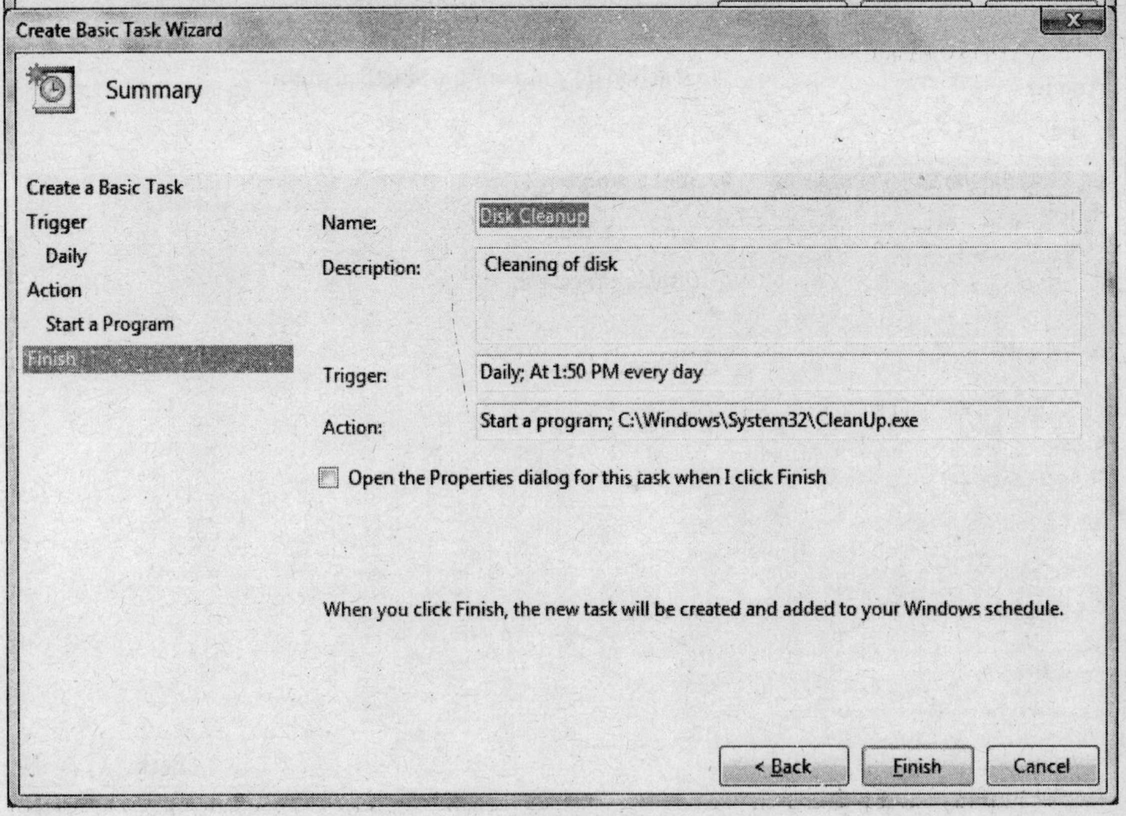
Create Basic Task Wizard
Summary
Create a Basic Task
Trigger
Daily
Action
Start a Program
Finish
Name:
Disk Cleanup
Description:
Cleaning of disk
Trigger:
Daily; At 1:50 PM every day
Action:
Start a program; C:\Windows\System32\CleanUp.exe
Open the Properties dialog for this task when I click Finish
When you click Finish, the new task will be created and added to your Windows schedule.
< Back
Finish
Cancel

same operation from the Hard disk checkup. You can check your hard disk or scan it for errors and correct them in case needed, you can do the following:

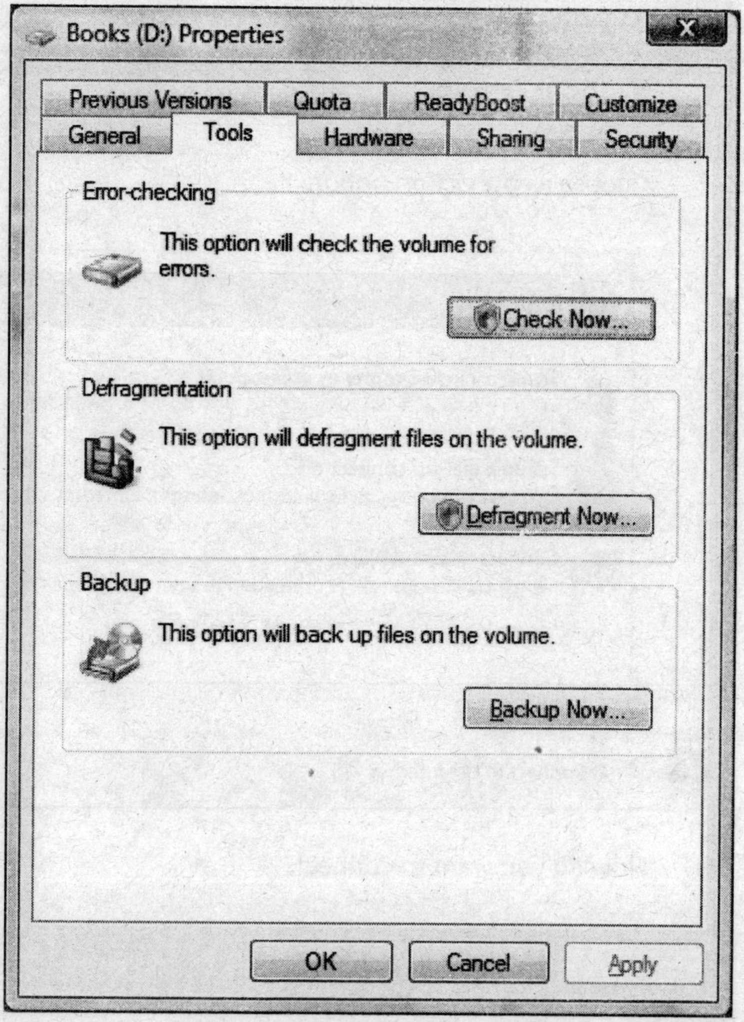

1. Open My Computer, and then select the local disk you want to check.
2. Right click the mouse, click Properties.
3. On the Tools tab, under Error-checking, click Check Now.
4. Under Check disk options, select the Scan for and attempt recovery of bad sectors check box.

Your disk will be checked in 2 phases and errors if any will be pointed out.

Automatically fix file system errors

Clearly, you want this option turned on, so that any problems Windows finds are taken care of automatically.

Scan for and attempt recovery of bad sectors

If you turn on this option, whenever the scan finds a damaged section of a drive, it moves any files located there elsewhere on the drive. Then the program surrounds that hard-disk area with the imaginary tape, so that Windows won't use the damaged area for storing files in the future.

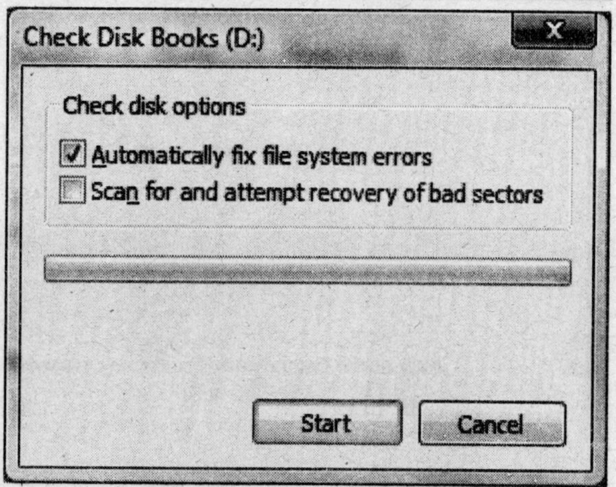

Networking and Internet

Now I will introduce you to Windows 7's ability to perform in a multitude of network configurations. In addition to working well with major network operating systems, Windows 7 has sophisticated 32-bit network components built-in, allowing Windows 7 to fulfil many network demands that you may want to place on it. With built-in sharing, printer sharing and access control, Windows 7 can operate as a high-performance **peer-to-peer network** operating system. Additionally Windows 7 can operate well as a client on a **client-server network**.

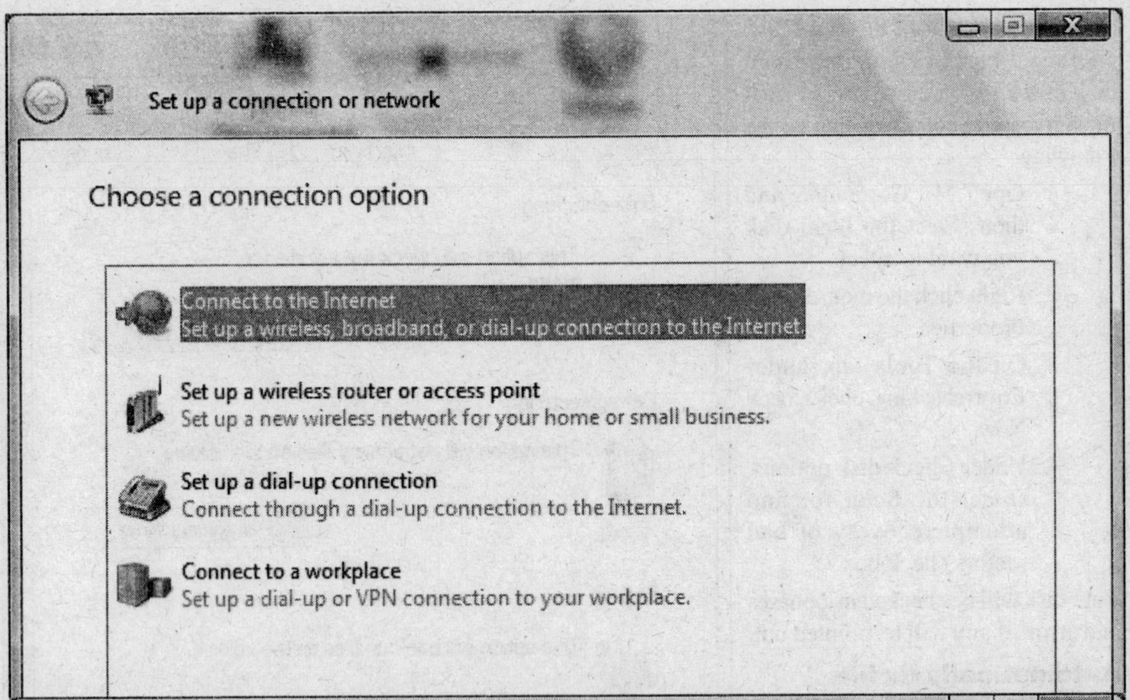
Set up a connection or network
Choose a connection option
Connect to the Internet
Set up a wireless, broadband, or dial-up connection to the Internet.
Set up a wireless router or access point
Set up a new wireless network for your home or small business.
Set up a dial-up connection
Connect through a dial-up connection to the Internet.
Connect to a workplace
Set up a dial-up or VPN connection to your workplace.

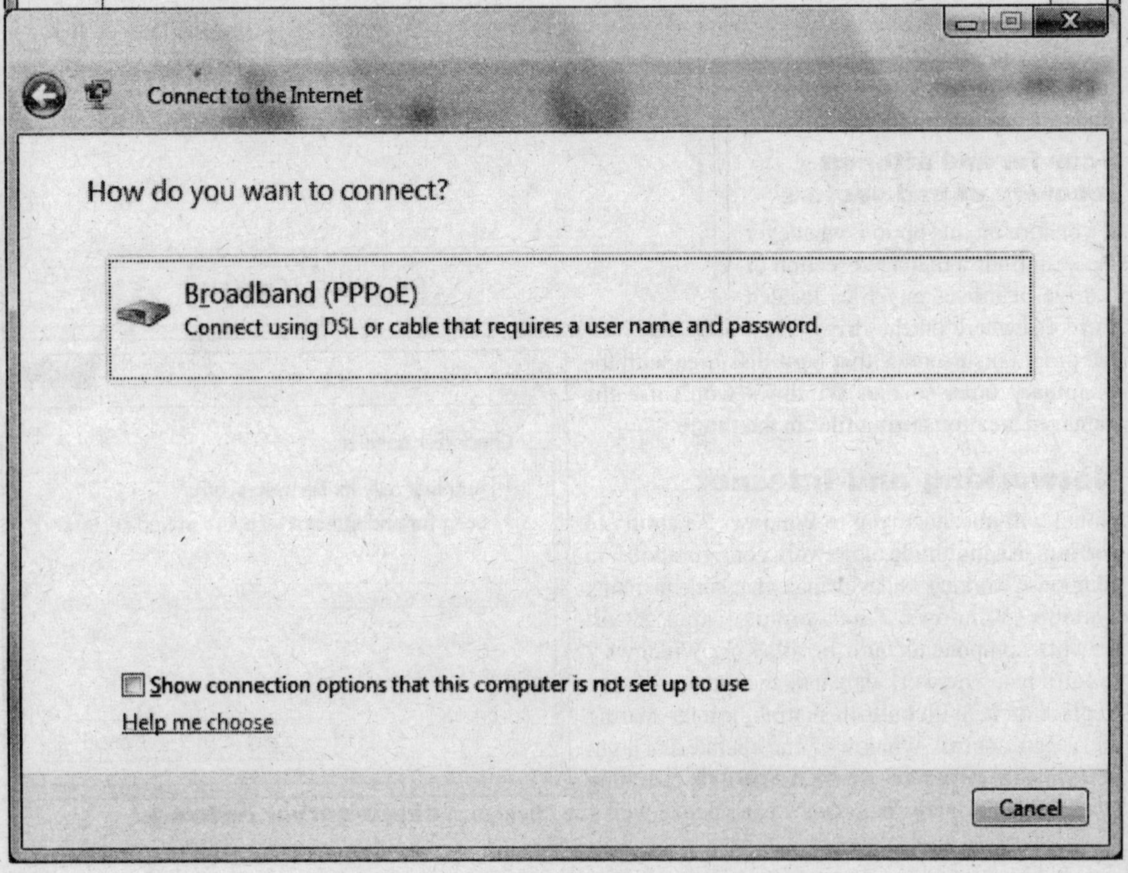
Connect to the Internet
How do you want to connect?
Broadband (PPPoE)
Connect using DSL or cable that requires a user name and password.
Show connection options that this computer is not set up to use
Help me choose
Cancel

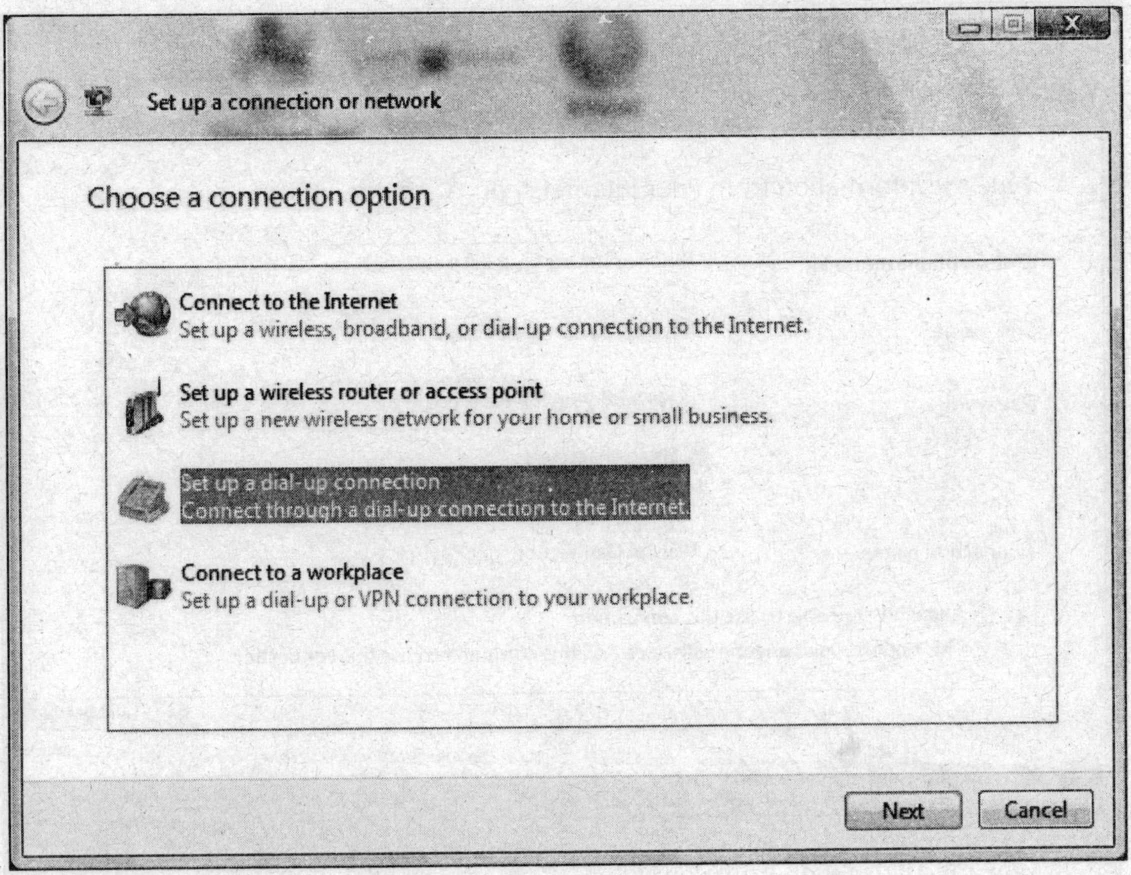

Peer-To-Peer Networking

The term peer-to-peer networking refers to a type of network where every computer connected to the network can share its resources with the rest of the network. In other words, every computer on the network can act like a file server and share its files and printers with other computers.

Setting up Network and Internet

Windows 7 allow you to set up Networking in a flash. It takes you through a set of wizards and once you have given all the answers correctly, your network is installed.

To set up networking do the following,

1. Click the **Start** button.
2. Select **Control Panel**.
3. Select **Network and Internet Connections**.
4. Click on the **Network Connections** icon.
5. From the Network Tasks click at **Connect to the Internet** task button.
6. The first wizard screen as shown below comes on screen.
7. Click Next to reach next screen.
8. Select among the options which you want to use. In our case, we would select Set up home or small office network.

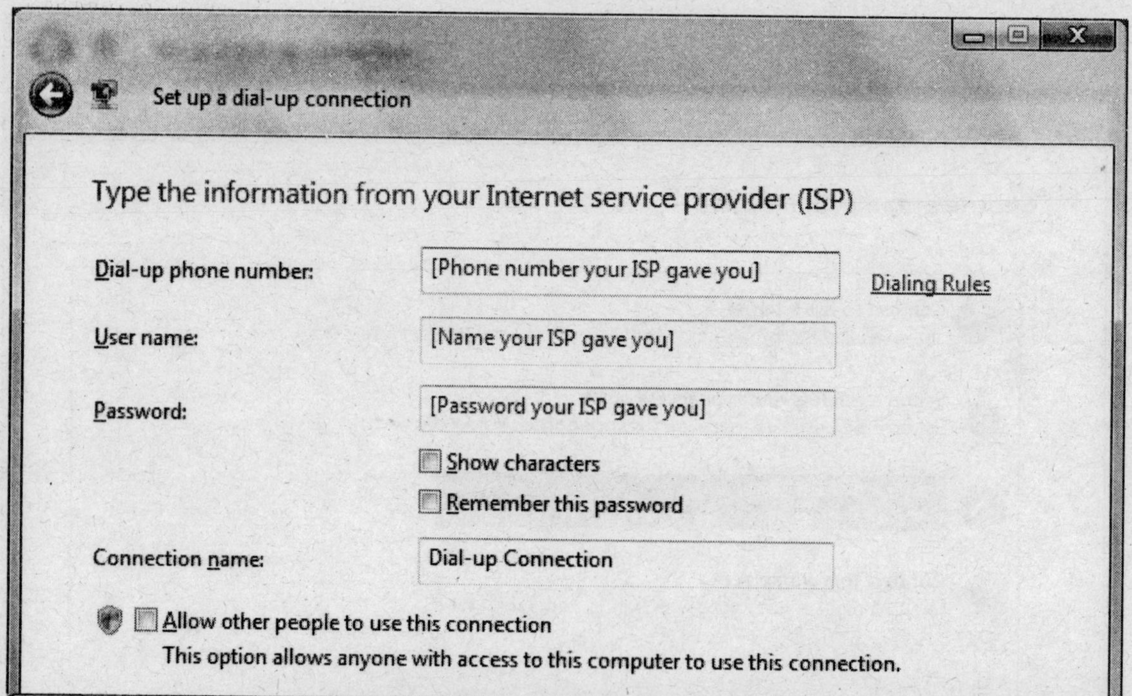
Set up a dial-up connection
Type the information from your Internet service provider (ISP)
Dial-up phone number:
[Phone number your ISP gave you]
Dialing Rules
User name:
[Name your ISP gave you]
Password:
[Password your ISP gave you]
Show characters
Remember this password
Connection name:
Dial-up Connection
Allow other people to use this connection
This option allows anyone with access to this computer to use this connection.

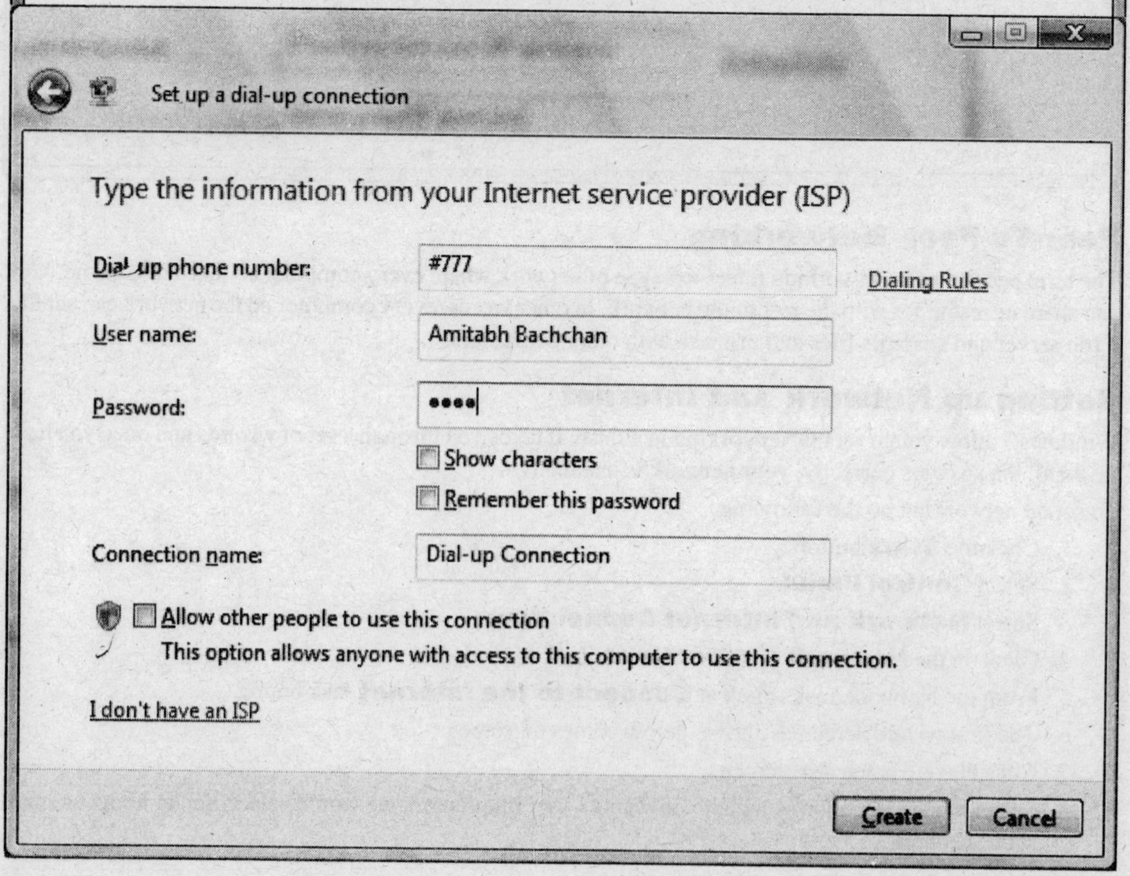
Set up a dial-up connection
Type the information from your Internet service provider (ISP)
Dial-up phone number:
#777
Dialing Rules
User name:
Amitabh Bachchan
Password:
••••
Show characters
Remember this password
Connection name:
Dial-up Connection
Allow other people to use this connection
This option allows anyone with access to this computer to use this connection.
I don't have an ISP
Create
Cancel

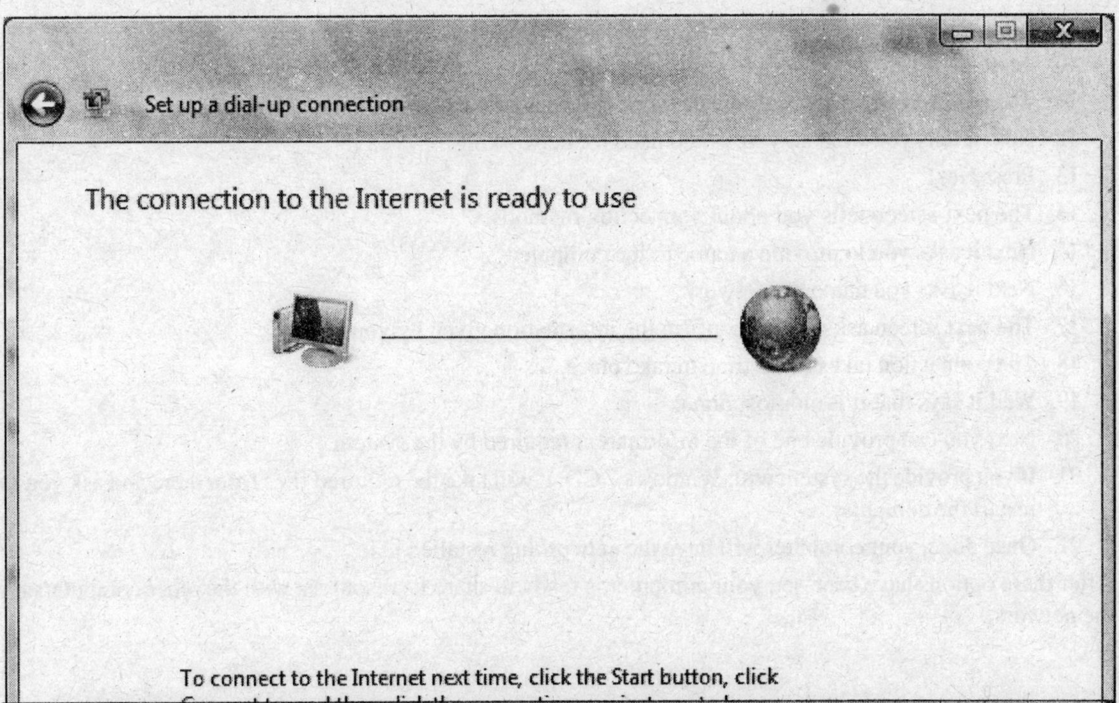
Set up a dial-up connection
The connection to the Internet is ready to use
To connect to the Internet next time, click the Start button, click

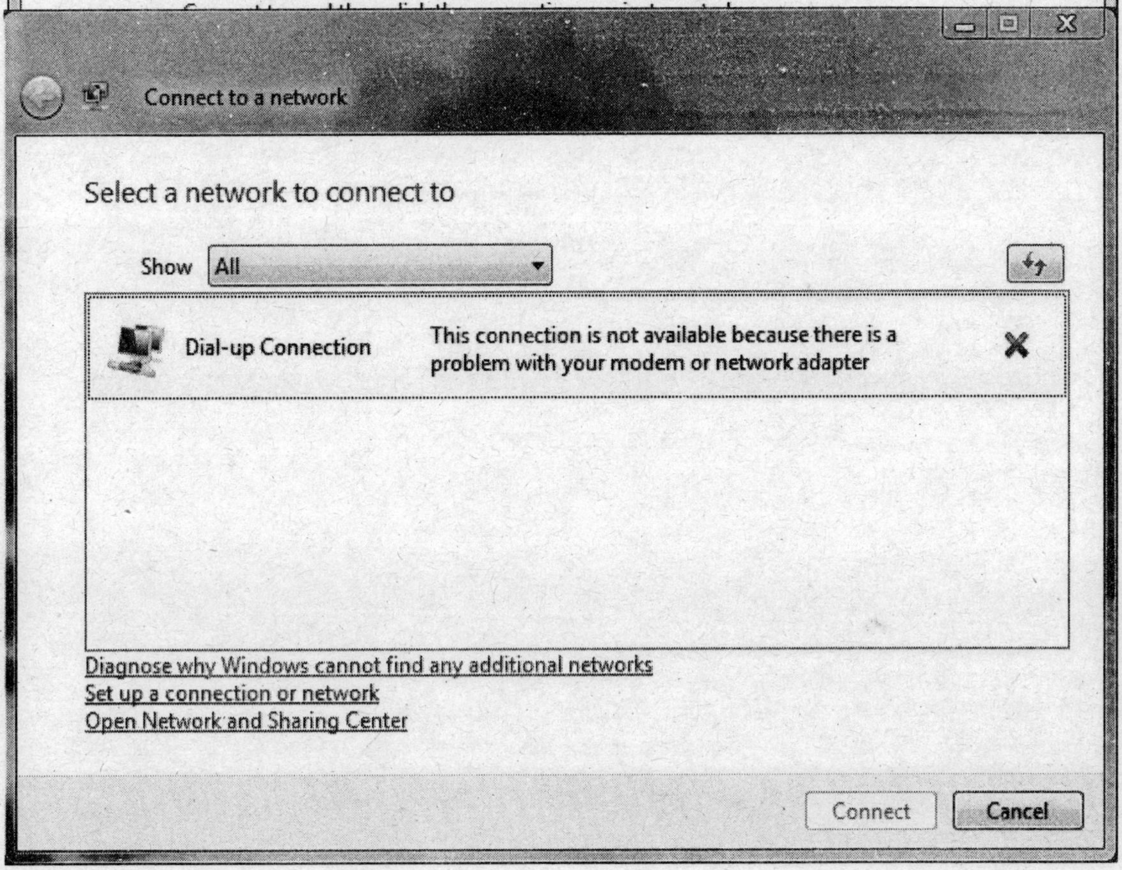
Connect to a network
Select a network to connect to
Show
All
Dial-up Connection
This connection is not available because there is a problem with your modem or network adapter
Diagnose why Windows cannot find any additional networks
Set up a connection or network
Open Network and Sharing Center
Connect
Cancel

9. Click at the option and press Next.
10. Another wizard screen would come on screen. Press Next to move further.
11. The next screen tells you that a network can be used for sharing files, printers, etc.
12. Next it tells you what all you would need for networking.
13. Press Next.
14. The next screen tells you about connection methods.
15. Next it asks you to provide a name to the computer.
16. Next it asks you name the network.
17. The next screen asks you to confirm the information given by you so far.
18. The connection takes some time to take place.
19. Well it says that it is alomost done.
20. Next you can provide one of the information required by the system.
21. If you provide the system with Windows 7 CD, it will take the required files from there and ask you to restart the computer.
22. Once done, your computer will have the networking installed in it.

After these options have been set, your computer is ready to share its resources with the other computers on the network.

6 Additional Commands of Windows 7

Understanding Security and Safe Computing

If you connect to the Internet, allow other people to use your computer, or share files with others, you should take steps to protect your computer from harm. Why? Because there are computer criminals (sometimes called hackers) who attack other people's computers. These people can attack directly, by breaking into your computer through the Internet and stealing your personal information, or indirectly, by creating malicious software to harm your computer.

Fortunately, you can help protect yourself by taking a few simple precautions.

Protect your computer

These are ways to help protect your computer against potential security threats:

- **Firewall**. A firewall can help protect your computer by preventing hackers or malicious software from gaining access to it.
- **Virus protection**. Antivirus software can help protect your computer against viruses, worms, and other security threats.
- **Spyware and other malware protection**. Antispyware software can help protect your computer from spyware and other potentially unwanted software.
- **Windows Update**. Windows can routinely check for updates for your computer and install them automatically.

Manage security settings with Action Center

Action Center is a central location for monitoring and managing firewall settings, Windows Update, anti-malware software settings, Internet security, and User Account Control settings. Action Center also monitors computer maintenance settings and provides links to troubleshooters and other tools that can help fix problems.

Use a firewall

A firewall is software or hardware that checks information coming from the Internet or a network and then either turns it away or allows it to pass through to your computer, depending on your firewall settings. In this way, a firewall can help prevent hackers and malicious software from gaining access to your computer.

Windows Firewall is built into Windows and is turned on automatically.

How a firewall works

If you run a program such as an instant messaging program or a multiplayer network game that needs to receive information from the Internet or a network, the firewall asks if you want to block or unblock (allow) the connection. If you choose to unblock the connection, Windows Firewall creates an exception so that the firewall won't bother you when that program needs to receive information in the future.

Use virus protection

Viruses, worms, and Trojan horses are programs created by hackers that use the Internet to infect vulnerable

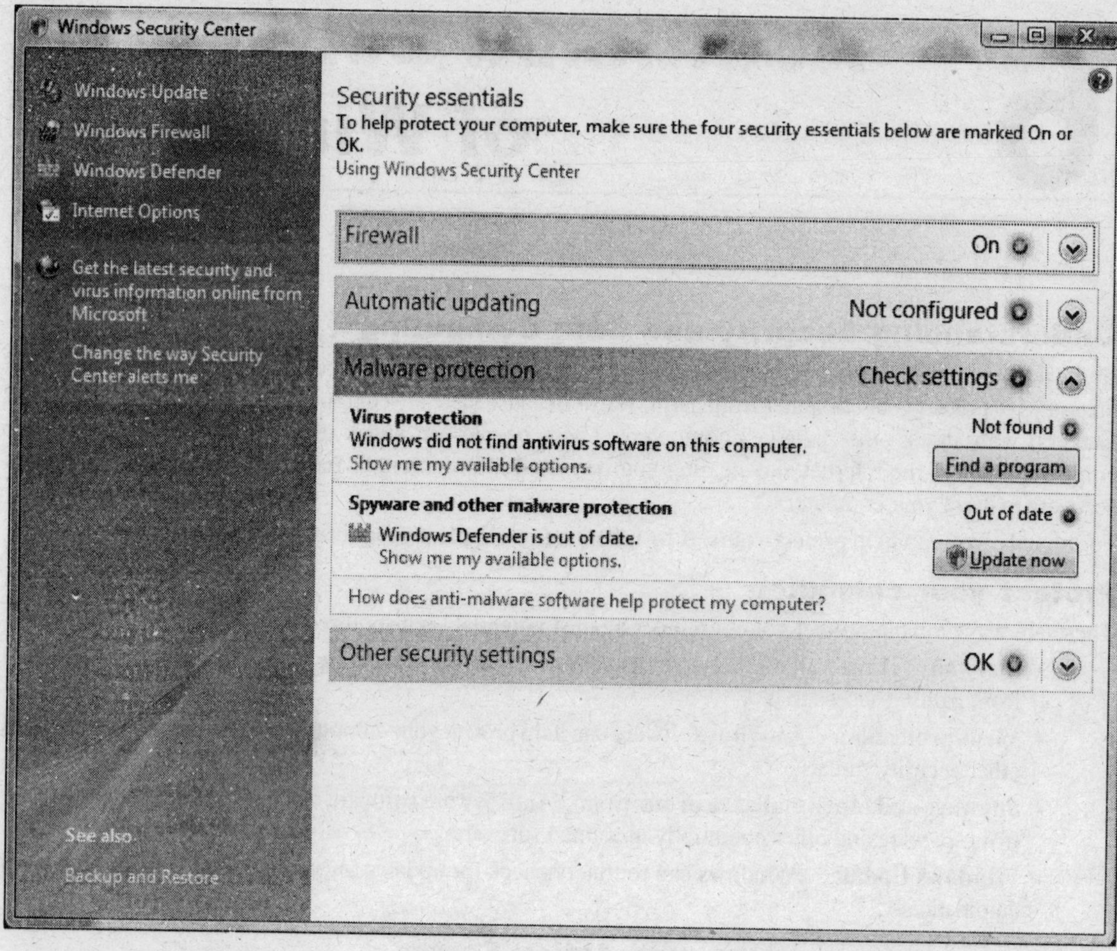

computers. Viruses and worms can replicate themselves from computer to computer, while Trojan horses enter a computer by hiding inside an apparently legitimate program, such as a screen saver. Destructive viruses, worms, and Trojan horses can erase information from your hard disk or completely disable your computer. Others don't cause direct damage, but worsen your computer's performance and stability.

Antivirus programs scan e mail and other files on your computer for viruses, worms, and Trojan horses. If one is found, the antivirus program either quarantines (isolates) it or deletes it entirely before it damages your computer and files.

Windows does not have a built-in antivirus program, but your computer manufacturer might have installed one. If not, go to the Windows 7 security software providers website to find an antivirus program.

Because new viruses are identified every day, it's important to use an antivirus program with an automatic update capability. When the program is updated, it adds new viruses to its list of viruses to check for, helping to protect your computer from new attacks. If the list of viruses is out of date, your computer is vulnerable to new threats. Updates usually require an annual subscription fee. Keep the subscription current to receive regular updates.

Use spyware protection

Spyware is software that can display advertisements, collect information about you, or change settings on your computer, generally without appropriately obtaining your consent. For example, spyware can install

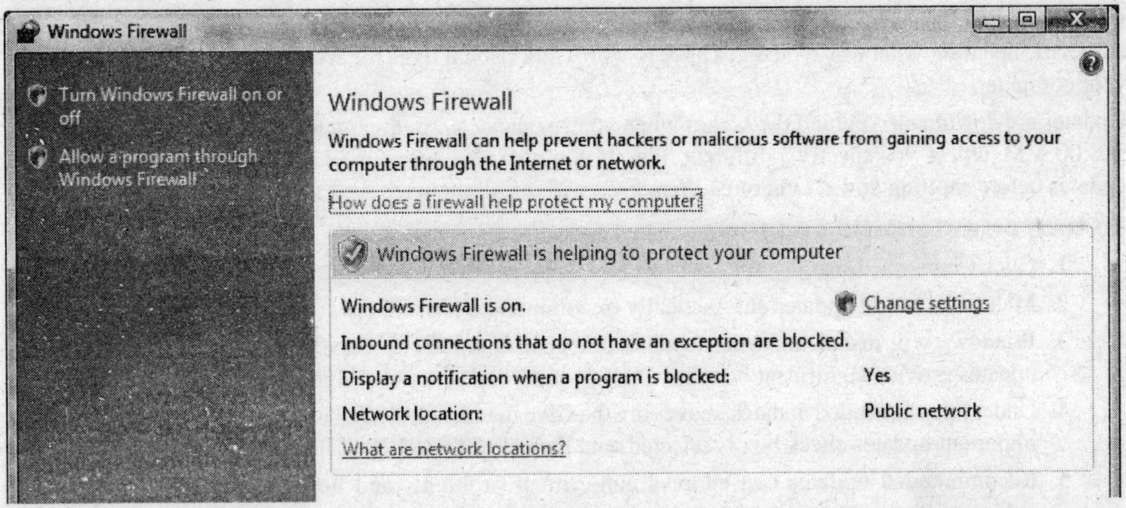

unwanted toolbars, links, or favorites in your web browser, change your default home page, or display pop-up ads frequently. Some spyware displays no symptoms that you can detect, but it secretly collects sensitive information, such as the websites you visit or the text you type. Most spyware is installed through free software that you download, but in some cases simply visiting a website results in a spyware infection.

To help protect your computer from spyware, use an antispyware program. This version of Windows has a built-in antispyware program called Windows Defender, which is turned on by default. Windows Defender alerts you when spyware tries to install itself on your computer. It also can scan your computer for existing spyware and then remove it.

Because new spyware appears every day, Windows Defender must be regularly updated to detect and guard against the latest spyware threats. Windows Defender is updated as needed whenever you update Windows. For the highest level of protection, set Windows to install updates automatically (see below).

Update Windows automatically

Microsoft regularly offers important updates to Windows that can help protect your computer against new

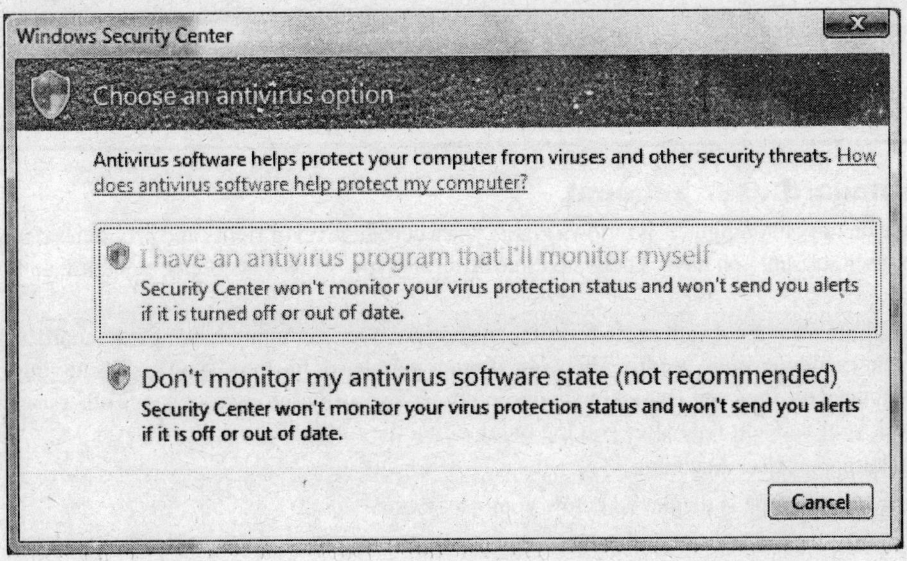

viruses and other security threats. To ensure that you receive these updates as quickly as possible, turn on automatic updating. That way, you don't have to worry that critical fixes for Windows might be missing from your computer.

Updates are downloaded behind the scenes when you're connected to the Internet. The updates are installed at 3:00 A.M. unless you specify a different time. If you turn off your computer before then, you can install updates before shutting down. Otherwise, Windows will install them the next time you start your computer.

To turn on automatic updating

1. Click Change settings.
2. Make sure Install updates automatically (recommended) is selected.
3. Windows will install important updates for your computer as they become available. Important updates provide significant benefits, such as improved security and reliability.
4. Under Recommended updates, make sure the Give me recommended updates the same way I receive important updates check box is selected, and then click OK.
5. Recommended updates can address non-critical problems and help enhance your computing experience If you're prompted for an administrator password or confirmation, type the password or provide confirmation.

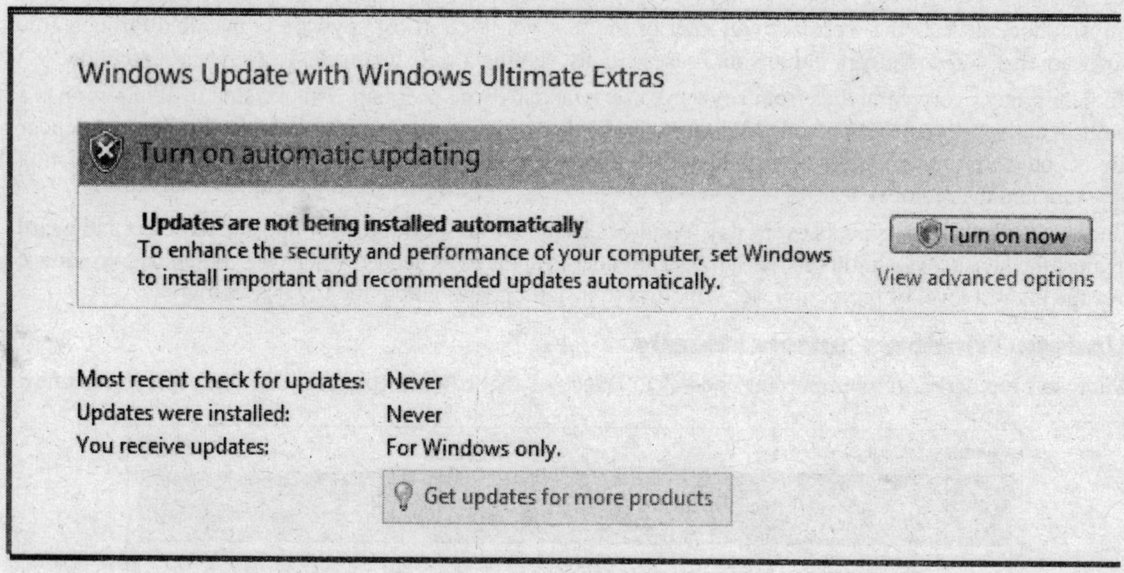

Use a standard user account

When you log on to your computer, Windows grants you a certain level of rights and privileges depending on what kind of user account you have. There are three different types of user accounts: standard, administrator, and guest.

Although an administrator account provides complete control over a computer, using a standard account can help make your computer more secure. That way, if other people (or hackers) gain access to your computer while you're logged on, they can't tamper with the computer's security settings or change other user accounts. You can check your account type after you log on by doing the following:

1. Click to open User Accounts.
2. Your account type is displayed below your user name.
3. Currently logged on user and user's account type

4. If your account type is Administrator, then you're currently logged on as an administrator.
5. You can view all of the user accounts on the computer by clicking Manage another account. If you're prompted for an administrator password or confirmation, type the password or provide confirmation.
6. All of the user accounts and the account types are displayed.
7. If you're currently using an administrator account, see Change a user's account type to learn how to change it to a standard account.

Tips for safely using e mail and the web

- Use caution when opening e mail attachments. E mail attachments (files attached to e mail messages) are a primary source of virus infection. Never open an attachment from someone you don't know. If you know the sender but weren't expecting an attachment, verify that the sender actually sent the attachment before you open it.
- Guard your personal information carefully. If a website asks for a credit card number, bank information, or other personal information, make sure you trust the website and verify that its transaction system is secure.
- Be careful when clicking hyperlinks in e mail messages. Hyperlinks (links that open websites when you click them) are often used as part of phishing and spyware scams, but they can also transmit viruses. Only click links in e mail messages that you trust.
- Only install add-ons from websites that you trust. Web browser add-ons allow webpages to display things like toolbars, stock tickers, video, and animation. However, add-ons can also install spyware or other malicious software. If a website asks you to install an add-on, make sure that you trust it before doing so.

BitLocker Drive Encryption

BitLocker Drive Encryption is an integral new security feature that provides considerable off-line data and operating system protection for your computer. BitLocker ensures that data stored on the computer is not revealed to anyone who tampers with the machine while the installed operating system is offline.

BitLocker Drive Encryption works with Trusted Platform Module (TPM) by encrypting the entire Windows volume, which assures early boot component integrity and data protection. BitLocker Drive Encryption is designed to provide a seamless end-user experience at startup with systems that have a compatible TPM microchip and BIOS.

TPM version 1.2 TPM with the appropriate BIOS modifications (to support the Static Root of Trust Measurement as defined by the Trusted Computing Group) is required to store the encryption keys on the computer. However, BitLocker Drive Encryption can be used on computers without a compatible version of TPM. Encryption keys are stored on an USB flash drive to validate the user's identity at startup.

Useful tools

This section describes the Microsoft Web site downloads and tools associated with this version of Windows that help you configure and manage BitLocker Drive Encryption.

Management Console

No Microsoft Management Console (MMC) snap-ins related to BitLocker Drive Encryption were available when this documentation was last updated.

Downloads

No BitLocker Drive Encryption-related downloads were available when this documentation was last updated.

Deployment

For information about deploying BitLocker Drive Encryption, go to the following resources on the Microsoft Web site:

Operations

For operational information about BitLocker Drive Encryption, go to the following resources on the Microsoft Web site:

Trusted Platform Module Services

Trusted Platform Module (TPM) Services is a new set of features in this version of Windows that is used to administer the TPM Security Hardware in your computer. TPM Services architecture provides the infrastructure for hardware-based security by providing access to and assuring application-level sharing of the TPM. This means that application-level sharing can be built in through software development and that the services can be administered through a graphical user interface.

Useful tools

This section describes the Microsoft Web site downloads and tools associated with this version of Windows that help you configure and manage TPM Services.

Management Console

You can find the Microsoft Management Console (MMC) snap-in for TPM Services in the following location: %windir%\System32\tpm.msc.

To open MMC with elevated privileges, click Start, click All Programs, and then click Accessories. Right-click Command Prompt and then click Run as administrator. If Windows displays a security message asking your permission to run this program, click Allow. In the command prompt that opens, type tpm.msc.

Downloads

No TMP Services-related downloads were available when this documentation was last updated.

Windows CardSpace

Microsoft Windows CardSpace™ is a system for creating relationships with websites and online services. Windows CardSpace manages the user names and passwords that you use to register with and log on to websites and online services with Information Cards.

Management Console

You can find Microsoft Management Console (MMC) snap-ins for Windows security in the following location: %windir%\System32*.msc.

To open MMC with elevated privileges, click Start, click All Programs, and then click Accessories. Right-click Command Prompt and then click Run as administrator. If Windows displays a security message asking your permission to run this program, click Allow. In the command prompt that opens, type mmc.exe to start MMC. In the console tree of MMC, click File, click Add/Remove Snap-in, and then select the appropriate snap-ins and click Add.

The following security snap-ins are available:

- Authorization Manager
- Certificate Templates
- Certificates
- Certification Authority
- IP Security Monitor
- IP Security Policy Management

- Security Configuration and Analysis
- Group Policy Management
- Group Policy Object Editor
- Network Access Protection
- Shared Folders
- Security Templates

Tips for creating a strong password

Passwords provide the first line of defense against unauthorized access to your computer. The stronger your password, the more protected your computer will be from hackers and malicious software. You should make sure you have strong passwords for all accounts on your computer.

What makes a password strong (or weak)?

A strong password:

- Is at least eight characters long.
- Does not contain your user name, real name, or company name.
- Does not contain a complete word.
- Is significantly different from previous passwords.
- Contains characters from each of the following four categories:

<table>
<tr><th>Character category</th><th>Examples</th></tr>
<tr><td>Uppercase letters</td><td>A, B, C</td></tr>
<tr><td>Lowercase letters</td><td>a, b, c</td></tr>
<tr><td>Numbers</td><td>0, 1, 2, 3, 4, 5, 6, 7, 8, 9</td></tr>
<tr><td>Symbols found on the keyboard (all keyboard characters not defined as letters or numerals) and spaces</td><td>‘ ~ ! @ # $ % ^ & * ( ) _ - + = { } [ ] \ | : ; “ ‘ < > , . ? /</td></tr>
</table>

A password might meet all the criteria above and still be a weak password. For example, Hello2U! meets all the criteria for a strong password listed above, but is still weak because it contains a complete word. H3ll0 2 U! is a stronger alternative because it replaces some of the letters in the complete word with numbers and also includes spaces.

Help yourself remember your strong password by following these tips:

- Create an acronym from an easy-to-remember piece of information. For example, pick a phrase that is meaningful to you, such as My son’s birthday is 12 December, 2004. Using that phrase as your guide, you might use Msbi12/Dec,4 for your password.
- Substitute numbers, symbols, and misspellings for letters or words in an easy-to-remember phrase. For example, My son’s birthday is 12 December, 2004 could become Mi$un’s Brthd8iz 12124 (it’s OK to use spaces in your password).
- Relate your password to a favorite hobby or sport. For example, I love to play badminton could become ILuv2PlayB@dm1nt()n.

If you feel you must write down your password in order to remember it, make sure you don’t label it as your password, and keep it in a safe place.

Windows Mail

Don't be shocked by this new term. It is the new name for Outlook Express.

Getting started with e mail

E mail (short for electronic mail) is a fast and convenient way to communicate with others. You can use e mail to:

- Send and receive text messages. You can send an e mail message to any person with an e mail address. The message arrives in the recipient's e mail inbox within seconds or minutes—whether he or she is your next-door neighbor or lives halfway around the world.

E mail is two-way. You can receive messages from anyone who knows your e mail address, and then read and reply to those messages.

- Send and receive files. Besides text, you can send almost any type of · file in an e mail message, including documents, pictures, and music. A file sent in an e mail message is called an attachment.
- Send messages to groups of people. You can send an e mail message to many people simultaneously. Recipients can reply to the whole group, allowing for group discussions.
- Forward messages. When you receive an e mail message, you can forward it to others without retyping it.

One advantage of e mail over the telephone or regular mail is its convenience: You can send a message at any time of day or night. If the recipients aren't in front of their computers and online (connected to the Internet) when you send the message, they'll find it waiting for them the next time they check their e mail. If they are online, you might get a reply within minutes.

E mail is also free. Unlike sending a regular letter, no stamp or fee is required, no matter where the recipient lives. The only charges that apply are those that you pay for an Internet connection.

What do I need before I can use e mail?

To use e mail, you need three things:

- An Internet connection. To connect your computer to the Internet, you must first sign up with an Internet service provider (ISP). An ISP provides you with access to the Internet, usually for a monthly fee. You also need a modem.
- An e mail program or web-based service. You can use Windows Mail, an e mail program included with Windows. You can also use any other e mail program, once you install it on your computer.

  If you prefer, you can sign up instead with a free web-based e mail service, such as Gmail, MSN Hotmail, or Yahoo! Mail. These services allow you to check your e mail with a web browser from any computer connected to the Internet.
- An e mail address. You get an e mail address from your ISP or web-based e mail service when you sign up. An e mail address consists of a user name (a nickname you choose, not necessarily your real name), the @ sign, and the name of your ISP or web-based e mail provider—for example, someone@example.com.

Setting up Windows Mail

Once you have an e mail address and an Internet connection, you're ready to send and receive e mail. To use e mail in Windows Mail, you must first set up an e mail account. Before you add an account, you'll need to get some information from your ISP: your e mail address, password, the names of your incoming and outgoing e mail servers, and certain other details. See Where to find your e mail account information.

To add an e mail account in Windows Mail

1. Click to open Windows Mail.

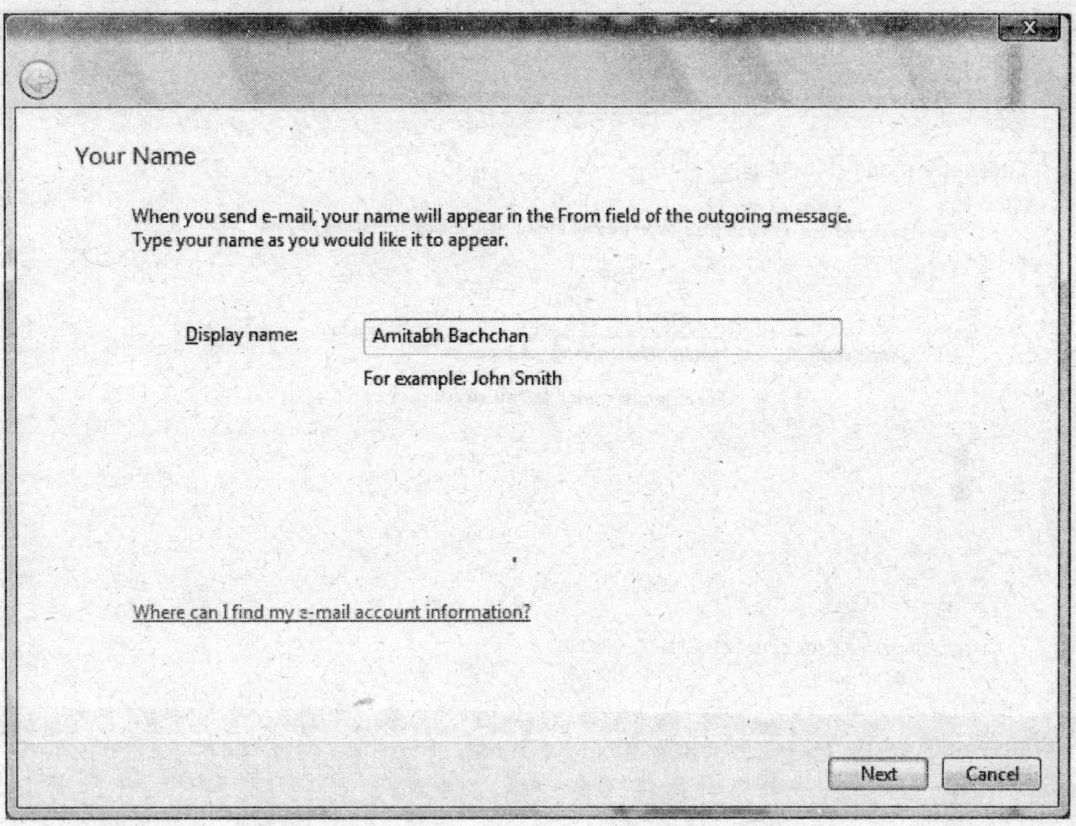

2. On the Tools menu, click Accounts.
3. Click Add, click e mail Account, click Next, and then follow the instructions.

During setup, you'll be asked to pick a display name. This is the name that recipients will see when you send them an e mail message.

Reading e mail messages

Windows Mail checks to see if you've received e mail whenever you start the program and every 30 minutes after that. E-mail you receive appears in your Inbox. The Inbox is one of several folders that hold e mail.

To see a list of e mail you've received, click Inbox in the Folders list. Your e mail messages appear in the message list. The list shows who sent the mail, the subject, and when it was received.

To read a message, click it in the message list. The contents of the message appear below the message list in the Preview pane. To read the message in a separate window, double-click it in the message list.

To reply to a message, click the Reply button. To learn how to write and send a reply, see "Creating and sending an e mail message" in this article.

Creating and sending e mail messages

To create a new e mail message in Windows Mail, click the Create Mail button. A new message window opens.

Here's how to fill out the message window in Windows Mail and most other e mail programs:

1. In the To box, type the e mail address of at least one recipient. If you're sending the message to multiple recipients, type a semicolon (;) between e mail addresses.
2. In the Cc box, you can type the e mail addresses of any secondary recipients—people who should

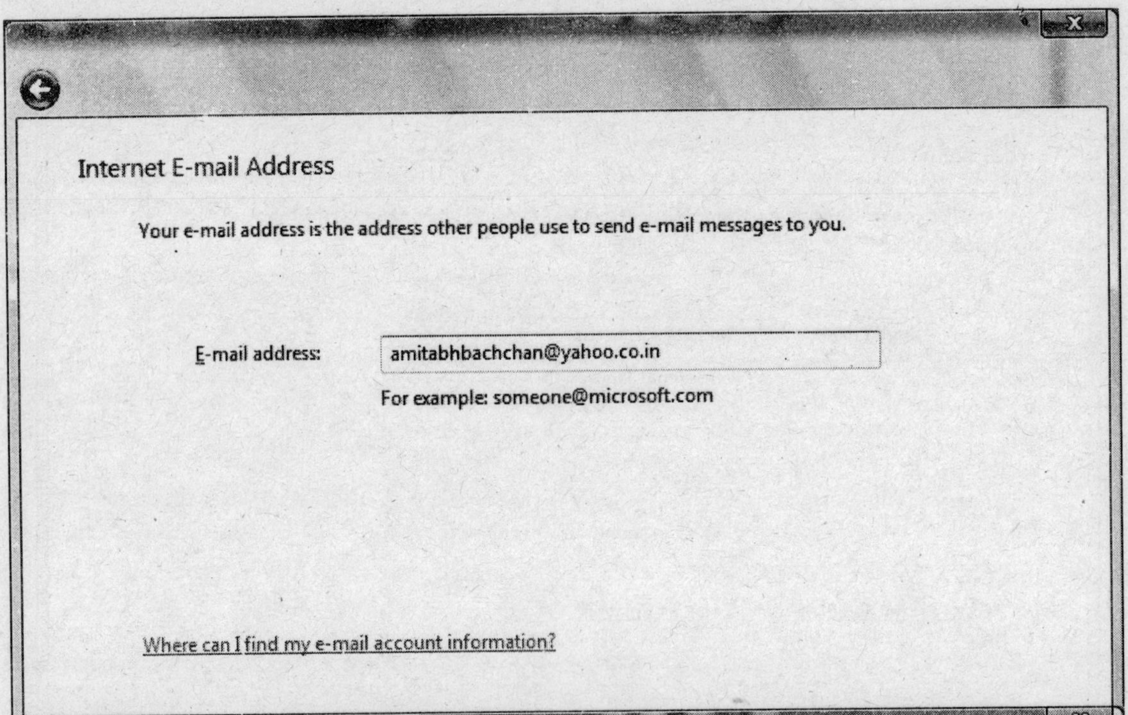
Internet E-mail Address
Your e-mail address is the address other people use to send e-mail messages to you.
E-mail address:
amitabhbachchan@yahoo.co.in
For example: someone@microsoft.com
Where can I find my e-mail account information?

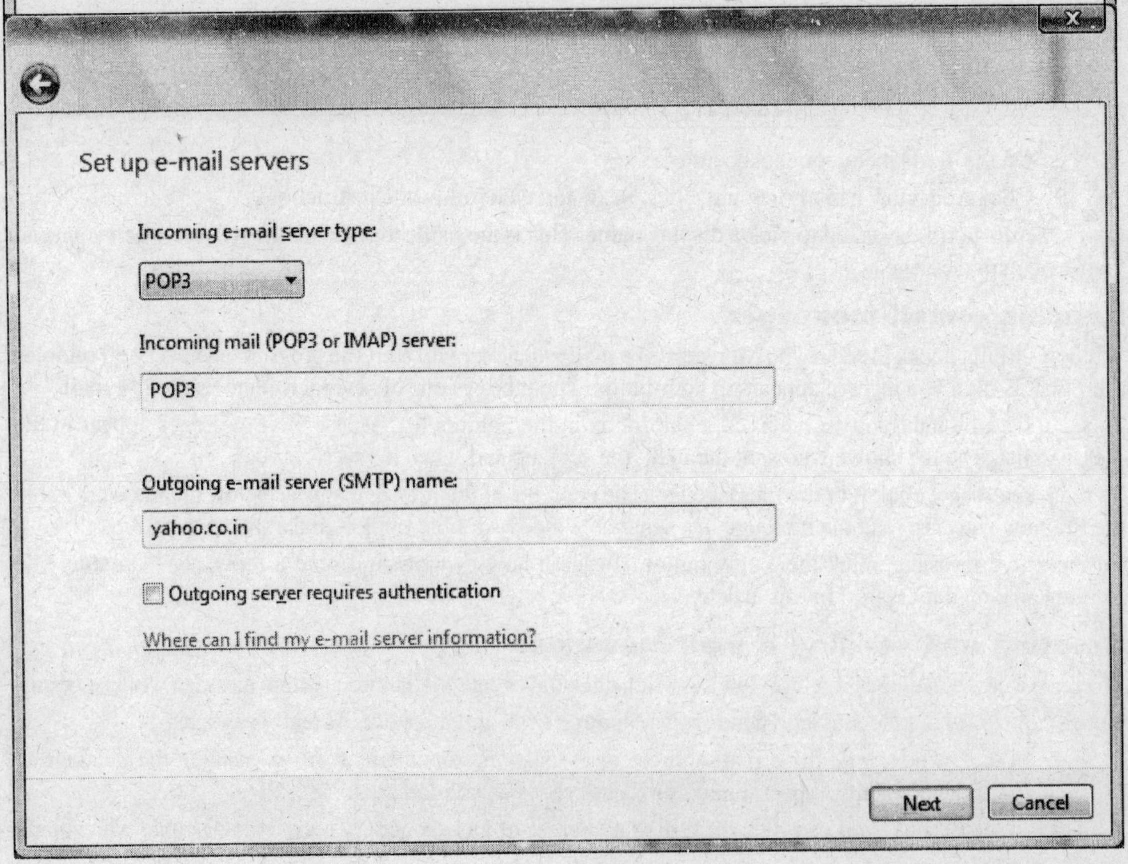
Set up e-mail servers
Incoming e-mail server type:
POP3
Incoming mail (POP3 or IMAP) server:
POP3
Outgoing e-mail server (SMTP) name:
yahoo.co.in
Outgoing server requires authentication
Where can I find my e-mail server information?
Next
Cancel

know about the message but don't need to act on it. They'll receive the same message as the people in the To box. If there are no secondary recipients, leave this box blank.

3. In the Subject box, type a title for your message.
4. In the large blank area, type your message.

To attach a file to the message, click the Attach File to Message button on the toolbar (located just below the menu bar). Locate the file, select it, and then click Open. The file now appears in the Attach box in the message header.

- To change the style, font, size, or color of the text, select the text, and then click one of the buttons on the formatting bar (located just above the message area).

E mail etiquette

Like telephone conversations and face-to-face communication, e mail communication has certain implied rules of behavior. These rules are referred to as e mail etiquette or netiquette (a combination of "Internet" and "etiquette"). For effective communication, follow these guidelines:

- Be careful with humor and emotion. E mail does not convey emotion well, so the recipient might not understand your intended tone. Sarcastic humor is particularly risky because the recipient might interpret it literally and take offense. To convey emotion, consider using emoticons (see "Using emoticons" in this article).
- Think before you send. Writing and sending an e mail message is fast and easy—sometimes too easy. Make sure you've thought out your message first, and avoid writing when you're angry. Once you send the message, you can't get it back.

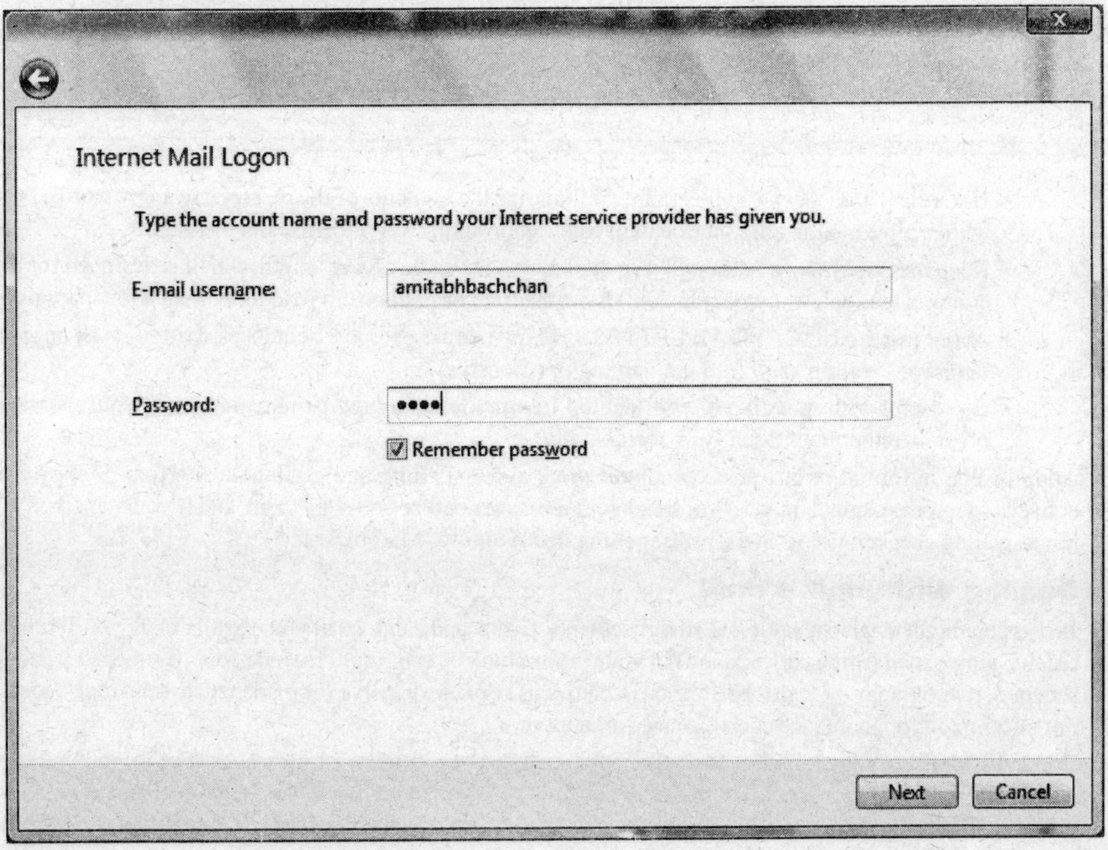

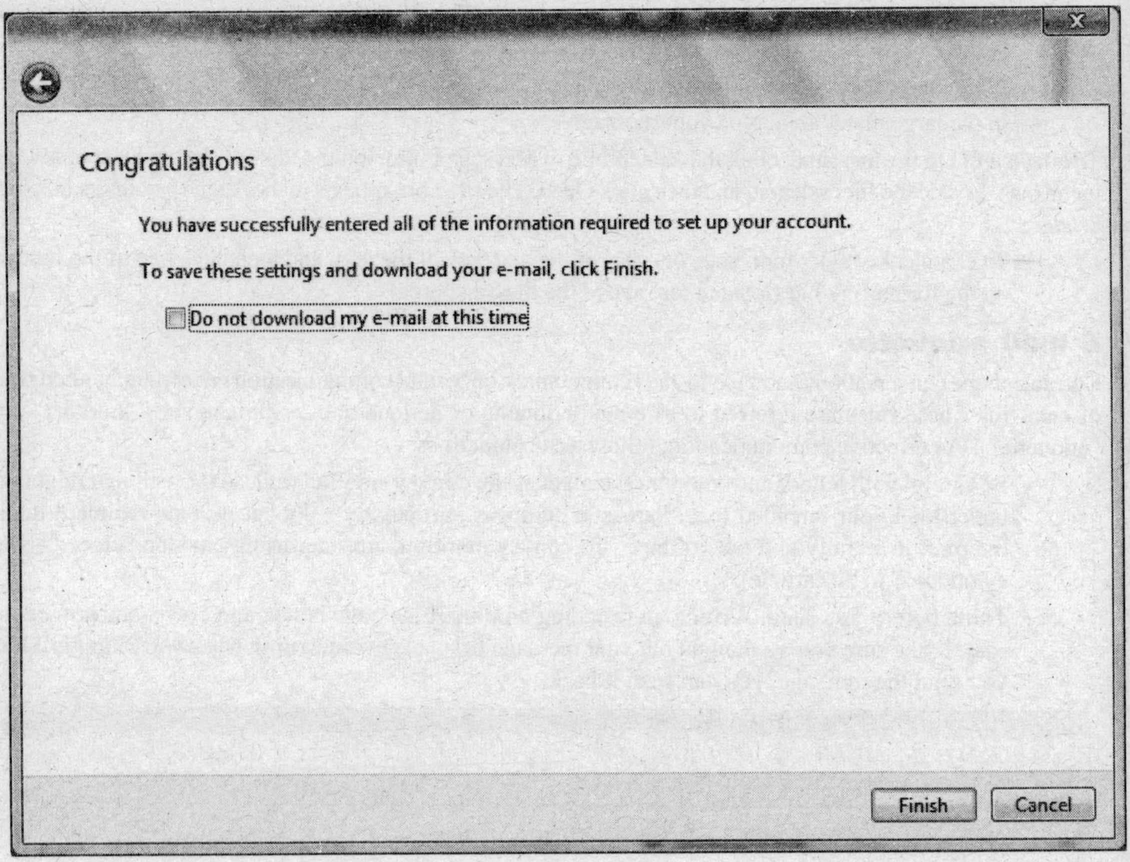

- Use a clear and concise subject line. Summarize the contents of the message in a few words. People who receive a large amount of e mail can use the subject to prioritize the message.
- Keep messages short. Although an e mail message can be of any length, e mail is designed for quick communication. Many people don't have the time or patience to read more than a few paragraphs.
- Avoid using ALL CAPITAL LETTERS. Many people perceive sentences written in all uppercase letters as "yelling" and find it annoying or offensive.
- Be careful with sensitive or confidential information. Any recipient can forward your message to others—either intentionally or accidentally.

Additionally, in formal or business communication, avoid spelling and grammatical errors. Sloppy e mail conveys an unprofessional image. Proofread your messages before you send them, and if your e mail program has a spelling checker, use it. See Check spelling in a Windows Mail message.

Dealing with junk e mail

Just as you might receive unsolicited advertisements, flyers, and catalogs in your regular mail, you'll probably receive junk e mail (often called spam) in your Inbox. Junk e mail might include advertisements, fraudulent schemes, pornography, or legitimate offers. Because it's very inexpensive for marketers to send junk e mail, it's not uncommon for people to receive a large amount of it.

Windows Mail includes a junk e mail filter that analyzes the content of messages sent to you and moves suspicious messages to a special junk e mail folder, where you can view or delete them at any time. And if a junk e mail message slips past the filter into your Inbox, you can specify that any future messages from the

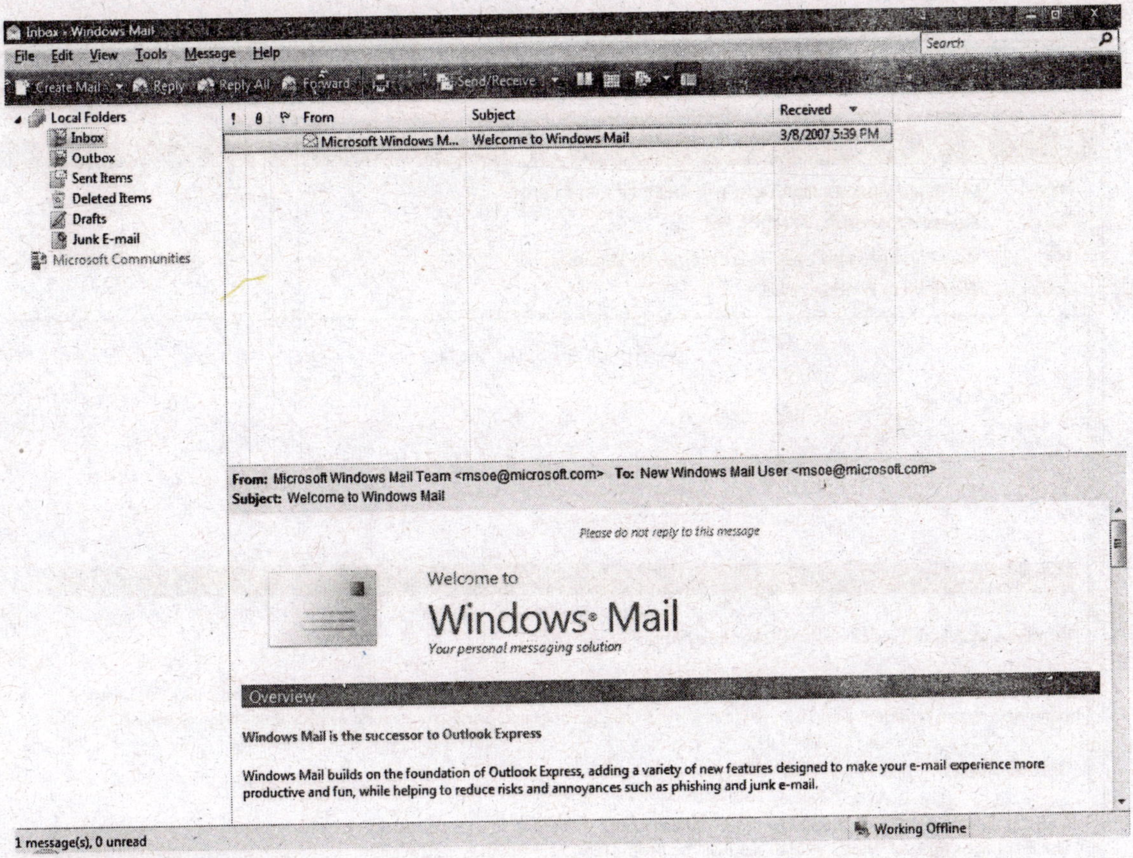

sender be automatically moved to the junk e mail folder. See Block spam and other unwanted e mail.

To help prevent junk e mail:

- Use caution in giving out your e mail address. Avoid publishing your real e mail address in newsgroups, on websites, or in other public areas of the Internet.
- Before you give your e mail address to a website, check the site's privacy statement to be sure it does not permit the disclosure of your e mail address to other companies.
- Never reply to a junk e mail message. The sender will know that your e mail address is valid and might sell it to other companies. You're then likely to receive even more junk e mail.

Using emoticons

Because it's often difficult to convey emotion, intent, or tone through text alone, early Internet users invented emoticons (a combination of "emotion" and "icons")—sequences of keyboard characters that symbolize facial expressions. For example, :) looks like a smiling face when you look at it sideways. Below are some examples of emoticons.

Emoticon	*Meaning*
:) or :-)	Smiling, happy, or joking
:(or :-(	Frowning or unhappy
;-)	Winking
:-|	Indifferent or ambivalent

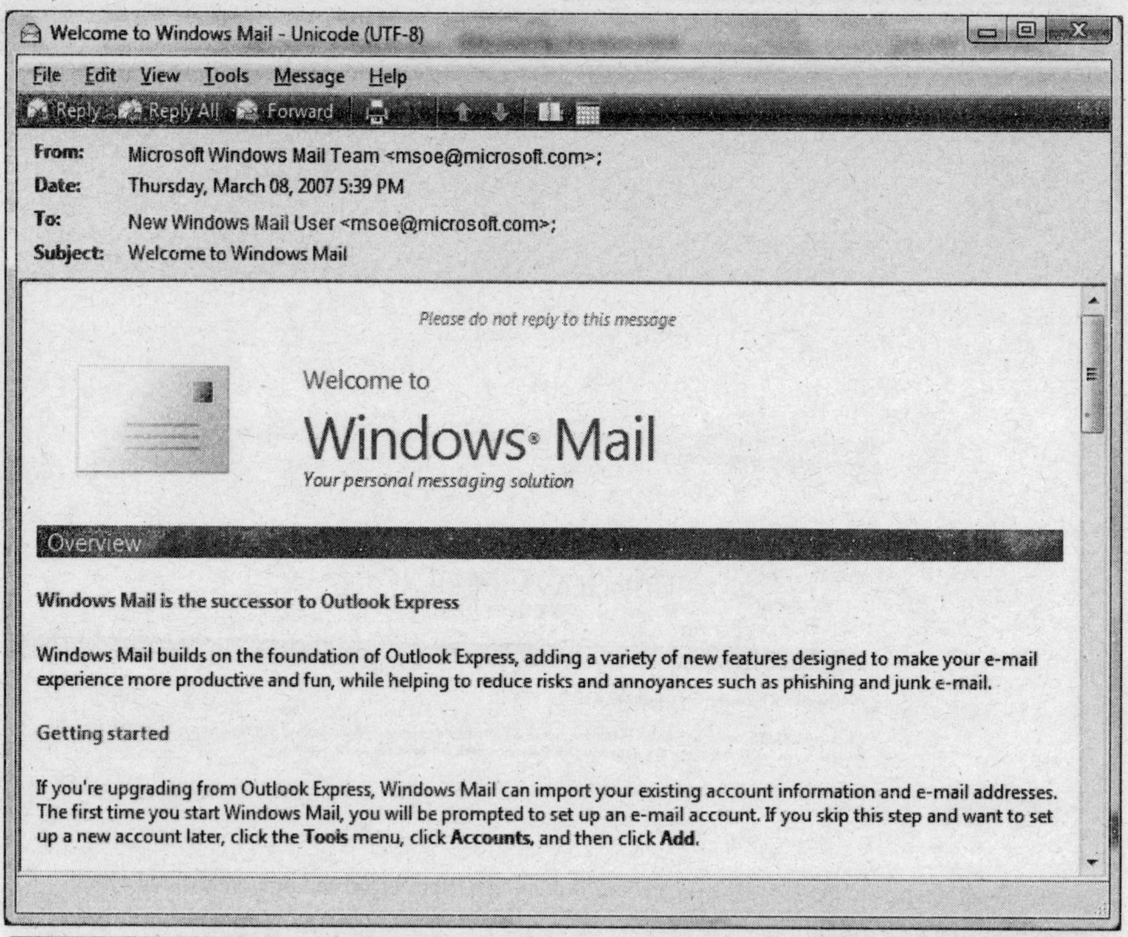
Welcome to Windows Mail - Unicode (UTF-8)
File Edit View Tools Message Help
Reply Reply All Forward
From: Microsoft Windows Mail Team <msoe@microsoft.com>;
Date: Thursday, March 08, 2007 5:39 PM
To: New Windows Mail User <msoe@microsoft.com>;
Subject: Welcome to Windows Mail
Please do not reply to this message
Welcome to
Windows® Mail
Your personal messaging solution
Overview
Windows Mail is the successor to Outlook Express
Windows Mail builds on the foundation of Outlook Express, adding a variety of new features designed to make your e-mail experience more productive and fun, while helping to reduce risks and annoyances such as phishing and junk e-mail.
Getting started
If you're upgrading from Outlook Express, Windows Mail can import your existing account information and e-mail addresses. The first time you start Windows Mail, you will be prompted to set up an e-mail account. If you skip this step and want to set up a new account later, click the Tools menu, click Accounts, and then click Add.

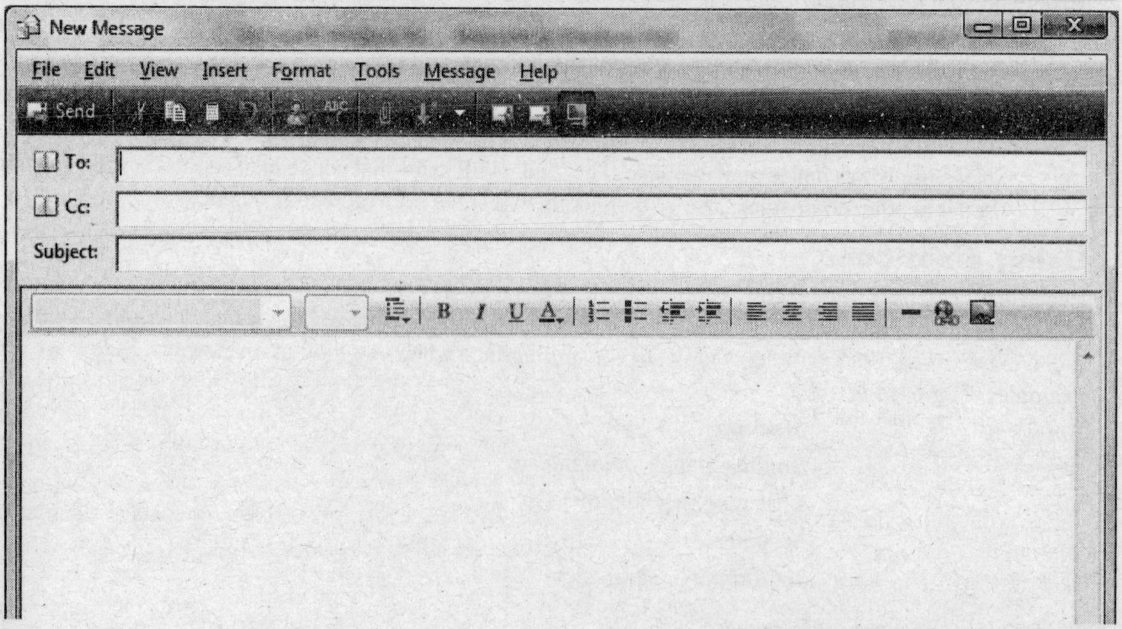
New Message
File Edit View Insert Format Tools Message Help
Send
To:
Cc:
Subject:

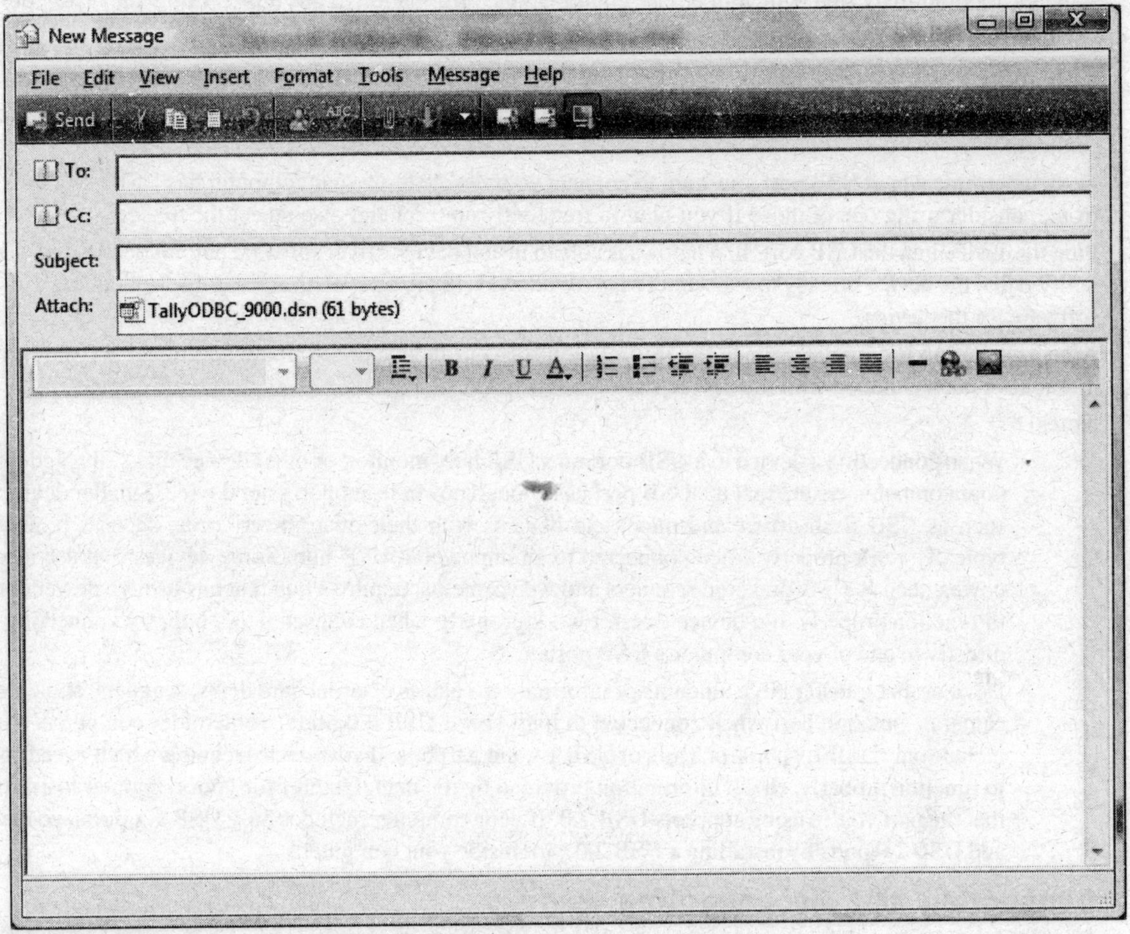

:-o	Surprised or concerned
:-x	Not saying anything
:-p	Sticking out your tongue (usually in fun)
:-D	Laughing

Install a USB device

The first time you connect a device that plugs into a universal serial bus (USB) port, Windows automatically installs driver software for that device. After driver software is installed, you can disconnect and reconnect the device without performing any additional steps.

Before you install your device

Check the instructions included with the device to determine whether driver software should be installed before you connect the device. Typically, Windows detects a new device after you connect it, and then installs the driver software automatically. However, some devices require you to install the driver software before plugging the device in.

Also, while most devices that have power switches should be turned on before you connect them, others require that you turn them on during the installation process. Because of issues like this, it's a good idea to read the instructions included with a new device before you connect it.

If the instructions that came with your device contradict the information in this topic, follow the instructions that came with the device.

Plugging your device in

If your USB device uses a power cord, you should connect the device to a power source and turn it on before connecting it.

Next, determine which USB port you want to connect your device to. If your computer has USB ports on the front, consider using one of those if you plan to frequently connect and disconnect the device.

Plug the device into the USB port. If Windows is able to install device driver software automatically, you'll be notified that the device is ready to use. Otherwise, Windows will prompt you to insert a disc containing driver software for the device.

After installation is complete, check the information for your device to see if any additional software that might have been included with the device should be installed.

Notes

- When connecting a device to a USB port on a USB hub, monitor, or other device that's plugged into your computer, ensure that the USB port has enough power to support your device. Smaller devices, such as USB flash drives and mice, and devices with their own power cords, such as printers, typically work properly when connected to an unpowered USB hub. Some devices that use more power, such as USB-powered scanners and web cameras, require a hub that has its own power cord to function properly. If a device doesn't work properly when connected to a hub, try connecting it directly to one of your computer's USB ports.
- Devices that transfer large amounts of information, such as external hard disks, scanners, and video cameras, function best when connected to high-speed USB 2.0 ports. Some older computers may include only USB 1.x ports, or a mix of USB 1.x and 2.0 ports. If your device requires a high-speed port to function properly, check information provided by the manufacturer for your computer to ensure that the port you're using supports USB 2.0. If your computer includes only USB 1.x ports, you can add USB 2.0 ports by installing a USB 2.0 card inside your computer.

Connecting and disconnecting devices

Most USB devices can be removed and unplugged at will. When unplugging storage devices, such as USB flash drives, you should be sure that the computer has finished saving any information to the device before removing it. If the device has an activity light, wait for a few seconds after the light has finished flashing before unplugging it.

If you see the Safely Remove Hardware icon in the notification area at the far right of the taskbar, you can use this to ensure that devices have finished all operations in progress and are ready to remove. Click the icon and you'll see a list of devices. Click the device you want to remove.

You can use any USB port when plugging in a device that you've previously installed. However, the first time you plug a device into a particular port, Windows will install the driver software for that device again.

Windows Contacts

It is a new feature in Windows 7; a central directory for phone numbers, email addresses, and mailing addresses. It is not so much a program as a specialized Explorer window, complete with individual icons that represent the people in your social circle.

Managing your contacts

You can use Windows to keep track of people and organizations by creating contacts for them in Windows Contacts. Each contact contains the information for one person or organization.

When you need to look up a friend's e mail address or phone number, you can open your Contacts folder and find it there. When you want to take notes about a business contact, you can store them in the Contacts folder. No matter what type of contact information you want to remember about someone, you can put it in the Contacts folder—even a picture.

The Contacts folder also functions as the address book for Windows Mail. When you create an e mail message in Windows Mail, you select the recipient from your Contacts folder. Even if you don't use Windows Mail as your e mail program, you can still use Windows Contacts to store information about people and organizations. Use Windows Contacts to keep track of all the people and organizations you communicate with

What's in a contact?

You can store as much or as little information as you like about each contact, including any of the following:

- E mail addresses. Store as many e mail addresses as you want for a contact, and set one as the preferred address. (The preferred e mail address is what Windows Mail will use if you want to send someone e mail quickly without selecting from a list of all their addresses.)
- A picture. Adding a picture of a contact can help you remember the person.
- Phone numbers. You can store home, work, cell, and fax phone numbers for a contact.
- Street addresses. You can store both home and work street addresses for a contact.
- Family information. You can enter information here about a contact's spouse or partner, children, gender, birthday, and anniversary.
- Website addresses. You can store both home and work website addresses for a contact.
- Notes. Type any other information about a contact.

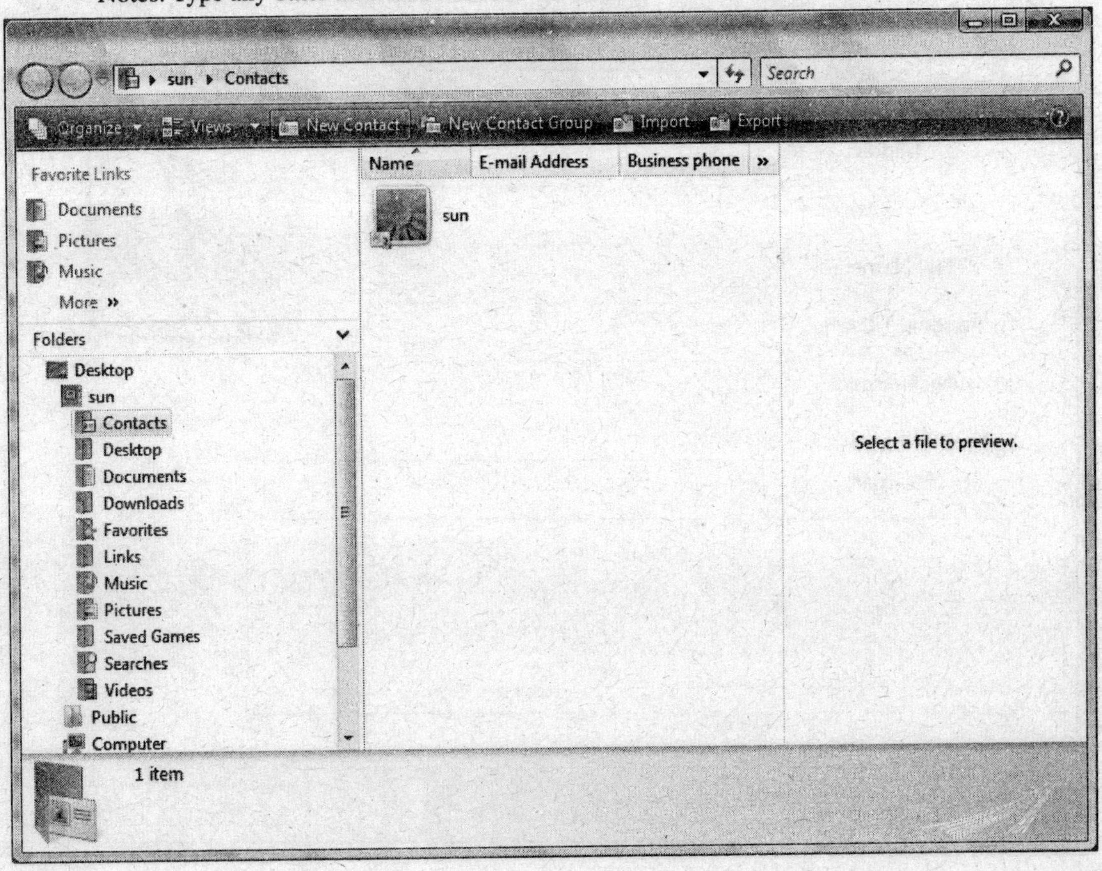

Finding the Contacts folder

Click to open Windows Contacts.

- You can find the Contacts folder yourself by clicking the Start button , clicking All Programs, and then clicking Windows Contacts.

Adding a contact

1. Click to open Windows Contacts.
2. Click New Contact, and then type the information you want for the contact in any of the boxes on the available tabs. You don't have to fill in all the boxes; just enter as much information as you want about the contact.

Adding information to a contact

1. Click to open Windows Contacts.
2. Double-click the contact you want to change.
3. Click the tab where you want to add information, and then type in any of the available boxes.

Adding a new picture to a contact

1. Click to open Windows Contacts.

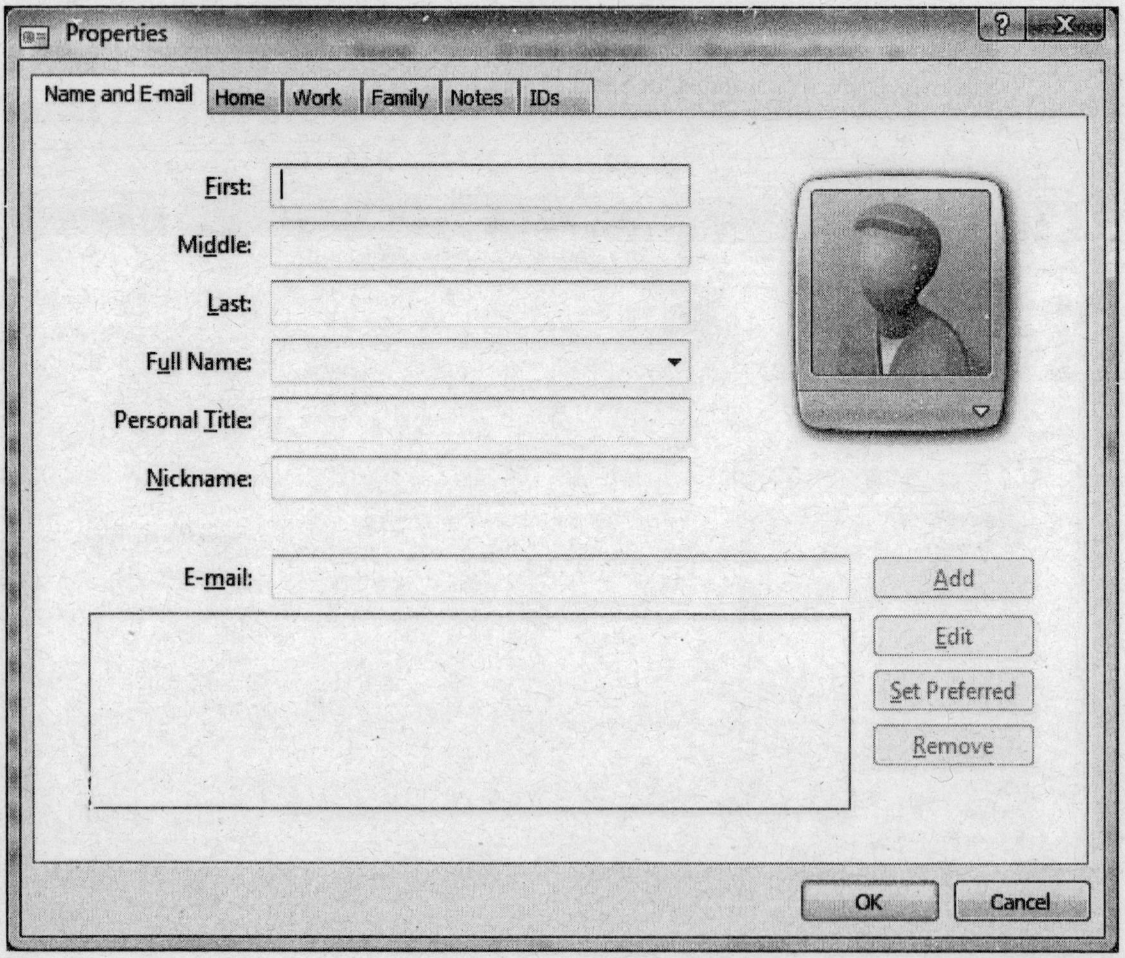

2. Double-click the contact with the picture you want to change. (Windows adds a default image for each contact which you can change to any picture or graphic you want.)
3. On the Name and e mail tab, click the contact picture, and then do one of the following:

- To add a new picture, click Change picture, locate the picture you want to use for the contact, click it, and then click Open.
- To remove an existing picture, click Remove picture. The picture will revert to the default contact image used by Windows. (You cannot remove this default image.)

Creating contact groups (mailing lists)

You can also create contact groups, which combine multiple individual contacts into a single group. Creating a contact group enables you to send e mail to many people at once. If you send an e mail message to a contact group, it will be sent to everyone you added to the group. Sending e mail to a contact group can be a lot easier than adding names one at a time to an e mail message, especially if you often send messages to the same group of people.

Sending contacts to other people

In addition to using Windows Contacts to address e mail messages and store information about people and organizations, you can also send contacts to other people. This is useful if you want to send someone contact information about yourself or someone else. There's no need to type a bunch of phone numbers, addresses, and other contact information into an e mail message—just send them a contact with the information you want to share.

To send a contact to someone who is not using this version of Windows, you may first need to export the contact to another format. For more information, see Import, export, or change the format for contacts.

Note

- If you upgrade to this version of Windows from Windows XP, each of your contacts in the Windows Address Book will be automatically stored in Windows Contacts.

Windows DVD Maker

DVD Maker, a new program, debuts with Windows 7, and then only iwth the Premium or Ultimate editions. You can export your finished Movie Maker project as a digital file, or save it to a good old VHS cassette. But preserving your work on a DVD gives you a boatload of benefits, including better durability than tape, dramatically better quality than a movie file, no need for rewinding, duplication without quality loss, and cheaper shipping.

Burn a DVD-Video disc

You can create DVDs quickly and easily using Windows DVD Maker. You can add video, pictures, and audio, make slide shows for your DVD, or add your Windows Movie Maker projects. Once you add files, you can burn your DVD with one click, or, if you prefer, you can choose from several menu styles and slide show options to make your DVD special before you burn it, or customize your DVD menus and write the DVD menu text yourself.

After you create a DVD, you can play the DVD in a DVD player and watch your movies and slide shows on TV. The following steps explain how to use Windows DVD Maker to burn a DVD.

To open Windows DVD Maker

- Click Start, click All Programs, and then click Windows DVD Maker.

Note

- You can also open Windows DVD Maker by inserting a blank recordable or rewriteable DVD into your DVD burner. When the AutoPlay dialog appears automatically, click Burn a DVD video disc using Windows DVD Maker.

To add and arrange items on a DVD

1. On the Add pictures and video to the DVD page, click Add items.
2. Locate and select the video files, pictures, and Windows Movie Maker project files that you want to include on your DVD, and then click Add.
3. To arrange items and specify the order that the different items will play from the DVD, click the video, picture, or slide show that you want to move, and then click Move up or Move down. You can also move items by dragging them up or down in the list.
4. To remove an item from the DVD, select the item you want to remove, and then click Remove items.

To choose a DVD burner and enter a DVD title

1. If you have more than one DVD burner installed on your computer, on the Add pictures and video to the DVD page, select the DVD burner that you want to use from the DVD burner list.
2. If you want to set different options for your DVD, click Options. For information about the different options you can specify when burning a DVD, see Change DVD-Video settings.
3. Click the Disc title box, and then type a title for the DVD.

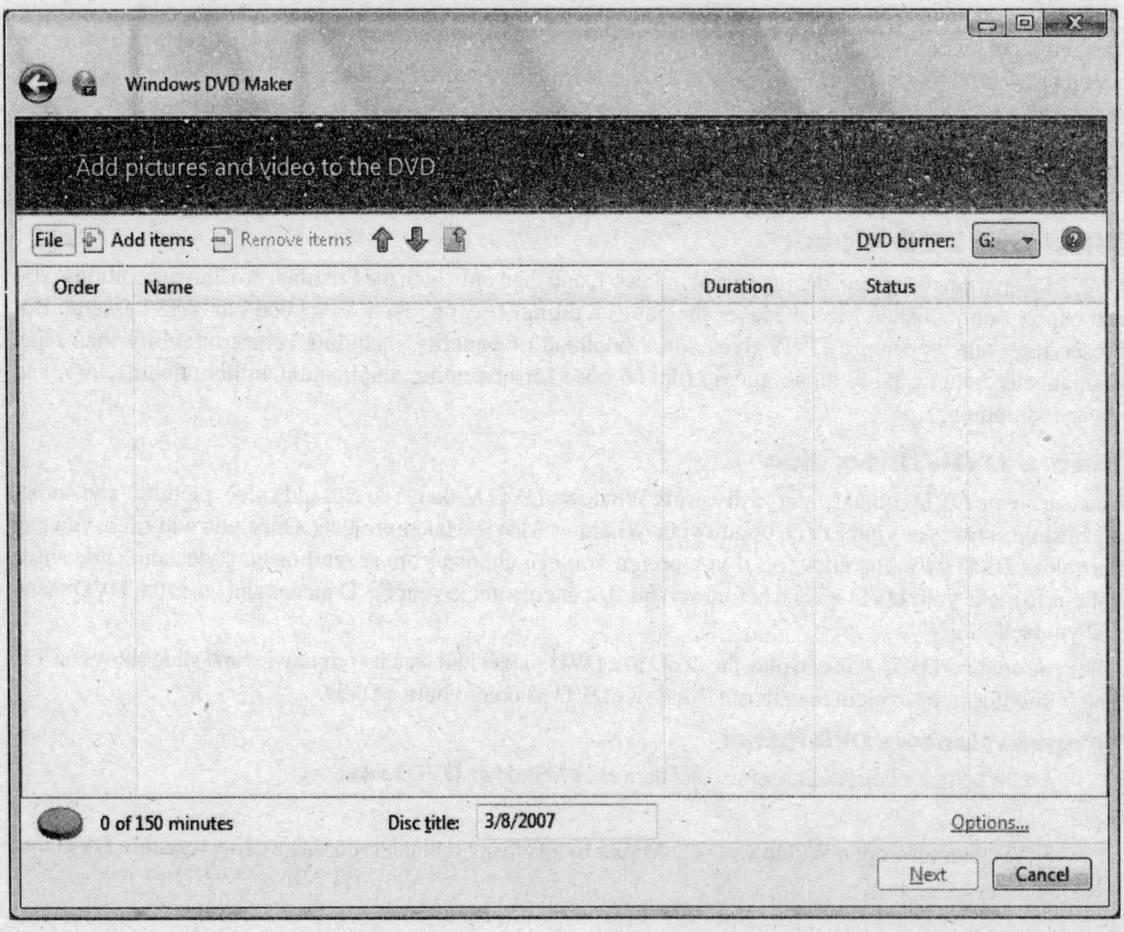

To change the menu text for your DVD

1. Once you've added all of your files and chosen the burner and title, click Next.
2. To customize the text for the DVD menu, click Menu text, and then do one or more of the following:

- Click the Font box, and then select the font for the menu text.
- Click the Font Color, Bold, or Italics buttons to select the font color and formatting.
- In the Disc title box, type the title you want to use for your DVD.
- In the Play button box, type a label for the button that plays your DVD.
- In the Scenes button box, type a label for the button that will display the different scenes on the DVD.
- In the Notes button box, type a label for the button that will display any notes you enter for the DVD.
- In the Notes box, type any notes that you want to appear on your DVD.
  The Notes button and Notes page only appear on the DVD if you include information in these fields.
- Click Change Text.
- You can see a static preview of your settings in the preview pane at the right side of the screen. Or, to see how the menu text will look when you burn your DVD, click Preview.

To customize the menu style for your DVD

1. To customize the menu style for your DVD, click one of the DVD menu styles along the right side of the screen, or click Customize menu and then do one or more of the following:

- Click the Font box, and then select a font.
- Click the Font Color, Bold, or Italic buttons to select the font color and formatting.
- If you've chosen a menu style with both foreground and background video options, near Foreground video, click Browse, locate the video that you want to appear in the foreground, and then click Open.
- To have a picture or video appear as the background for the main DVD menu, near Background video, click Browse, locate the video that you want to appear in the background, and then click Open.
- To add a digital media audio file to play as background music while the menu is displayed for your DVD, near Menu audio, click Browse, locate the audio file that you want to use, and then click Open.
- Click the Scenes button styles box, and then select the shape for the scenes buttons on your DVD.
- If you want to see the menu as it will appear when you play your DVD, click Preview.

2. If you want to save the customized DVD menu settings as a new DVD menu style, click Save as new style. In the Style name name box, type a name for the customized menu style, and then click OK. You can then choose to use this customized DVD menu style for the current DVD and for other DVDs you create using Windows DVD Maker.
3. If you did not save the style as a new style, click Change Style to save the changes you made for this DVD and to return to the previous page.

To choose the settings for a slide show on the DVD

1. To set the photo settings for the slide show on your DVD, click Slide show.
2. On the Change your slide show settings page, do one or more of the following:

- Click Add Music, navigate to the music files you want to add, and then click Open.
- Depending on the length and settings for the slide show, you might want to add additional audio files. To do so, repeat the previous step.
- If you added more than one audio file and you want to change the order in which the music files play in the slide show, click an audio file that you want to move, and then click Move Up or Move Down.

- To remove an audio file from the list, in the Music for slide show list, select the audio file, and then click Remove.
- To automatically change the slide show length so it matches the duration of the music you have added, select the Change slide show length to match music length check box.
- To specify the duration for each picture to display in the slide show, select the duration (in seconds) from the Picture length box.
- To choose the kind of transitions you want to use between pictures, select a transition type from the Transition box.
- To add pan-and-zoom effects to the pictures you include in your slide show, click Use pan-and-zoom effects for pictures.

3. Click Change Slide Show to save the changes you made and to go to the previous page.

To burn your DVD

1. When you've finished adding files and customizing your DVD menus, click Burn.
2. After the DVD disc has been successfully burned, you can do one or more of the following on the Your disc is ready page:
    - To make another copy of the current DVD, remove the completed DVD, insert a new recordable DVD, and then click Make another copy of this disc.
    - To close Windows DVD Maker, click Close.

Windows Photo Gallery

Photo Gallery approaches digital photo management as a four-step process; importing the photos to your Picture folder; organizing, tagging, and rating them; editing them; and sharing them (via prints, onscreen slideshows, design DVD slideshows, email, screen saver, and so on).

Find a picture on your computer

The easiest way to locate and view pictures on your computer is by using Windows Photo Gallery. By default, Photo Gallery shows all the pictures and videos that are located in the Pictures folder, but you can add other folders to Photo Gallery. You can search for pictures and videos by typing in the Search box or by clicking tags, ratings, or dates in the Navigation pane.

Click to open Windows Photo Gallery.

To browse and view pictures

To	*Do this*
See all your pictures and videos in Photo Gallery	In the Navigation pane, click All Pictures and Videos. All Pictures and Videos in the Navigation pane
See all pictures or all videos, but not both	In the Navigation pane, under All Pictures and Videos, click either Pictures or Videos.
See a larger preview of a picture thumbnail	Rest the mouse pointer over a picture thumbnail.
See the picture in a larger view	Double-click the picture.
Return to the thumbnail view	Click Back to Gallery.

To find pictures

To	*Do this*
Find a picture by tag	In the Navigation pane, under Tags, click a tag to see all of the pictures and videos using that tag.Tags in the Navigation pane

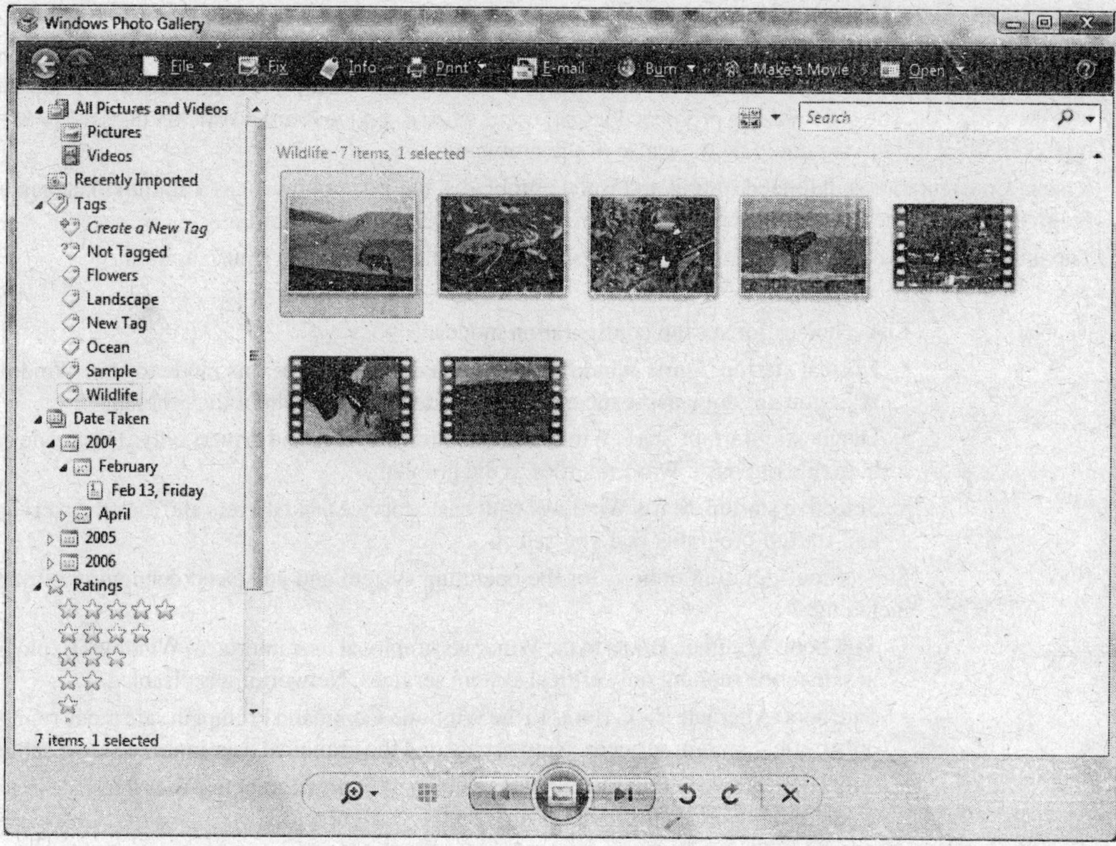

Find a picture by multiple tags	Press the CTRL key and click multiple tags to see all of the pictures and videos that include any of those tags.
Find a picture by file name or tag	Type the name of the file or tag in the Search box. You can type the entire name, or just the first few letters. The Search box
Find a picture by file extension	Type the file extension in the Search box to quickly limit the results to certain file formats, such as .jpg, .tif, or .wmv.
Find a picture by year, month, or date taken	In the Navigation pane, under Date Taken, click a year to see all of the pictures and videos taken during that year, or expand the year to select a month or date.
Find a picture by multiple dates	Press CTRL and click multiple dates to see all of the pictures and videos taken on any of those dates.
Find a picture by rating	In the Navigation pane, under Ratings, click a set of stars (from Not Rated to five stars) to see all of the pictures and videos that have been marked with that star rating.
Find a picture by multiple ratings	Press CTRL and click multiple sets of star ratings to see all pictures and videos that have been marked with any of those star ratings.

System Configuration

System Configuration is an advanced tool that can help identify problems that might prevent Windows from starting correctly. You can start Windows with common services and startup programs turned off and then turn them back on, one at a time. If a problem does not occur when a service is turned off, but does occur when turned on, then the service could be the cause of the problem.

System Configuration is intended to find and isolate problems, but it is not meant as a startup management program. To permanently remove or turn off programs or services that run at startup.

The following table describes the tabs and options that are available in System Configuration:

Tab	*Description*
General	Lists choices for startup configuration modes: • Normal startup. Starts Windows in the usual manner. Use this mode to start Windows after you are done using the other two modes to troubleshoot the problem. • Diagnostic startup. Starts Windows with basic services and drivers only. This mode can help rule out basic Windows files as the problem. • Selective startup. Starts Windows with basic services and drivers and the other services and startup programs that you select.
Boot	Shows configuration options for the operating system and advanced debugging settings, including: • Safe boot: Minimal. Boots to the Windows graphical user interface (Windows Explorer) in safe mode running only critical system services. Networking is disabled. • Safe boot: Alternate shell. Boots to the Windows Command Prompt in safe mode running only critical system services. Networking and the graphical user interface are disabled. • Safe boot: Active Directory repair. Boots to the Windows graphical user interface in safe mode running critical system services and Active Directory. • Safe boot: Network. Boots to the Windows graphical user interface in safe mode running only critical system services. Networking is enabled. • No GUI boot. Does not display the Windows splash screen when booting. • Boot log. Stores all information from the boot process in the file %SystemRoot%Ntbtlog.txt. • Base video. Boots to the Windows graphical user interface in minimal VGA mode. This loads standard VGA drivers instead of display drivers specific to the video hardware on the computer. • OS boot information. Shows driver names as drivers are being loaded during the boot process. • Make all settings permanent. Does not track changes made in System Configuration. Options can be changed later using System Configuration, but must be changed manually. When this option is selected, you cannot roll back your changes by selecting Normal startup on the General tab.
Services	Lists all of the services that start when the computer boots, along with their current status (Running or Stopped). Use the Services tab to enable or disable individual services at boot time to troubleshoot which services might be contributing to boot problems. Select Hide all Microsoft services to show only third-party applications in the services list. Clear the check box for a service to disable it on your next boot. If you have chosen Selective startup on the General tab, you must either choose Normal startup on the General tab or select the service's check box to start it again at boot time.

Warning

- Disabling services that normally run at boot time might cause some programs to malfunction or result in system instability. Do not disable services in this list unless you know they are not essential to your computer's operation. Selecting Disable all will not disable some secure Microsoft services required for the operating system to start.

Startup — Lists applications that run when the computer boots, along with the name of their publisher, the path to the executable file, and the location of the registry key or shortcut that causes the application to run.

Clear the check box for a startup item to disable it on your next boot. If you have chosen Selective startup on the General tab, you must either choose Normal startup on the General tab or select the startup item's check box to start it again at boot time.

If you suspect an application has been compromised, examine the Command column to review the path to the executable file.

- Disabling applications that normally run at boot time might result in related applications starting more slowly or not running as expected.

Tools — Provides a convenient list of diagnostic tools and other advanced tools that you can run.

To start Windows in Diagnostic startup mode

1. Click to open System Configuration. If you are prompted for an administrator password or confirmation, type the password or provide confirmation.
2. Click the General tab, click Diagnostic startup, click OK, and then click Restart.
3. If the problem occurs, then basic Windows files or drivers might be corrupted. For more information, search Windows Help and Support for "Startup Repair."
4. If the problem does not occur, then use Selective startup mode to try to find the problem by turning individual services and startup programs on or off.

To start Windows in Selective startup mode

1. Click to open System Configuration. If you are prompted for an administrator password or confirmation, type the password or provide confirmation.
2. Click the General tab, click Selective startup, and then clear the Load system services and Load startup items check boxes.
3. Select the Load system services check box, click OK, and then click Restart.
4. If the problem occurs after restarting, do one or both (if necessary) of the following tasks:

Identify the system service that is causing the problem

1. Click the Services tab, click Disable all, select the check box for the first service that is listed, and then restart the computer. If the problem does not occur, then you can eliminate the first service as the cause of the problem.
2. With the first service selected, select the second service check box, and then restart the computer.
3. Repeat this process until you reproduce the problem. If you cannot reproduce the problem, then you can eliminate system services as the cause of the problem. Perform the following task:

Identify the startup item that is causing the problem

1. Click the General tab, and then select the Load startup items check box.
2. Click the Startup tab, click Disable all, select the check box for the first startup item that is listed, and then restart the computer. If the problem does not occur, then you can eliminate the first startup item as the cause of the problem.

3. With the first startup item selected, select the second startup item check box, and then restart the computer. Repeat this process until you reproduce the problem.

Windows Calender

In addition to using Windows Calendar as your primary calendar, you can use it to subscribe to web calendars from any participating organization's website or to share your schedule with others. It has the following features:

- It can automate the process of entering repeating events, such as weekly staff meeting or gym workout dates.
- Calender can give you a gentle nudge, with a dialog box and a sound, if you like; when an important appointment is approaching.
- You can "publish" your calendar on the Internet, so all your family members/classmates/baseball team members/downtrodden employees know the schedule. For example, you can susbscribe to your spouse's calender, thereby finding out when you have been committed to after-dinner drinks on the night the big game's on TV.

To open Windows Calendar

1. Click to open Windows Calendar.

To change the calendar view

You can view your calendar by day, work week, week, or month.

- Click the View menu, and then click the view you want. A check mark appears next to the view you select.

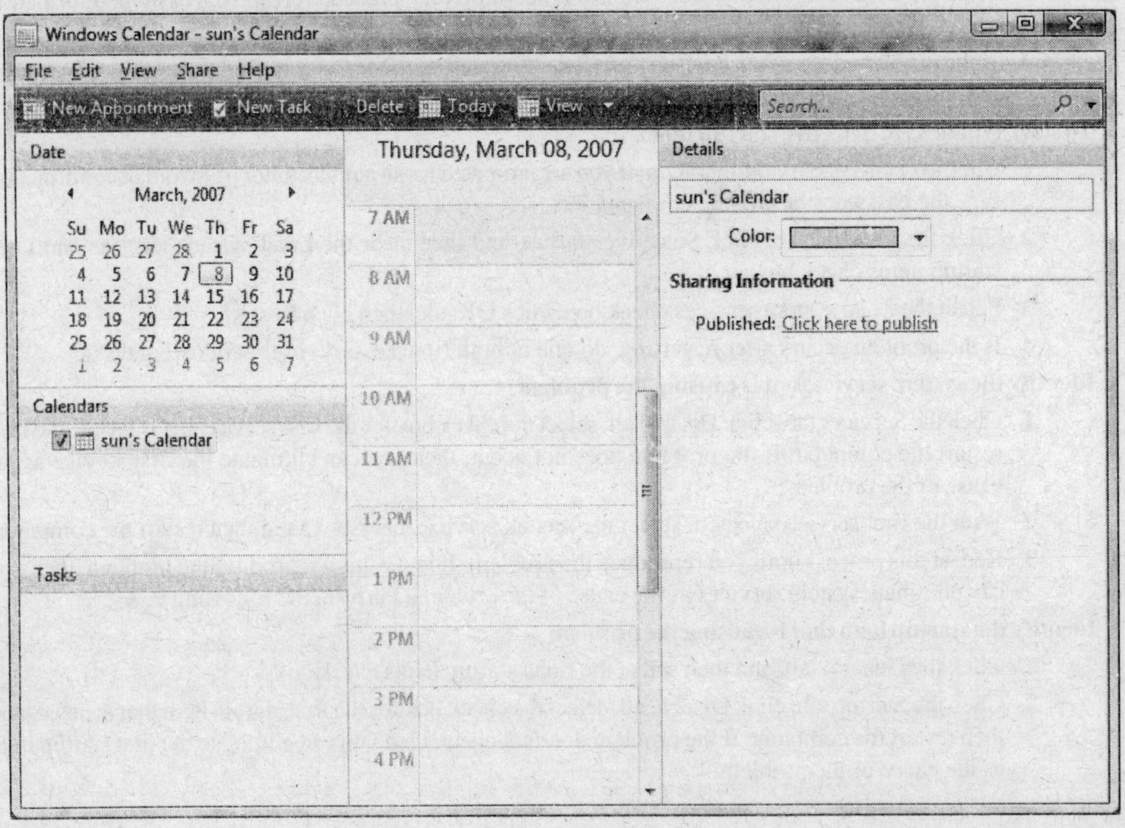

To view the details pane

- If you can't see the details of a task, date, or calendar, click the View menu, and then click Details Pane so that a check mark appears. To close the Details pane, click Details Pane again, so that the check mark disappears.

To create a calendar

1. Click the File menu, and then click New Calendar.
2. In the New Calendar box, type the name you want for the calendar, and then press ENTER.
3. To choose the color of your appointments, in the Details pane, click Color, and then click the color you want.

To create an appointment

1. On the toolbar, click New Appointment.
2. In the New Appointment box, type a description of the appointment.
3. In the Location box on the Details pane, type the location of the appointment.
4. In the Calendar list, click the calendar where you want the appointment to appear.
5. To make an all-day appointment, select the All-day Appointment check box.
6. Enter start and end times.
7. To make the appointment recur, in the Recurrence list, click the type of recurrence you want.
8. To set a reminder, in the Reminder list, click how long before the appointment you want to be reminded.
9. To invite someone, in the Attendees list, type the e mail address of the person you want to invite, press ENTER, click the e mail address in the Invite list, and then click Invite.

Note

- To edit an appointment, double-click it, and then type over the existing text with your changes.

To create a task

1. On the toolbar, click New Task.
2. In the New Task box, type a description of the task.
3. In the Calendar list on the Details pane, click the calendar where you want the task to appear.
4. In the Priority list, click the priority you want: low, medium, or high.
5. Enter the start and due dates.
6. To set a reminder, in the Reminder list, click On date, and enter the date and time you want to be reminded.

To search for appointments or tasks based on letters, words, or other text

- In the Search box, type letters or words from the appointment you want to find. The results appear as you type. The more you type, the more precise the results are.

To subscribe to a calendar

Many major sports teams, television and radio shows, and academic institutions offer calendars on the Internet. When you subscribe to one of these calendars, you can set how often your personal calendar is updated with the subscription calendar's event dates. Windows Calendar works with calendars in the iCalendar format (.ics).

- On the toolbar, click Subscribe, and then follow the instructions.

Note

- To see a list of calendars that you can subscribe to online, click Windows Calendar website.

To publish a calendar

You can publish your own calendar on the Internet through a web host so that others can see and share it. If you want, you can publish your personal schedule with password protection, so that you can choose who can access and view it.

1. Click the Share menu, and then click Publish.
2. In the Calendar name box, type the calendar name that you want to share.
3. In the Location to publish calendar box, enter the location (such as a website) where you want to publish the calendar.
4. Select any other options you want, and then click Publish.

Note

- To see locations where you can publish your calendar online, click Where can I publish this calendar?

To print a calendar

You can print your calendar by day, work week, week, or month.

1. On the toolbar, click Print.
2. Under Print Style, click one of the following: Day, Work Week, Week, or Month, and then click OK.

Windows Meeting Space

Windows Meeting Space gives you the ability to share documents, programs, or your desktop with other people. Some advantages are:

- You can share your desktop or any program with other meeting participants.
- You and other meeting participants can distribute and co-edit documents.
- You can pass notes to other participants.
- You can connect to a network projector to give a presentation.

Windows Meeting Space uses peer-to-peer technology and automatically sets up an ad hoc network if it can't find an existing network. So you can use it in a conference room, a favorite hotspot, or a place where no network exists. You can join a meeting that someone else sets up, or you can start a new meeting and invite other people to join it.

Join a meeting using Windows Meeting Space

With Windows Meeting Space, you can collaborate and share documents, programs, or your desktop with other people on the Internet, a local network, or a wireless ad hoc network.

You can join a meeting by double-clicking the invitation file that you receive from someone in the meeting. You can also join a meeting by following these steps:

1. Click to open Windows Meeting Space.

   If this is the first time you open Windows Meeting Space, you will be prompted to turn on some services and sign in to People Near Me. If you are prompted for an administrator password or confirmation, type the password or provide confirmation.
2. Click Join a meeting near me, type the password for the meeting, and then click the arrow.

Windows Search

Every computer offers a way to find files. And every system offers several differnt ways to open them. But Search, a star feature of 7 combines these two functions in a way that's so fast, so efficient, and so spectular, it reduces much of time. Its important to note, though, that you can search for files on your Pc using the superfast Search box in two different places:

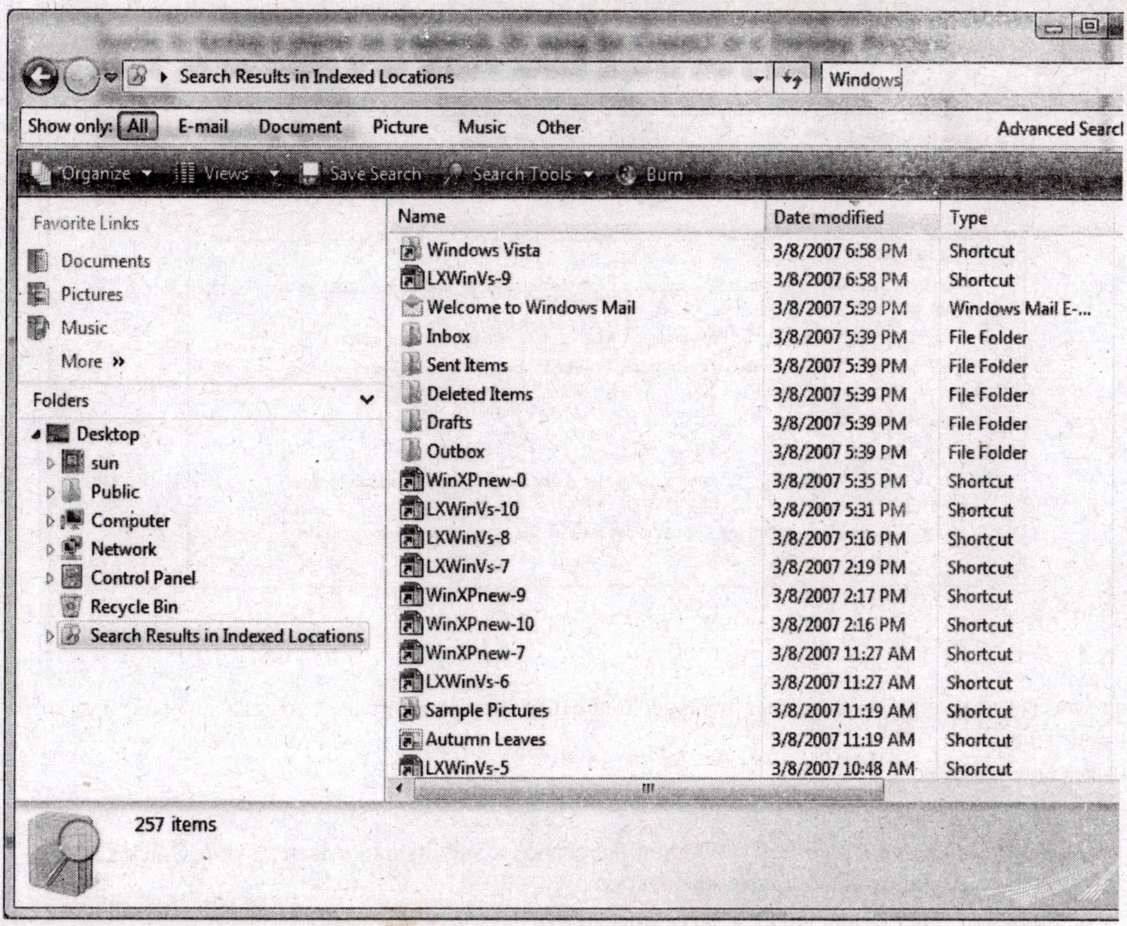

- The Start Menu The Start Search box at the bottom of the Start menu searches everywhere on your computer.
- Explorer windows The Search box at the top of every desktop window searches only that window, including folders within it. You can expand it, too, into something called the Search pane—a way to limit the scope of your search to certain file types or date ranges, for example.

Search boxes also appear in the Control Panel window, Internet Explorer, Windows Mail, Windows Media Player, and other spots where it is useful to perform small-time, limited searches.

Snipping Tool

Snipping tool takes pictures of your PC's screen.

You can use Snipping Tool to capture a screen shot, or snip, of any object on your screen and then annotate, save, or share the image. Simply use a mouse or tablet pen to capture any of the following types of snips:

- Free-form Snip. Draw an irregular line, such as a circle or a triangle, around an object.
- Rectangular Snip. Draw a precise line by dragging the cursor around an object to form a rectangle.
- Window Snip. Select a window, such as a browser window or dialog box, that you want to capture.
- Full-screen Snip. Capture the entire screen when you select this type of snip.

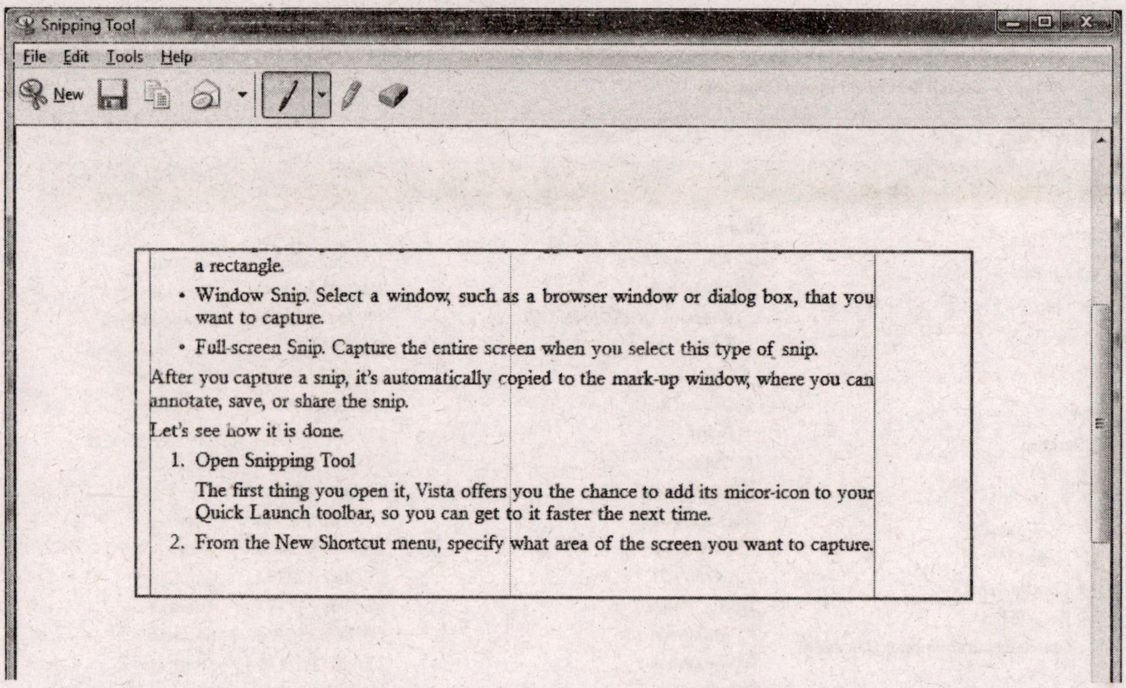

After you capture a snip, it's automatically copied to the mark-up window, where you can annotate, save, or share the snip.

Let's see how it is done.

1. Open Snipping Tool

   The first thing you open it, 7 offers you the chance to add its micor-icon to your Quick Launch toolbar, so you can get to it faster the next time.

2. From the New Shortcut menu, specify what area of the screen you want to capture.

   Your choces are as mentioned above.

What you do with your finished graphic is up to you. For example,

- Paste it. The edited image may be in the window in front of you, but the original, unedited image is also on your invisible Windows Clipboard. Close the editing window without saving changes, pop into your graphics, word processing, or email program, and paste what you have copied. Often, that is exactly what you will want to do.
- Send it. The little envelope button on the eidting-window toolbar automatically prepares an outgoing email message with your graphic alrady pasted in for, if your email program is set to send plain, unformatted text message only, as an attachment.
- Save it. If your intention is to save the capture as a file, click the Save icon, or choose File, Save, or press Ctrl+S. When the Save As dialog box appears type a name for your graphic, choose a file format for it pop-up men, specify a folder location, and then click Save.

Windows Media Player

The new Windows Media Player is not only meant for listing to songs, copying them, burning them, etc., it can also be used for seeing the various types of videos and DVDs. Once you start using Media Player, you would like to use the various keyboard commands too for easy and fast actions.

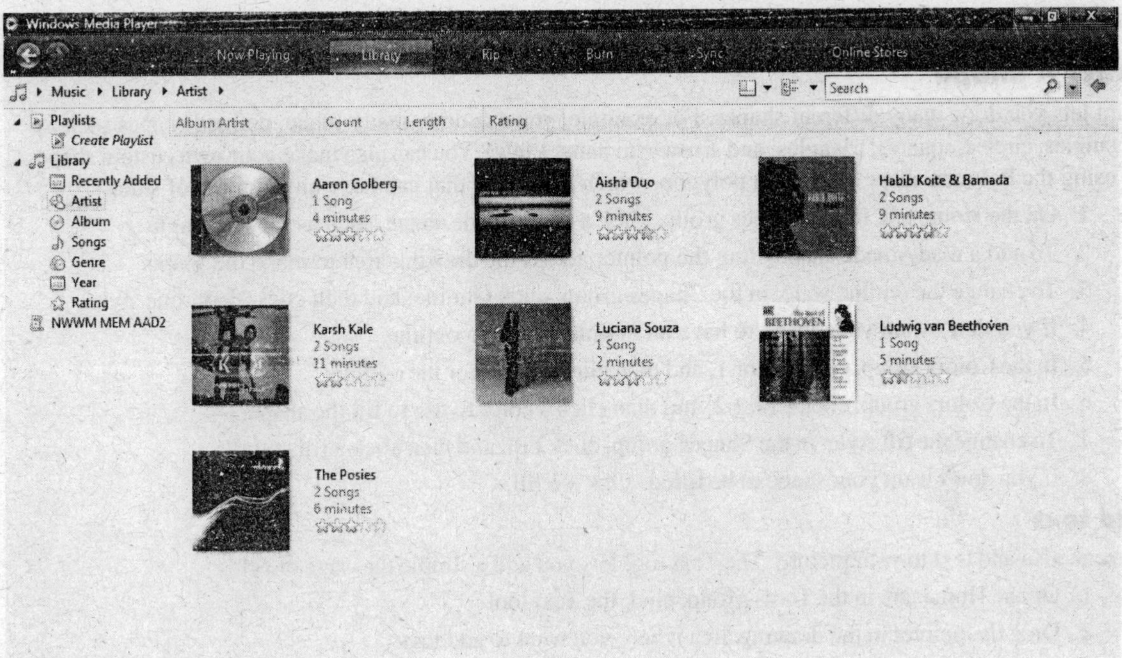

Working with Paint

Paint is a feature in Windows that you can use to draw, color, and edit pictures. You can use Paint like a digital sketchpad to make simple pictures, creative projects, or to add text and designs to other pictures, such as those taken with your digital camera.

The parts of Paint

When you start Paint, you'll see an empty window; drawing and painting tools are located in the ribbon at the top of the window. The following illustration shows the different parts of the Paint window:

Working with tools

The ribbon in Paint includes a handy collection of drawing tools. You can use these tools to create freehand drawings and add a variety of shapes to your pictures.

Draw a line

Some tools and shapes, such as the Pencil, Brush, Line, and Curve, let you make a variety of straight, curved, and squiggly lines. What you draw is determined by how you move the mouse as you draw. You can use the Line to draw a straight line, for example.

1. On the Home tab, in the Shapes group, click the Line
2. In the Colors group, click Color 1, and then click the color you want to use.
3. To draw, drag the pointer across the drawing area.

Draw a squiggly line

Your drawings don't have to be composed of only straight lines. The Pencil and Brushes can be used to make completely random, free-form shapes.

1. On the Home tab, in the Tools group, click the Pencil tool
2. In the Colors group, click Color 1, and then click the color you want to use.
3. To draw, drag the pointer across the drawing area and make a squiggly line.

- If you want to make a line that has a different appearance, use one of the Brushes, instead.

Draw a shape

Paint lets you draw many different shapes. For example, you can draw ready-made, defined shapes such as rectangles, circles, squares, triangles, and arrows (to name a few). You can also make your own custom shape by using the Polygon shape to draw a polygon, which is a shape that can have any number of sides.

1. On the Home tab, in the Shapes group, click a ready-made shape, such as the Rectangle .
2. To add a ready-made shape, drag the pointer across the drawing area to make the shape.
3. To change the outline style, in the Shapes group, click Outline, and then click an outline style.
4. If you don't want your shape to have an outline, click No outline.
5. In the Colors group, click Color 1, and then click a color for the outline.
6. In the Colors group, click Color 2, and then click a color to use to fill the shape.
7. To change the fill style, in the Shapes group, click Fill, and then click a fill style.
8. If you don't want your shape to be filled, click No fill.

Add text

You can also add text to your picture. The Text tool lets you add a simple message or title.

1. On the Home tab, in the Tools group, click the Text tool
2. Drag the pointer in the drawing area where you want to add text.
3. Under Text Tools, on the Text tab, click the font face, size, and style in the Font group.

The Font group

1. In the Colors group, click Color 1, and then click a color. This is the text color.
2. Type the text that you want to add.

Erase part of your picture

If you make a mistake or need to change part of a picture, use the eraser. By default, the eraser changes any area you erase to white, but you can change the eraser color. For example, if you set the background color to yellow, anything you erase turns to yellow.

1. On the Home tab, in the Tools group, click the Eraser tool .
2. In the Colors group, click Color 2, and then click the color that you want to erase with. If you want to erase with white, you don't have to select a color.
3. Drag the pointer over the area you want to erase.

Saving a picture

Save your picture frequently so you don't accidentally lose your work. To save, click the Paint button, and then click Save. This saves all of the changes made to the picture since the last time you saved.

The very first time that you save a new picture, you will need to give your picture a file name. Follow these steps:

1. Click the Paint button , and then click Save.
2. In the Save as type box, select the file format you want.
3. In the File name box, type a name, and then click Save.

What is the Aero desktop experience?

The Aero desktop experience features a translucent glass design with subtle window animations and new window colors.

It includes distinctive visual styles that combine the appearance of lightweight, translucent windows with powerful graphic advances. You can enjoy visually appealing effects and appearance and also benefit from better access to your programs.

Glass effects

One of the more visually obvious features is glass window borders, which let you focus on the contents of your open windows. Window behavior has also been redesigned, with subtle animations accompanying the minimizing, maximizing, and repositioning of windows to appear more smooth and effortless.

You can even fine-tune the color and appearance of windows, the Start menu, and the taskbar by tinting your translucent windows. Select one of the provided colors, or create your own custom color using the color mixer.

Switching between programs

The Aero desktop experience also includes taskbar previews for your open windows. When you point to a taskbar button, you'll see a thumbnail-sized preview of the window, whether the content of the window is a document, a photo, or even a running video.

When you press Alt+Tab to switch between windows, you can see live previews of the windows for each open program.

Aero is not included in Windows 7 Home Basic or Windows 7 Starter. You can find out which edition of Windows 7 you have on your computer by opening System in Control Panel.

The edition of Windows 7 you're running is displayed under Windows edition near the top of the window.

You also need to use a Windows theme to display Aero graphics. If you are using an Ease of Access theme, some elements such as transparency and thumbnail previews will not appear. To view which theme you are using, open Personalization in Control Panel.

Your computer's hardware and video card must meet hardware requirements to able to display Aero graphics. Check that your computer meets the minimum hardware requirements for running Aero:

- 1-gigahertz (GHz) 32-bit (x86) or 64-bit (x64) processor
- 1 gigabyte (GB) of random access memory (RAM)
- 128-megabyte (MB) graphics card

Aero also requires a DirectX 9 class graphics processor that supports a Windows Display Driver Model Driver, Pixel Shader 2.0 in hardware, and 32 bits per pixel.

For best results, you might also want to follow these graphics processor recommendations:

- 64 MB of graphics memory to support a single monitor with a resolution that is less than 1,310,720 pixels (for example, a 17–inch flat panel LCD monitor that has a 1280 × 1024 resolution)
- 128 MB of graphics memory to support a single monitor with a resolution from 1,310,720 to 2,304,000 pixels (for example, a 21.1–inch flat panel LCD monitor that has up to a 1600 × 1200 resolution)
- 256 MB of graphics memory to support a single monitor with a resolution greater than 2,304,000 pixels (for example, a 30–inch wide-screen flat panel LCD monitor that has up to a 2560 × 1600 resolution)

To enable the Aero desktop experience in Windows Server 2008 R2, you'll need to install the Desktop Experience feature, enable the Themes service, and then select an Aero theme.

- You might need to update your video card driver to run Aero. If your hardware does not support Aero, you can select the Windows 7 Basic color scheme, which does not include transparency or other Aero effects.

To install Desktop Experience in Windows Server 2008 R2

1. Click Start, click Control Panel, and then, under Programs, click Turn Windows Features on or off. If you're prompted for an administrator password or confirmation, type the password or provide confirmation.

2. In the Features Summary section, click Add Features.
3. Select the Desktop Experience check box. If you are prompted to install additional features, click Add Required Features, and then click Next.
4. Click Install. You might be prompted to restart your computer.

To enable the Themes service in Windows Server 2008 R2

1. Click Start, point to Administrative Tools, and then click Services. If you're prompted for an administrator password or confirmation, type the password or provide confirmation.
2. Double-click Themes.
3. In the Startup type list, select Automatic, and then click Apply.
4. Under Service status, click Start, and then click OK.

To select an Aero theme

1. Right-click an open area of the desktop, and then click Personalize.
2. Click Themes.
3. Under Aero Themes, click an Aero theme.

The Taskbar

The taskbar is the long horizontal bar at the bottom of your screen. Unlike the desktop, which can get obscured by open windows, the taskbar is almost always visible. It has three main sections:

- The Start button , which opens the Start menu.
- The middle section, which shows you which programs and files you have open and allows you to quickly switch between them.
- The notification area, which includes a clock and icons (small pictures) that communicate the status of certain programs and computer settings.

You're likely to use the middle section of the taskbar the most, so let's look at it first.

Keep track of your windows

If you open more than one program or file at a time, you can quickly start piling up open windows on your desktop. Because windows often cover each other or take up the whole screen, it's sometimes hard to see what else is underneath or remember what you've already opened.

That's where the taskbar comes in handy. Whenever you open a program, folder, or file, Windows creates a corresponding button on the taskbar. The button shows an icon that represents the open program. In the picture below, two programs are open—Calculator and Minesweeper—and each has its own button on the taskbar.

Notice how the taskbar button for Minesweeper is highlighted. That indicates that Minesweeper is the active window, meaning that it's in front of any other open windows and is ready for you to interact with.

To switch to another window, click its taskbar button. In this example, clicking the taskbar button for Calculator brings its window to the front.

Clicking taskbar buttons is one of several ways to switch between windows.

Minimize and restore windows

When a window is active (its taskbar button is highlighted), clicking its taskbar button minimizes the window. That means that the window disappears from the desktop. Minimizing a window doesn't close it or delete its contents—it temporarily removes it from the desktop.

In the picture below, Calculator is minimized, but not closed. You can tell it's still running because it has a button on the taskbar.

You can also minimize a window by clicking the minimize button in the upper-right corner of the window.

To restore a minimized window (make it show up again on the desktop), click its taskbar button.

See previews of your open windows

When you move your mouse pointer to a taskbar button, a small picture appears that shows you a miniature version of the corresponding window. This preview, also called a thumbnail, is especially useful. And if one of your windows has video or animation playing, you'll see it playing in the preview.

The notification area

The notification area, at the far right of the taskbar, includes a clock and a group of icons. It looks like this.

These icons communicate the status of something on your computer or provide access to certain settings. The set of icons you see depends on which programs or services you have installed and how your computer manufacturer set up your computer.

When you move your pointer to a particular icon, you will see that icon's name or the status of a setting. For example, pointing to the volume icon shows the current volume level of your computer. Pointing to the network icon displays information about whether you are connected to a network, the connection speed, and the signal strength.

Double-clicking an icon in the notification area usually opens the program or setting associated with it. For example, double-clicking the volume icon opens the volume controls. Double-clicking the network icon opens Network and Sharing Center.

Occasionally, an icon in the notification area will display a small pop-up window (called a notification) to notify you about something. For example, after adding a new hardware device to your computer, you might see this.

The notification area displays a message after new hardware is installed

Click the Close button in the upper-right corner of the notification to dismiss it. If you don't do anything, the notification will fade away on its own after a few seconds.

To reduce clutter, Windows hides icons in the notification area when you haven't used them in a while. If icons become hidden, click the Show hidden icons button to temporarily display the hidden icons.

Click the Show hidden icons button to display all icons in the notification area

Customize the taskbar

There are many ways to customize the taskbar to suit your preferences. For example, you can move the entire taskbar to the left, right, or top edge of the screen. You can make the taskbar larger, have Windows automatically hide it when you're not using it, and add toolbars to it.

Working with files and folders

A file is an item that contains information—for example, text or images or music. When opened, a file can look very much like a text document or a picture that you might find on someone's desk or in a filing cabinet. On your computer, files are represented with icons; this makes it easy to recognize a type of file by looking at its icon. Here are some common file icons:

A folder is a container you can use to store files in. If you had thousands of paper files on your desk, it would be nearly impossible to find any particular file when you needed it. That's why people often store paper files in folders inside a filing cabinet. On your computer, folders work the same way. Here are some typical folder icons:

Folders can also store other folders. A folder within a folder is usually called a subfolder. You can create any number of subfolders, and each can hold any number of files and additional subfolders.

Using libraries to access your files and folders

When it comes to getting organized, you don't need to start from scratch. You can use libraries, a feature new to this version of Windows, to access your files and folders, and arrange them in different ways. Here's a list of the four default libraries and what they're typically used for:

- Documents library. Use this library to organize and arrange word-processing documents, spreadsheets, presentations, and other text-related files.

  By default, files that you move, copy, or save to the Documents library are stored in the My Documents folder.

- Pictures library. Use this library to organize and arrange your digital pictures, whether you get them from your camera, scanner, or in e mail from other people.

  By default, files that you move, copy, or save to the Pictures library are stored in the My Pictures folder.

- Music library. Use this library to organize and arrange your digital music, such as songs that you rip from an audio CD or that you download from the Internet.

  By default, files that you move, copy, or save to the Music library are stored in the My Music folder.

- Videos library. Use this library to organize and arrange your videos, such as clips from your digital camera or camcorder, or video files that you download from the Internet.

  By default, files that you move, copy, or save to the Videos library are stored in the My Videos folder.

To open the Documents, Pictures, or Music libraries, click the Start button , and then click Documents, Pictures, or Music.

You can open common libraries from the Start menu

Understanding the parts of a window

When you open a folder or library, you see it in a window. The various parts of this window are designed to help you navigate around Windows or work with files, folders, and libraries more easily. Here's a typical window and each of its parts:

- **Navigation pane** Use the navigation pane to access libraries, folders, saved searches, and even entire hard disks. Use the Favorites section to open your most commonly used folders and searches; use the Libraries section to access your libraries. You can also expand Computer to browse folders and subfolders.
- **Back and Forward buttons** Use the Back button and the Forward button to navigate to other folders or libraries you've already opened without closing the current window. These buttons work together with the address bar; after you use the address bar to change folders, for example, you can use the Back button to return to the previous folder.
- **Toolbar** Use the toolbar to perform common tasks, such as changing the appearance of your files and folders, burning files to a CD, or starting a digital picture slide show. The toolbar's buttons change to show only the tasks that are relevant. For example, if you click a picture file, the toolbar shows different buttons than it would if you clicked a music file.
- **Address bar** Use the address bar to navigate to a different folder or library or to go back to a previous one. For more information, see Navigate using the address bar.
- **Library pane** The library pane appears only when you are in a library (such as the Documents library). Use the library pane to customize the library or to arrange the files by different properties. For more information, see Working with libraries.
- **Column headings** Use the column headings to change how the files in the file list are organized. For example, you can click the left side of a column heading to change the order the files and folders

are displayed in, or you can click the right side to filter the files in different ways. (Note that column headings are available only in Details view.

- **File list** This is where the contents of the current folder or library are displayed. If you type in the search box to find a file, only the files that match your current view (including files in subfolders) will appear.
- **Search box** Type a word or phrase in the search box to look for an item in the current folder or library. The search begins as soon as you begin typing—so if you type "B," for example, all the files with names starting with the letter B will appear in the file list. For more information, see Find a file or folder.
- **Details pane** Use the details pane to see the most common properties associated with the selected file. File properties are information about a file, such as the author, the date you last changed the file, and any descriptive tags you might have added to the file.
- **Preview pane** Use the preview pane to see the contents of most files. If you select an e mail message, text file, or picture, for example, you can see its contents without opening it in a program. If you don't see the preview pane, click the Preview pane button in the toolbar to turn it on.

Viewing and arranging files and folders

When you open a folder or library, you can change how the files look in the window. For example, you might prefer larger (or smaller) icons or a view that lets you see different kinds of information about each file. To make these kinds of changes, use the Views button in the toolbar.

Each time you click the left side of the Views button, it changes the way your files and folders are displayed by cycling through five different views: Large Icons, List, a view called Details that shows several columns of information about the file, a smaller icon view called Tiles, and a view called Content that shows some of the content from within the file.

If you click the arrow on the right side of the Views button, you have more choices. Move the slider up or down to fine-tune the size of the file and folder icons. You can see the icons change size as you move the slider.

The Views options

1. In libraries, you can go a step further by arranging your files in different ways. For example, say you want to arrange the files in your Music library by genre (such as Jazz and Classical):
2. Click the Start button , and then click Music.
3. In the library pane (above the file list), click the menu next to Arrange by, and then click Genre.

Finding files

Depending on how many files you have and how they are organized, finding a file might mean browsing through hundreds of files and subfolders—not an easy task. To save time and effort, use the search box to find your file.

The search box

The search box is located at the top of every window. To find a file, open the folder or library that makes the most sense as a starting point for your search, click the search box, and start typing. The search box filters the current view based on the text that you type. Files are displayed as search results if your search term matches the file's name, tags or other properties, or even the text inside a text document.

If you're searching for a file based on a property (such as the file's type), you can narrow the search before you start typing by clicking the search box, and then clicking one of the properties just below the search box. This adds a search filter (such as "type") to your search text, which will give you more accurate results.

If you aren't seeing the file you're looking for, you can change the entire scope of a search by clicking one of the options at the bottom of the search results. For example, if you search for a file in the Documents library but you can't find it, you can click Libraries to expand the search to the rest of your libraries.

Copying and moving files and folders

Occasionally, you might want to change where files are stored on your computer. You might want to move files to a different folder, for example, or copy them to removable media (such as CDs or memory cards) to share with another person.

Most people copy and move files using a method called drag and drop. Start by opening the folder that contains the file or folder you want to move. Then, open the folder where you want to move it to in a different window. Position the windows side by side on the desktop so that you can see the contents of both. Next, drag the file or folder from the first folder to the second folder. That's all there is to it.

To copy or move a file, drag it from one window to another

When using the drag-and-drop method, you might notice that sometimes the file or folder is copied, and at other times it's moved. If you're dragging an item between two folders that are stored on the same hard disk, then the item is moved so that two copies of the same file or folder aren't created in the same location. If you drag the item to a folder that's in a different location (such as a network location) or to removable media like a CD, then the item is copied.

- The easiest way to arrange two windows on the desktop is to use Snap.
- If you copy or move a file or folder to a library, it will be stored in the library's default save location. To learn how to customize a library's default save location.
- Another way to copy or move a file is to drag it from the file list to a folder or library in the navigation pane so you don't need to open two separate windows.

Creating and deleting files

The most common way to create new files is by using a program. For example, you can create a text document in a word-processing program or a movie file in a video-editing program.

Some programs create a file as soon as you open them. When you open WordPad, for example, it starts with a blank page. This represents an empty (and unsaved) file. Start typing, and when you are ready to save your work, click the Save button . In the dialog box that appears, type a file name that will help you find the file again in the future, and then click Save.

By default, most programs save files in common folders like My Documents and My Pictures, which makes it easy to find the files again next time.

When you no longer need a file, you can remove it from your computer to save space and to keep your computer from getting cluttered with unwanted files. To delete a file, open the folder or library that contains the file, and then select the file. Press Delete on your keyboard and then, in the Delete File dialog box, click Yes.

When you delete a file, it's temporarily stored in the Recycle Bin. Think of the Recycle Bin as a safety net that allows you to recover files or folders that you might have accidentally deleted. Occasionally, you should empty the Recycle Bin to reclaim all of the hard disk space being used by your unwanted files. To learn how, see Permanently delete files from the Recycle Bin.

Opening an existing file

To open a file, double-click it. The file will usually open in the program that you used to create or change it. For example, a text file will open in your word-processing program.

That's not always the case, though. Double-clicking a picture file, for example, will usually open a picture viewer. To change the picture, you need to use a different program. Right-click the file, click Open with, and then click the name of the program that you want to use.

Manage your extras in Windows Media Center

Windows Media Center includes a number of extras that can be used within Media Center. Typically, these are games or Internet services made by companies other than Microsoft. You can manage how your extras are displayed in Media Center, including adding extras that you use regularly to the Windows Media Center Start screen.

Managing Extras

1. On the Windows Media Center start screen, scroll to Extras, click Extras library, and then click Manage extras.
2. Click Extras Library, and then do one of the following:
   - To hide an extra, clear the check box next to it.
   - To show a hidden extra, select the check box next to it.
3. Click Save.

To have an extra appear on the Start screen

1. On the Windows Media Center start screen, scroll to Extras, and then click Extras library.
2. Right-click the extra you want to appear, and then, on the context menu, click Add to Start Menu.
3. Click Yes. The item will now appear under Extras on the start screen.

To remove a extra from the Start screen

1. On the Windows Media Center start screen, scroll to Extras, and then click Extras library.
2. Right-click the program you want to remove from the Start screen, and then, on the context menu, click Remove from Start menu.

Add media files to Windows Media Center

The first time you start Windows Media Center, it looks for media files in the Music, Pictures, and Videos libraries on your computer. Through these libraries, you can control which songs, movies, and other media appear in Media Center.

There are two ways to do this:

- From outside of Media Center, add or remove folders in Windows libraries. When you add or remove a folder, the change is reflected in Media Center.
- From within Media Center, add or remove folders that you want Media Center to monitor for media files. When you add or remove a folder, the change is reflected in your Windows library.

The Media Library page in Media Center

Each time you open Media Center, it looks for media files in the your Music, Pictures, and Videos libraries, and in the Recorded TV library (usually located at C:\Users\Public). If you add or delete a file in any of those folders, the content that appears in Media Center is automatically updated.

To add media files to Media Center

1. Click the Start button, click All Programs, and then click Windows Media Center.
2. On the Windows Media Center start screen, scroll to Tasks, and then click Settings.
3. Click Media Libraries.
4. Click the type of media that you want to add (such as Music), and then click Next.

5. Click Add folders to the library, and then click Next.
6. Depending on where your media files are stored, click one of the options under Where are the folders you want to add?, and then click Next.
7. Navigate to the folders that you want to add by clicking the Plus or Minus buttons, and then select the check box next to each folder. (Files in subfolders will be included in your selection.)
8. When you've selected all the folders that you want Media Center to monitor, click Next, click Yes, use these locations, and then click Finish.
8. After you've finished adding files, it might take several minutes for the files to appear in the libraries.

- Under Where are the folders you want to add?, if you select On another computer to add a folder from a network, and Media Center doesn't detect the folder, try mapping the folder as a network drive.
- If you delete an album from your Music library in Media Center, but choose the Library Only option when deleting, the album will only be removed from Media Center—it will not be deleted from where it's stored. You can add the album back to Media Center by removing the parent folder from the Music library then adding it again.

To import media from a digital camera or other removable device

1. If you have media on a removable device, such as a USB flash drive or a digital camera, you can import the media directly to your computer. When you do this, the files will be stored in the My Pictures folder in Windows.
2. Click the Start button , click All Programs, and then click Windows Media Center.
3. If Media Center is not in full-screen mode, click the Maximize button .
4. Connect your removable device to your computer. (Cameras and most other removable devices are usually connected to a USB port.)
5. In the dialog that appears, click Import pictures and videos.
6. If you want to change the name of the folder where your media will be stored, type a new name.
7. Click Import. Media Center will copy the files to your My Pictures folder.

- If you have video files in addition to pictures on your removable device, they'll be imported to the My Pictures folder. To see them in the Video library in Media Center, you'll need to manually move them to the My Videos or Public Videos folder in Windows Explorer.
- If you store media on certain types of removable drives (such as external USB hard drives), you'll need to add them manually to see them in Media Center.

Listen to music in Windows Media Center

Most people think of watching and recording TV when they think of Windows Media Center, but did you know that Media Center is also a great way to listen to music?

You can use Windows Media Center to play your favorite songs, create playlists for parties, and even watch a slide show of your pictures while the music plays.

Media Center is best experienced using a compatible Media Center remote control. If you don't have a Media Center remote control, you can scroll left or right through your digital media collection by moving the mouse to the edge of the screen or by using the left and right arrow keys on your keyboard.

To find and play music

1. Click the Start button , click All Programs, and then click Windows Media Center.
2. On the Windows Media Center start screen, scroll to Music, and then click Music library.
3. Click a grouping (such as Albums or Artists), and then click the music that you want to listen to.

4. Find the song, album, or playlist that you want to play, and then click Play.
   - If you already have music playing and you want to add a song, album, or playlist to the song list (queue) to play afterward, right-click the item, and then click Add to Song List.
   - To search your Media Center music library from the Windows Media Center start screen, scroll to Music, scroll to the right, click Search, and then enter your search criteria.

To rate and play your favorite music

1. You can rate individual songs so you can keep track of your favorites, and then play only your favorite music.
2. Click the Start button , click All Programs, and then click Windows Media Center.
3. On the Windows Media Center start screen, scroll to Music, and then click Music library.
4. Click Songs, right-click a song that you want to rate, and then click the Rating button (five stars in a row) multiple times until it displays the desired rating.
5. Click the green Start button to return to the Windows Media Center start screen, scroll to Music, and then click Play favorites.
6. By default, Media Center uses ratings to determine which songs are your favorites. To change the Favorite Music settings, from the Media Center start screen, scroll to Tasks, click Settings, click Music, click Favorite Music, make any adjustments you like, and then click Save.

To display your favorite pictures while playing music

1. You can create a special presentation of your favorite pictures to display when your music is playing.
2. When music is playing, on the Windows Media Center start screen, scroll to Now Playing, and then click the icon.
3. Click Play Pictures to start the presentation of your favorite pictures.
   - By default, Media Center determines which pictures are your favorites by each picture's rating. To change the rating for a picture, or to change the Favorite Pictures settings, see · View pictures and videos in Windows Media Center.

To view and edit the song list (queue)

1. When music is playing, on the Windows Media Center start screen, scroll to Now Playing, and then click the icon.
2. Click View Song List, click Edit List, and then do one of the following:
   - To move a song up or down in the list, click the Up arrow or Down arrow .
   - To remove a song from the list, click the Delete button .
3. Click Done.

To save the song list (queue) as a playlist

1. You can save the songs that are queued in your song list as a permanent playlist to play again. Playlists are a great way to customize your listening experience. By creating a playlist, you can group any combination of songs into a list that you can then quickly play or burn to a CD. To learn how to burn music, see Burn a CD or DVD in Windows Media Center.
2. After adding music to your song list, on the Windows Media Center start screen, scroll to Now Playing, and then click the icon.
3. Click View List, and then click Save As Playlist.
4. Type a name for the playlist, and then click Save.

5. When you save the song list (queue) as a playlist, it's added to your permanent set of playlists. You can access your playlists in the Music library under Playlists.

To delete music from your computer

1. If you delete a song, album, or playlist from within Media Center, it's deleted from the Music library and the computer permanently.
2. Click the Start button , click All Programs, and then click Windows Media Center.
3. On the Windows Media Center start screen, scroll to Music, and then click Music library.
4. Click Album, Song, or Playlist, right-click a title or name, and then click Delete.
5. Click Yes to confirm the deletion.

To turn on visualizations while playing music

1. While music is playing, on the Windows Media Center start screen, scroll to Now Playing, and then click the icon.
2. Click Visualize.

- You can cycle through the various visualizations using the left and right arrow keys on the keyboard.

To have a visualization always start when music plays

1. Click the Start button , click All Programs, and then click Windows Media Center.
2. On the Windows Media Center start screen, scroll to Tasks, click Settings, and then click Music.
3. Click Now Playing Options, and then select the Start visualizations automatically check box.
4. Under Show song information during visualizations, select an option, and then click Save.

Edit pictures in Windows Media Center

You can make changes to your digital pictures in Windows Media Center, such as rotating a picture or removing red eye. You can also print pictures and delete pictures.

To rotate a picture

1. Click the Start button, click All Programs, and then click Windows Media Center.
2. On the Windows Media Center start screen, scroll to Pictures + Videos, and then click Picture library.
3. To rotate the picture clockwise 90 degrees, right-click the picture, and then click Rotate. If you click the picture more than once, the picture rotates 90 degrees clockwise every time you click Rotate.

- When you rotate a picture, you alter the original picture file, not just how it displays in Media Center.

To touch up a picture

1. Click the Start button , click All Programs, and then click Windows Media Center.
2. On the Windows Media Center start screen, scroll to Pictures + Videos, and then click Picture library.
3. Right-click the picture you want to edit, click Picture Details, click Touch Up, and then do one of the following:

- To remove red eye, click Red Eye.
- To increase the contrast, click Contrast.
- To adjust the cropping, click Crop, and then click the buttons below the picture to move, enlarge, shrink, or rotate the cropping boundaries.
- To preview any changes you've made at full screen, click Preview. When you're done, click the Back button.

4. When you're finished making changes to the picture, click Save.

- When you touch up a picture, you alter the original picture file, not just how it displays in Media Center.

To print a picture

1. Click the Start button , click All Programs, and then click Windows Media Center.
2. On the Windows Media Center start screen, scroll to Pictures + Videos, and then click Picture library.
3. Navigate to the picture you want to print, right-click the picture, and then click Picture Details.
4. To print the picture, click Print, and then click Print again.

To delete a picture from your computer

1. On the Windows Media Center start screen, scroll to Pictures + Videos, and then click Picture library.
2. Navigate to the picture you want to delete, right-click the picture, click Delete, and then click Yes.

- You can also edit pictures while a slide show is playing by right-clicking a picture during a slide show. When you're finished, on the Picture details screen, click Resume slide show to pick up where you left off.
- While viewing a picture at full screen, you can zoom in on it by pressing Enter.

View pictures and videos in Windows Media Center

With Windows Media Center, you can play home videos and view your digital photos in a number of fun ways.

Media Center is best experienced using a compatible Media Center remote control. If you don't have a Media Center remote control, you can scroll left or right through your pictures and videos by moving the mouse to the edge of the screen, or by using the left and right arrow buttons on your keyboard.

To find and view a picture

1. If you can't find a particular picture, try changing the way Media Center groups your pictures.
2. Click the Start button , click All Programs, and then click Windows Media Center.
3. On the Windows Media Center start screen, scroll to Pictures + Videos, and then click Picture library.
4. Click Folders to sort your folders and files alphabetically, click Date taken to sort folders and files by date, or click Tags to sort files by tags that have been applied.
5. Click the picture that you want to view.

To view or import pictures or videos from a removable device

1. If you have pictures on a removable device, such as a USB flash drive or a digital camera, you can view the pictures in Media Center or import them directly to your computer.
2. Click the Start button , click All Programs, and then click Windows Media Center.
3. If Media Center is not in full-screen mode, click the Maximize button .
4. Connect your removable device to your computer. (Cameras and most other removable devices are usually connected to a USB port.)
5. In the dialog that appears, do one of the following:

- Click Import pictures and videos, and then follow the instructions to copy all the pictures and videos on your device to the My Pictures folder on your computer. To see imported videos in Media Center, you'll need to manually move them to the My Videos or Public Videos folder in Windows Explorer.
- Click View pictures or View videos to access the pictures or videos on the device without copying them to your computer.

- If you store media on certain types of removable drives (such as external USB hard drives), you'll need to add them manually to see them in Media Center.

To create a slide show

1. A slide show is a way to view a group of photos one-by-one at full screen. You can create your own slide show complete with pictures and music of your choice, and then save it for easy access later.
2. Click the Start button , click All Programs, and then click Windows Media Center.
3. On the Windows Media Center start screen, scroll to Pictures + Videos, and then click Picture library.
4. Click Slide shows, click Create Slide Show, and then follow the instructions to add pictures and music to your slide show.
5. On the Review & Edit Slide Show page, click Add More to add additional pictures and music, and when you're finished, click Create.
6. On the Picture library page, click the slide show you want to play, and then click Play slide show.

- You can quickly play slide shows without creating a custom slide show. On the Picture library page, click a folder, and then click Play slide show.

To play a slide show

1. On the Windows Media Center start screen, scroll to Pictures + Videos, and then click Picture library.
2. On the Picture library page, click Slide shows, click the slide show you want to play, and then click Play slide show.
3. While your slide show is playing, move the mouse to make the playback controls appear, and then do any of the following:

- Click the Left arrow button or the Right arrow button to go back or forward one picture in the slide show.
- Click the Pause button to pause the music and the slide show.
- Click the Skip Forward button or the Skip Backward button to go ahead to the next song or go back to the previous song.
- Click the Mute button to mute the sound.
- Click the Volume Increase button or the Volume Decrease button to change the volume.
- Click the Stop button to stop the slide show. (The music will continue playing, but the pictures won't appear.)
- You can also control playback of a slide show with a Media Center remote control, or by using keyboard shortcuts.

To customize settings for slide shows

There are many options for customizing the presentation of your slide shows. You can specify the order in which pictures are shown, the duration of the transitions, and other aspects of a slide show presentation.

1. Click the Start button, click All Programs, and then click Windows Media Center.
2. On the Windows Media Center start screen, scroll to Tasks, click Settings, click Pictures, and then click Slide Shows. You can customize your slide show using the options on this screen.
3. Click Save to save the new settings.

To rate and play your favorite pictures

You can rate individual pictures so you can keep track of your favorites, and then play a special presentation of only your favorite pictures.

1. Click the Start button, click All Programs, and then click Windows Media Center.

2. On the Windows Media Center start screen, scroll to Pictures + Videos, and then click Pictures library.
3. Right-click a picture that you want to rate, and then click the Rating button (five stars in a row) multiple times until it displays the desired rating.
4. Click the green Start button to return to the Windows Media Center start screen, scroll to Pictures + Videos, and then click Play favorites.
5. By default, Media Center uses ratings to determine which pictures are your favorites. To change the Favorite Picture settings, from the Media Center start screen, scroll to Tasks, click Settings, click Pictures, click Favorite Pictures, make any adjustments you like, and then click Save.

To find and play a video file

If you're having trouble finding a particular video file, try changing the way that Media Center groups your videos.

1. Click the Start button , click All Programs, and then click Windows Media Center.
2. On the Windows Media Center start screen, scroll to Pictures + Videos, and then click Video library.
3. Click Folders to sort your folders and files alphabetically, or click Date taken to sort them by date.
4. Find the video that you want to watch, and then click the video file to play it.
   - If you can't find the video you're looking for, you might need to tell Media Center where the file is located.

To slow down, speed up, or rewind a video file

1. Click the Start button , click All Programs, and then click Windows Media Center.
2. On the Windows Media Center start screen, scroll to Pictures + Videos, and then click Video library.
3. Find the video that you want to watch, and then click the video file to play it.
4. Click the Pause button , and then do one of the following:
   - Click the Fast Forward button once to play the video in slow motion.
   - Click the Fast Forward button four times to speed up playback of the video.
   - Click the Rewind button one, two, three, or four times to play the video backwards at different speeds.
   - Click the Play button to resume playback at normal speed.

To change the video background color

If an unchanging image stays on the screen for too long, sometimes a faint remnant of the image will stay on the screen even after a new image has replaced it. This is called screen burn. To avoid screen burn during video playback in Media Center, you can change the shade of black that might appear on the left and right or on the top and bottom of your video.

1. Click the Start button , click All Programs, and then click Windows Media Center.
2. On the Windows Media Center start screen, scroll to Tasks, click Settings, click General, and then click Visual and Sound Effects.
3. Under Video background color, click the Plus or Minus button to change the color. The default color is black—you can change it to different shades of gray, or to solid white.
4. Click Save.

Install a program

You can do a lot with the programs and features included in Windows, but you might want to install other programs.

How you add a program depends on where the installation files for the program are located. Typically, programs are installed from a CD or DVD, from the Internet, or from a network.

To install a program from a CD or DVD

- Insert the disc into your computer, and then follow the instructions on your screen. If you're prompted for an administrator password or confirmation, type the password or provide confirmation.

If a program doesn't begin installation automatically, check the information that came with the program. This information will likely provide instructions for installing the program manually. If you can't access the information, you can also browse through the disc and open the program setup file, usually called Setup.exe or Install.exe. If your program was written for an earlier version of Windows.

To install a program from the Internet

In your web browser, click the link to the program.

Do one of the following:

- To install the program immediately, click Open or Run, and then follow the instructions on your screen. If you're prompted for an administrator password or confirmation, type the password or provide confirmation.
- To install the program later, click Save, and then download the installation file to your computer. When you're ready to install the program, double-click the file, and then follow the instructions on your screen. This is a safer option because you can scan the installation file for viruses before you proceed.
- When downloading and installing programs from the Internet, be sure you trust the publisher of the program and the website that's offering the program.

Uninstall or change a program

You can uninstall a program from your computer if you no longer use it or if you want to free up space on your hard disk. You can use Programs and Features to uninstall programs or to change a program's configuration by adding or removing certain options.

Go to the Windows website to watch the video. (1:16)

To uninstall or change a program

1. Click to open Programs and Features.
2. Select a program, and then click Uninstall. Some programs include the option to change or repair the program in addition to uninstalling it, but many simply offer the option to uninstall. To change a program, click Change or Repair. If you're prompted for an administrator password or confirmation, type the password or provide confirmation.

- If the program you want to uninstall isn't listed, it might not have been written for this version of Windows. To uninstall the program, check the information that came with the program.
- To learn more about turning off programs and features that are included with Windows.

Turn Windows features on or off

Some programs and features included with Windows, such as Internet Information Services, must be turned on before you can use them. Certain other features are turned on by default, but you can turn them off if you don't use them.

1. To turn a feature off in earlier versions of Windows, you had to uninstall it completely from your computer. In this version of Windows, the features remain stored on your hard disk so you can turn

them back on if you want to. Turning off a feature does not uninstall the feature, and it does not reduce the amount of hard disk space used by Windows features.

2. To turn Windows features on or off, follow these steps:
3. Click the Start button , click Control Panel, click Programs, and then click Turn Windows features on or off. If you're prompted for an administrator password or confirmation, type the password or provide confirmation.
4. To turn a Windows feature on, select the check box next to the feature. To turn a Windows feature off, clear the check box. Click OK.
5. Folders can contain both checked and unchecked features
6. Some Windows features are grouped together in folders, and some folders contain subfolders with additional features. If a check box is partially checked or is dimmed, then some of the items inside the folder are turned on and some are turned off. To view the contents of a folder, double-click it.

- In Windows Server 2008 R2, use Server Manager to turn Windows features on or off.

Use Parental Controls in Windows Media Center

You can use Parental Controls in Windows Media Center to prevent children from watching objectionable TV shows and movies.

When you turn on Parental Controls, you'll be asked to create an access code that you can use later to access restricted content or to change parental control settings. Only TV shows and movies that don't exceed the maximum allowed rating can be viewed without the access code. Not all TV shows and movies are rated, so you can also configure Parental Controls to block unrated content.

To set Parental Controls

On the Windows Media Center start screen, scroll to Tasks, click Settings, click General, and then click Parental Controls.

If this is the first time you've accessed Parental Controls, you'll be asked to type and confirm a 4-digit number to use as your access code. We recommend that you write this code down for future reference.

Do one of the following:

- To set Parental Controls for TV programs, click TV Ratings, select the Turn on TV blocking check box, and then use the plus (+) and minus (-) buttons to select a maximum allowed rating. If you want to restrict content that's not rated, select the Block unrated TV programs check box (this is optional). Click Save.
- To adjust the settings by content in addition to rating, click Advanced. There are five areas that you can set restrictions for: fantasy violence, suggestive dialogue, offensive language, sexual content, and violence.
- To set Parental Controls for DVDs and movies, click Movie/DVD Ratings, select the Turn on movie blocking check box, and then use the plus (+) and minus (-) buttons to select a rating. If you want to restrict content that's not rated, select the Block unrated movies check box (this is optional). Click Save.

To change the access code

1. On the Windows Media Center start screen, scroll to Tasks, click Settings, click General, click Parental Controls, and then type your current access code.
2. Click Change Access Code.
3. Type and confirm a new 4-digit access code, and then click OK.

To reset Parental Controls

1. On the Windows Media Center start screen, scroll to Tasks, click Settings, click General, click Parental Controls, and then type your current access code.
2. Click Reset Parental Controls.
3. Click Yes to remove the access code and disable all restrictions.

- Parental Controls aren't available in some countries or regions.
- Media Center uses the ratings from the TV broadcast signal to determine which shows to block. In rare cases, the Guide rating might not match the rating information received from the TV broadcast signal.

7 Keyboard Shortcuts of Windows 7

Introduction

Keyboard shortcuts are combinations of two or more keys that, when pressed, can be used to perform a task that would typically require a mouse or other pointing device. Keyboard shortcuts can make it easier to interact with your computer, saving you time and effort as you work with Windows and other programs.

Most programs also provide accelerator keys that can make it easier to work with menus and other commands. Check the menus of programs for accelerator keys. If a letter is underlined in a menu, that usually means that pressing the Alt key in combination with the underlined key will have the same effect as clicking that menu item.

Pressing the Alt key in some programs, such as Paint and WordPad, shows commands that are labeled with additional keys that you can press to use them.

You can also create new keyboard shortcuts to open programs.

The following table contains keyboard shortcuts that can help make your computer easier to use.

Press this key	*To do this*
Right Shift for eight seconds	Turn Filter Keys on and off
Left Alt+Left Shift+PrtScn (or PrtScn)	Turn High Contrast on or off
Left Alt+Left Shift+Num Lock	Turn Mouse Keys on or off
Shift five times	Turn Sticky Keys on or off
Num Lock for five seconds	Turn Toggle Keys on or off
Windows logo key +U	Open the Ease of Access Center

General keyboard shortcuts

The following table contains general keyboard shortcuts.

Press this key	*To do this*
Fl	Display Help
Ctrl+C (or Ctrl+Insert)	Copy the selected item
Ctrl+X	Cut the selected item
Ctrl+V (or Shift+Insert)	Paste the selected item
Ctrl+Z	Undo an action

Ctrl+Y	Redo an action
Delete (or Ctrl+D)	Delete the selected item and move it to the Recycle Bin
Shift+Delete	Delete the selected item without moving it to the Recycle Bin first
F2	Rename the selected item
Ctrl+Right Arrow	Move the cursor to the beginning of the next word
Ctrl+Left Arrow	Move the cursor to the beginning of the previous word
Ctrl+Down Arrow	Move the cursor to the beginning of the next paragraph
Ctrl+Up Arrow	Move the cursor to the beginning of the previous paragraph
Ctrl+Shift with an arrow key	Select a block of text
Shift with any arrow key	Select more than one item in a window or on the desktop, or select text within a document
Ctrl with any arrow key+Spacebar	Select multiple individual items in a window or on the desktop
Ctrl+A	Select all items in a document or window
F3	Search for a file or folder
Alt+Enter	Display properties for the selected item
Alt+F4	Close the active item, or exit the active program
Alt+Spacebar	Open the shortcut menu for the active window
Ctrl+F4	Close the active document (in programs that allow you to have multiple documents open simultaneously)
Alt+Tab	Switch between open items
Ctrl+Alt+Tab	Use the arrow keys to switch between open items
Ctrl+Mouse scroll wheel	Change the size of icons on the desktop
Windows logo key +Tab	Cycle through programs on the taskbar by using Aero Flip 3-D
Ctrl+Windows logo key +Tab	Use the arrow keys to cycle through programs on the taskbar by using Aero Flip 3-D
Alt+Esc	Cycle through items in the order in which they were opened
F6	Cycle through screen elements in a window or on the desktop
F4	Display the address bar list in Windows Explorer
Shift+F10	Display the shortcut menu for the selected item

Ctrl+Esc	Open the Start menu
Alt+underlined letter	Display the corresponding menu
Alt+underlined letter	Perform the menu command (or other underlined command)
F10	Activate the menu bar in the active program
Right Arrow	Open the next menu to the right, or open a submenu
Left Arrow	Open the next menu to the left, or close a submenu
F5 (or Ctrl+R)	Refresh the active window
Alt+Up Arrow	View the folder one level up in Windows Explorer
Esc	Cancel the current task
Ctrl+Shift+Esc	Open Task Manager
Shift when you insert a CD	Prevent the CD from automatically playing
Left Alt+Shift	Switch the input language when multiple input languages are enabled
Ctrl+Shift	Switch the keyboard layout when multiple keyboard layouts are enabled
Right or Left Ctrl+Shift	Change the reading direction of text in right-to-left reading languages

Dialog box keyboard shortcuts

The following table contains keyboard shortcuts for use in dialog boxes.

Press this key	*To do this*
Ctrl+Tab	Move forward through tabs
Ctrl+Shift+Tab	Move back through tabs
Tab	Move forward through options
Shift+Tab	Move back through options
Alt+underlined letter	Perform the command (or select the option) that goes with that letter
Enter	Replaces clicking the mouse for many selected commands
Spacebar	Select or clear the check box if the active option is a check box
Arrow keys	Select a button if the active option is a group of option buttons
F1	Display Help

F4	Display the items in the active list
Backspace	Open a folder one level up if a folder is selected in the Save As or Open dialog box

Windows logo key keyboard shortcuts

The following table contains keyboard shortcuts that use the Windows logo key .

Press this key	*To do this*
Windows logo key	Open or close the Start menu.
Windows logo key +Pause	Display the System Properties dialog box.
Windows logo key +D	Display the desktop.
Windows logo key +M	Minimize all windows.
Windows logo key +Shift+M	Restore minimized windows to the desktop.
Windows logo key +E	Open Computer.
Windows logo key +F	Search for a file or folder.
Ctrl+Windows logo key +F	Search for computers (if you're on a network).
Windows logo key +L	Lock your computer or switch users.
Windows logo key +R	Open the Run dialog box.
Windows logo key +T	Cycle through programs on the taskbar.
Windows logo key +number	Start the program pinned to the taskbar in the position indicated by the number. If the program is already running, switch to that program.
Shift+Windows logo key +number	Start a new instance of the program pinned to the taskbar in the position indicated by the number.
Ctrl+Windows logo key +number	Switch to the last active window of the program pinned to the taskbar in the position indicated by the number.
Alt+Windows logo key +number	Open the Jump List for the program pinned to the taskbar in the position indicated by the number.
Windows logo key +Tab	Cycle through programs on the taskbar by using Aero Flip 3-D.
Ctrl+Windows logo key +Tab	Use the arrow keys to cycle through programs on the taskbar by using Aero Flip 3-D.
Ctrl+Windows logo key +B	Switch to the program that displayed a message in the notification area.
Windows logo key +Spacebar	Preview the desktop.
Windows logo key +Up Arrow	Maximize the window.
Windows logo key +Left Arrow	Maximize the window to the left side of the screen.

Windows logo key +Right Arrow	Maximize the window to the right side of the screen.
Windows logo key +Down Arrow	Minimize the window.
Windows logo key +Home	Minimize all but the active window.
Windows logo key +Shift+Up Arrow	Stretch the window to the top and bottom of the screen.
Windows logo key +Shift+Left Arrow or Right Arrow	Move a window from one monitor to another.
Windows logo key +P	Choose a presentation display mode.
Windows logo key +G	Cycle through gadgets.
Windows logo key +U	Open Ease of Access Center.
Windows logo key +X	Open Windows Mobility Center.

Windows Explorer keyboard shortcuts

The following table contains keyboard shortcuts for working with Windows Explorer windows or folders.

Press this key	*To do this*
Ctrl+N	Open a new window
Ctrl+W	Close the current window
Ctrl+Shift+N	Create a new folder
End	Display the bottom of the active window
Home	Display the top of the active window
F11	Maximize or minimize the active window
Ctrl+Period (.)	Rotate a picture clockwise
Ctrl+Comma (,)	Rotate a picture counter-clockwise
Num Lock+Asterisk (*) on numeric keypad	Display all subfolders under the selected folder
Num Lock+Plus Sign (+) on numeric keypad	Display the contents of the selected folder
Num Lock+Minus Sign (-) on numeric keypad	Collapse the selected folder
Left Arrow	Collapse the current selection (if it's expanded), or select the parent folder
Alt+Enter	Open the Properties dialog box for the selected item
Alt+P	Display the preview pane
Alt+Left Arrow	View the previous folder
Backspace	View the previous folder
Right Arrow	Display the current selection (if it's collapsed), or select the first subfolder
Alt+Right Arrow	View the next folder

Alt+Up Arrow	View the parent folder
Ctrl+Shift+E	Display all folders above the selected folder
Ctrl+Mouse scroll wheel	Change the size and appearance of file and folder icons
Alt+D	Select the address bar
Ctrl+E	Select the search box
Ctrl+F	Select the search box

Taskbar keyboard shortcuts

The following table contains keyboard shortcuts for working with items on the taskbar.

Press this key	*To do this*
Shift+Click on a taskbar button	Open a program or quickly open another instance of a program
Ctrl+Shift+Click on a taskbar button	Open a program as an administrator
Shift+Right-click on a taskbar button	Show the window menu for the program
Shift+Right-click on a grouped taskbar button	Show the window menu for the group
Ctrl+Click on a grouped taskbar button	Cycle through the windows of the group

Magnifier keyboard shortcuts

The following table contains keyboard shortcuts for working with Magnifier.

Press this key	*To do this*
Windows logo key + Plus Sign (+) or Minus Sign (-)	Zoom in or out
Ctrl+Alt+Spacebar	Preview the desktop in full-screen mode
Ctrl+Alt+F	Switch to full-screen mode
Ctrl+Alt+L	Switch to lens mode
Ctrl+Alt+D	Switch to docked mode
Ctrl+Alt+I	Invert colors
Ctrl+Alt+arrow keys	Pan in the direction of the arrow keys
Ctrl+Alt+R	Resize the lens
Windows logo key + Esc	Exit Magnifier

Remote Desktop Connection keyboard shortcuts

The following table contains keyboard shortcuts for working with Remote Desktop Connection.

Press this key	*To do this*
Alt+Page Up	Move between programs from left to right.

Alt+Page Down	Move between programs from right to left.
Alt+Insert	Cycle through programs in the order that they were started in.
Alt+Home	Display the Start menu.
Ctrl+Alt+Break	Switch between a window and full screen.
Ctrl+Alt+End	Display the Windows Security dialog box.
Alt+Delete	Display the system menu.
Ctrl+Alt+Minus Sign (-) on the numeric keypad	Place a copy of the active window, within the client, on the Terminal server clipboard (provides the same functionality as pressing Alt+PrtScn on a local computer).
Ctrl+Alt+Plus Sign (+) on the numeric keypad	Place a copy of the entire client window area on the Terminal server clipboard (provides the same functionality as pressing PrtScn on a local computer).
Ctrl+Alt+Right Arrow	"Tab" out of the Remote Desktop controls to a control in the host program (for example, a button or a text box). Useful when the Remote Desktop controls are embedded in another (host) program.
Ctrl+Alt+Left Arrow	"Tab" out of the Remote Desktop controls to a control in the host program (for example, a button or a text box). Useful when the Remote Desktop controls are embedded in another (host) program.

Paint keyboard shortcuts

The following table contains keyboard shortcuts for working with Paint.

Press this key	***To do this***
Ctrl+N	Create a new picture
Ctrl+O	Open an existing picture
Ctrl+S	Save changes to a picture
F12	Save the picture as a new file
Ctrl+P	Print a picture
Alt+F4	Close a picture and its Paint window
Ctrl+Z	Undo a change
Ctrl+Y	Redo a change
Ctrl+A	Select the entire picture
Ctrl+X	Cut a selection
Ctrl+C	Copy a selection to the Clipboard

Ctrl+V	Paste a selection from the Clipboard
Right Arrow	Move the selection or active shape right by one pixel
Left Arrow	Move the selection or active shape left by one pixel
Down Arrow	Move the selection or active shape down by one pixel
Up Arrow	Move the selection or active shape up by one pixel
Esc	Cancel a selection
Delete	Delete a selection
Ctrl+B	Bold selected text
Ctrl++	Increase the width of a brush, line, or shape outline by one pixel
Ctrl+-	Decrease the width of a brush, line, or shape outline by one pixel
Ctrl+I	Italicize selected text
Ctrl+U	Underline selected text
Ctrl+E	Open the Properties dialog box
Ctrl+W	Open the Resize and Skew dialog box
Ctrl+Page Up	Zoom in
Ctrl+Page Down	Zoom out
F11	View a picture in full-screen mode
Ctrl+R	Show or hide the ruler
Ctrl+G	Show or hide gridlines
F10 or Alt	Display keytips
Shift+F10	Show the current shortcut menu
F1	Open Paint Help

WordPad keyboard shortcuts

The following table contains keyboard shortcuts for working with WordPad.

Press this key	*To do this*
Ctrl+N	Create a new document
Ctrl+O	Open an existing document
Ctrl+S	Save changes to a document
F12	Save the document as a new file
Ctrl+P	Print a document

Alt+F4	Close WordPad
Ctrl+Z	Undo a change
Ctrl+Y	Redo a change
Ctrl+A	Select the entire document
Ctrl+X	Cut a selection
Ctrl+C	Copy a selection to the Clipboard
Ctrl+V	Paste a selection from the Clipboard
Ctrl+B	Make selected text bold
Ctrl+I	Italicize selected text
Ctrl+U	Underline selected text
Ctrl+=	Make selected text subscript
Ctrl+Shift+=	Make selected text superscript
Ctrl+L	Align text left
Ctrl+E	Align text center
Ctrl+R	Align text right
Ctrl+J	Justify text
Ctrl+1	Set single line spacing
Ctrl+2	Set double line spacing
Ctrl+5	Set line spacing to 1.5
Ctrl+Shift+>	Increase the font size
Ctrl+Shift+<	Decrease the font size
Ctrl+Shift+A	Change characters to all capitals
Ctrl+Shift+L	Change the bullet style
Ctrl+D	Insert a Microsoft Paint drawing
Ctrl+F	Find text in a document
F3	Find the next instance of the text in the Find dialog box
Ctrl+H	Replace text in a document
Ctrl+Left Arrow	Move the cursor one word to the left
Ctrl+Right Arrow	Move the cursor one word to the right
Ctrl+Up Arrow	Move the cursor to the line above
Ctrl+Down Arrow	Move the cursor to the line below
Ctrl+Home	Move to the beginning of the document

Ctrl+End	Move to the end of the document
Ctrl+Page Up	Move up one page
Ctrl+Page Down	Move down one page
Ctrl+Delete	Delete the next word
F10	Display keytips
Shift+F10	Show the current shortcut menu
F1	Open WordPad Help

Calculator keyboard shortcuts

The following table contains keyboard shortcuts for working with Calculator.

Press this key	***To do this***
Alt+1	Switch to Standard mode
Alt+2	Switch to Scientific mode
Alt+3	Switch to Programmer mode
Alt+4	Switch to Statistics mode
Ctrl+E	Open date calculations
Ctrl+H	Turn calculation history on or off
Ctrl+U	Open unit conversion
Alt+C	Calculate or solve date calculations and worksheets
F1	Open Calculator Help
Ctrl+Q	Press the M- button
Ctrl+P	Press the M+ button
Ctrl+M	Press the MS button
Ctrl+R	Press the MR button
Ctrl+L	Press the MC button
%	Press the % button
F9	Press the +/– button
/	Press the / button
*	Press the * button
+	Press the + button
-	Press the – button
R	Press the 1/× button
@	Press the square root button

0-9	Press the number buttons (0-9)
=	Press the = button
.	Press the . (decimal point) button
Backspace	Press the backspace button
Esc	Press the C button
Del	Press the CE button
Ctrl+Shift+D	Clear the calculation history
F2	Edit the calculation history
Up Arrow key	Navigate up in the calculation history
Down Arrow key	Navigate down in the calculation history
Esc	Cancel editing the calculation history
Enter	Recalculate the calculation history after editing
F3	Select Degrees in Scientific mode
F4	Select Radians in Scientific mode
F5	Select Grads in Scientific mode
I	Press the Inv button in Scientific mode
D	Press the Mod button in Scientific mode
Ctrl+S	Press the sinh button in Scientific mode
Ctrl+O	Press the cosh button in Scientific mode
Ctrl+T	Press the tanh button in Scientific mode
(	Press the (button in Scientific mode
)	Press the) button in Scientific mode
N	Press the ln button in Scientific mode
;	Press the Int button in Scientific mode
S	Press the sin button in Scientific mode
O	Press the cos button in Scientific mode
T	Press the tan button in Scientific mode
M	Press the dms button in Scientific mode
P	Press the pi button in Scientific mode
V	Press the F-E button in Scientific mode
X	Press the Exp button in Scientific mode
Q	Press the x^2 button in Scientific mode

Y	Press the x^y button in Scientific mode
#	Press the x^3 button in Scientific mode
L	Press the log button in Scientific mode
!	Press the n! button in Scientific mode
Ctrl+Y	Press the y”x button in Scientific mode
Ctrl+B	Press the 3"x button in Scientific mode
Ctrl+G	Press the 10x button in Scientific mode
F5	Select Hex in Programmer mode
F6	Select Dec in Programmer mode
F7	Select Oct in Programmer mode
F8	Select Bin in Programmer mode
F12	Select Qword in Programmer mode
F2	Select Dword in Programmer mode
F3	Select Word in Programmer mode
F4	Select Byte in Programmer mode
K	Press the RoR button in Programmer mode
J	Press the RoL button in Programmer mode
<	Press the Lsh button in Programmer mode
>	Press the Rsh button in Programmer mode
%	Press the Mod button in Programmer mode
(	Press the (button in Programmer mode
)	Press the) button in Programmer mode
|	Press the Or button in Programmer mode
^	Press the Xor button in Programmer mode
~	Press the Not button in Programmer mode
&	Press the And button in Programmer mode
A-F	Press the A-F buttons in Programmer mode
Spacebar	Toggles the bit value in Programmer mode
A	Press the Average button in Statistics mode
Ctrl+A	Press the Average Sq button in Statistics mode
S	Press the Sum button in Statistics mode
Ctrl+S	Press the Sum Sq button in Statistics mode

T	Press the S.D. button in Statistics mode
Ctrl+T	Press the Inv S.D. button in Statistics mode
D	Press the CAD button in Statistics mode

Windows Journal keyboard shortcuts

The following table contains keyboard shortcuts for working with Windows Journal.

Press this key	*To do this*
Ctrl+N	Start a new note
Ctrl+O	Open a recently used note
Ctrl+S	Save changes to a note
Ctrl+Shift+V	Move a note to a specific folder
Ctrl+P	Print a note
Alt+F4	Close a note and its Journal window
Ctrl+Z	Undo a change
Ctrl+Y	Redo a change
Ctrl+A	Select all items on a page
Ctrl+X	Cut a selection
Ctrl+C	Copy a selection to the Clipboard
Ctrl+V	Paste a selection from the Clipboard
Esc	Cancel a selection
Delete	Delete a selection
Ctrl+F	Start a basic find
Ctrl+G	Go to a page
F5	Refresh find results
F5	Refresh the note list
F6	Toggle between a note list and a note
Ctrl+Shift+C	Display a shortcut menu for column headings in a note list
F11	View a note in full-screen mode
F1	Open Journal Help

Windows Help viewer keyboard shortcuts

The following table contains keyboard shortcuts for working with the Help viewer.

Press this key	*To do this*
Alt+C	Display the Table of Contents
Alt+N	Display the Connection Settings menu
F10	Display the Options menu
Alt+Left Arrow	Move back to the previously viewed topic
Alt+Right Arrow	Move forward to the next (previously viewed) topic
Alt+A	Display the customer support page
Alt+Home	Display the Help and Support home page
Home	Move to the beginning of a topic
End	Move to the end of a topic
Ctrl+F	Search the current topic
Ctrl+P	Print a topic
F3	Move the cursor to the search box

8 Questions

Chapter 1 — Introduction to Windows 7

1. Describe what's new in Windows 7.

Chapter 2 — Exploring Desktop of Windows 7

1. Describe the various items of the Taskbar.
2. What is Computer used for? Describe its constituents.
3. Describe the process of copying of files.
4. How is Recycle Bin used in Windows 7?
5. Describe the process of creating a shortcut.

Chapter 3 — Control Panel of Windows 7

1. Describe the various tasks and icons available under:

   Action Center

   Adminstrative Tools

   AutoPlay

   Backup and Restore Centre

   BitLocker Drive Encryption

   Color Management

   Date and Time

   Default Programs

   Desktop Gadgets

   Device Manager

   Devices and Printers

   Display

   Ease of Access Center

   Folder Options

   Fonts

   Getting Started

   HomeGroup

   Indexing Options

Internet Options

Keyboard

Location and Other Sensors

Mail

Mouse

Nero BurnRights

Network and Sharing Centre

Notification Area Icons

Parental Controls

Performance Information

Personalize

Phone and Modem Options

Power Options

Program Updates

Printers

Problem Reports and Solutions

Programs and Features

Regional and Language Options

Sound

Speech Recognition

Sync Center

System

Taskbar and Start Menu

Troubleshooting

User Accounts

Windows CardSpace

Windows Defender

Windows Firewall

Windows Update

Chapter 4 — Accessories of Windows 7

1. Describe the various options available under the following Accessories heads.

   Calculator

   Command Prompt

   Connect to a Network Projector

   Getting Started

   Math Input Panel

Notepad

Paint

Remote Desktop Connection

Run

Snipping Tool

Sound Recorder

Sticky Notes

Sync Center

Windows Explorer

WordPad

Ease of Access

System Tools

Internet Explorer

System Information

System Restore

Task Scheduler

Windows Easy Transfer Reports

Tablet PC

Windows PowerShell

Chapter 5 — Configure and Maintain Your System

1. Describe the process of setting up of Date, Time and Regional Settings in Windows 7.
2. Describe the various options of Keyboard under Keyboard Settings.
3. How would you manage fonts on your computer? Describe.
4. How would you change passwords in your system?
5. How would you change Taskbar properties?
6. How would you change the various properties of Monitor Display?
7. What role does the Screen Saver plays?
8. What does Disk Fragmentation do? Explain.
9. What does Disk Cleanup do? Explain.
10. How would you tune up your system using Task Scheduler? Describe.
11. Describe the process of setting up Home Networking.
12. Describe the process of setting up of Internet on your computer.

Chapter 6 — Additional Commands of Windows 7

1. Describe the various security and privacy options in Windows 7.
2. Describe the working of Windows Mail?

3. How would you install a USB Drive?
4. What does Windows Contacts do?
5. How would you create a DVD using Windows DVD Maker?
6. What are the functions of Windows Photo Gallery?
7. What sort of calender in there in Windows Calender?
8. How would you search using Windows Search?
9. What is Snipping Tool used for?
10. What is new in Windows Media Player of Windows 7?